*Deliverance
From*
Demonic Covenants & Curses

Rev. James A. Solomon

Copyright © 2010 by Rev. James A. Solomon

Deliverance From Demonic Covenants And Curses
by Rev. James A. Solomon

Printed in the United States of America
ISBN 9781609573386
Registration Number/Date:
TXu001271815 / 2005-11-18

1st Printing – May 2006
2nd Printing – November 2007

All rights reserved solely by the author. The author guarantees all contents are original and do not infringe upon the legal rights of any other person or work. No part of this book may be reproduced, stored in a retrieval system, or transmitted in any form or by any means – electronic or mechanical, including photocopying, without permission in writing from the author. The views expressed in this book are not necessarily those of the publisher.

Unless otherwise indicated, all Scripture quotations are taken from the King James Version of the Bible. Used by permission. All emphases within quotations are the author's additions

www.xulonpress.com

Copyright Claimant: James Solomon
Type of Work: Text
Date of Creation: 1987
Rights And Permissions:
Rights & Permissions Info. on Original Appl. in C. O.
Copyright Note: cataloged from appl. only
Names: Solomon, James

+++

The Library of Congress
United States Copyright Office
101 Independence Ave, S.E.
Washington, D.C. 20559-6000
202-707-3000

Printed in the United States of America

Published By:

JESUS PEOPLE PUBLICATIONS
P.O. Box 930640
Norcross, GA 30003
United States of America
Phone: 770-817-1376
Website: www.jesuspeople1.net
Email: jesuspeople@aol.com

List of other books by Rev. James A. Solomon are on the back cover.

To purchase copies of this and other books, please use the following contact information or contact the author directly at:

USA
Jesus People Publications
P.O. Box 930640
Norcross, GA 30003
Tel: 770-817-1376
Email: jesuspeople@aol.com

UNITED KINGDOM
C/O Abtax
1b – 2b Cobalt House
Center Court
1 Sir Thomas Longley Road
Rochester, Kent ME2 4BQ
Tel: 01795 509 131

Purchase a copy online at
www.jesuspeople1.net

Acknowledgements

Discovering the importance of people in the pursuit of greatness is one of the best discoveries we can make in life. It is important to note that from the cradle to the grave we will always need people who will help us succeed and fulfill our divine destiny.

I want to express my appreciation to some people whom God has placed in my life to assist me in my journey toward greatness. This book is a joint effort of people who have believed in my vision and have contributed immensely in one area or another to make it a reality.

I want to thank my father in the Lord, **Rev. Dr. James Boyejo**. Your life and ministry has greatly impacted my life for good, and I just can't forget you, Sir. **Pastor Enoch Adeboye**, the General Overseer of the Redeemed Christian Church of God (worldwide), my mentor whose life and ministry have been perfect examples to me at all times. Sir, I love and appreciate the opportunity given to me to be a blessing to the body of Christ in the Redeemed Christian Church of God worldwide. Thanks a lot for always being there for me.

I would like to express my appreciation to my faithful friends:
Rev. Kayode Kolawole of Power House of Jesus Ministries, Ibadan (Nigeria);
Pastor Bayo Adeyokunnu of The Redeemed Christian Church of God – Victory Temple, Bowie, Maryland (USA);

Pastor Ade Okonrende of The Redeemed Christian Church of God – Redemption Parish, Houston, Texas (USA);
Pastor Andrew Adeleke of The Redeemed Christian Church of God – Lighthouse Fellowship Parish, London (UK);
Evangelist Mike Okuo – AIG (Retired) who is always a source of encouragement to me;
To my special friend **Rev. Dr. Omomokuyo** of Christ Anointed Kingdom Church, Lagos (Nigeria).

I sincerely appreciate those who have sacrificed their time to work on this book to make it excellent. These faithful brethren in the Lord include: **Sister Denise Santana, Sister Angela Rivers, Sister Roli Buwa-Tossoukpe, Sister Wunmi Ogunleye, Sister Marquise Book, Pastor Sola Olorunfemi, Sister Bola, Sister Deborah** and my big son in the Lord, **Pastor David Adeboye**. You are such a wonderful blessing here in our midst in America.

I cannot forget all my faithful pastors who are committed to the vision of **Jesus People's Revival Ministries** and **Jesus Family Chapel** in Nigeria, in the United Kingdom, and in the United States of America.
Words cannot express my thanks to my wonderful wife, **Rev. Mrs. Florence James** – the **"Power House"** of this ministry. I want to say that I appreciate your prayers and support at all times as well as your mature understanding; I love you so much. I appreciate my children: **Felicia, Joseph, David, and Ruth**; you are all so wonderful to me. May the Lord lift up your heads in life, in Jesus' name.

God Bless you all
James Solomon

Dedication

This book is dedicated to the Holy Spirit,
The Helper of my soul
And the One behind all the revelations
shared in this book.
To Him alone be glory, honor, and power
Forever and ever, Amen.

TABLE OF CONTENTS

Acknowledgements v
Dedication vii
Table of Contents.. ix
Introduction xiii

SECTION A: THE FOUNDATIONS

1. My Testimony In The Demonic World 17
2. Faulty Foundations.. 34
3. Demonic Covenants and Possession 44

SECTION B: ANCESTRAL YOKES

4. Inherited Family Curses... 59
5. Demonic Initiations And Dedications 71
6. Witchcraft And Spiritual Manipulators............................... 77
7. Demonic Diaries 82

SECTION C: SECRETS OF THE DARK KINGDOM

8. Resurrecting Your Star.. 97
9. Dreams And Demonic Manipulations 110

SECTION D: BELIEVERS AND SATANIC ATTACKS

10. Why Do Some Christians Die Young 126
11. Causes And Cure Of Backsliding................................... 142

SECTION E: VICTORY OVER UNSEEN FORCES

12. Unseen Forces Fighting Against Us 159
13. Unseen Forces Fighting For Us 172
14. Pulling Down The Walls 186

SECTION F: KEYS TO COMPLETE DELIVERANCE

15. The Process of Deliverance 192
16. How To Receive Your Deliverance 203
17. How To Keep Your Deliverance 216
18. Power In The Blood Of Jesus 223
19. Biblical Curses 226
20. Prayers Of Preparation Before Deliverance ... 229
21. Renouncing Declarations And Scriptures 231
22. Scriptures For Deliverance
    And Spiritual Warfare 235
23. Warfare Prayers For Self-Deliverance 236
    - I. Repentance And Confession 239
    - II. Breaking Evil Covenants And Curses From
      The Bloodline 244
    - III. Renouncing Evil Initiations, Dedications,
      And Occultism 247
    - IV. Deliverance From Generational Curses .. 250
    - V. Renouncing All Memberships Of Evil
      Associations 253
    - VI. Prayers Against The Manipulation Of
      Familiar Spirits And Witchcraft 255
    - VII. Deliverance From The Spirit, Husband,
      Or Wife 258
    - VIII. Renouncing All Hidden And General Curses 261
    - IX. Binding And Loosing 265
    - X. Lord Enthrone My Esther: Break Conspiracy
      And Instigate Promotion 268
    - XI. Lord Fight For Me 270
    - XII. Scriptural Declaration Of Victory Through
      The Blood Of Jesus 275
    - XIII. Possessing Your Possessions ....

XIV.	Re-Aligning Yourself Back Into God's Presence	278
XV.	Intercessory Prayers For The Body Of Christ	279
XVI.	Daily Scriptural Declarations And Confessions	280

About The Author 285

List of Book Titles by **Rev. James Solomon** 287

Introduction

"... In meekness instructing those that oppose themselves; if God peradventure will give them repentance to the acknowledging of the truth;
And that they may recover themselves out of the snare of the devil, who are taken captive by him at his will."
(2 Timothy 2:25-26)

I feel very strongly that giving an account of my life and background in the demonic world before Christ is a testimony to the glory of God and a proof to His might which is able to set all people free no matter how bad or far gone they are in their activities for the enemy.

The facts in this book are true-life experiences of what I have gone through, plus the testimony of others who have been set free through the ministration of the power of God. The demonic kingdom is real in every culture, every tribe, and every tongue on the face of the earth. Witches, wizards, mermaids, and other marine or water spirits, snake spirits, etc., exist everywhere on earth – from the fall of man to the death of Jesus – after all, the entire world is controlled by Satan. How they manifest in different cultures and continents is what makes them different. The demonic world is very real, very active, and powerful, set to steal, kill and destroy. The power of the enemy, however, is powerless in the lives of believers who have acquired the knowledge (in Christ Jesus) to break themselves loose from the stronghold and bondage of the enemy.

There are many believers who have received Christ and yet are still struggling with demonic oppressions, bondages, and curses; and after many prayers, they are yet to see any change or victory over their situations. The Word of God says many are held captive due to their lack of knowledge.

> *"My people are destroyed for lack of knowledge: because thou hast rejected knowledge, I also will reject thee, that thou shalt be no priest to me: seeing thou hast forgotten the law of thy God, I will also forget thy children."* **(Hosea 4:6)**

There is a reason behind everything you are going through. This book will shed some light on certain areas of your life – especially your foundations – because nothing happens without a reason. There is a reason behind your failures and lack of progress in life. The Bible says that curse comes with a reason.

> *"As the bird by wandering, as the swallow by flying, so the curse causeless shall not come."* **(Proverbs 26:2)**

By the time you finish reading this book, I trust that the Lord will enable you to identify the sources of your problems. There are a lot of revelations in this book, so you need to take time to read and understand.

There is a workbook available for those who truly want to fight zealously for their freedom and that of others as well. Information on how to get the workbook is available at the back of this book.

I pray that the words in this book will illuminate your understanding and that the light of God will go forth and set you free from all demonic entanglements, evil covenants, curses, strongholds and bondages, in Jesus' Name. Amen!

> *"A wise man in strong; yea, a man of knowledge increaseth strength."* **(Proverbs 24:5)**

SECTION A

The Foundations

*If the foundations be destroyed,
What can the righteous do?*
(Psalm 11:3)

CHAPTER 1

My Testimony In The Demonic World

"Therefore if any man be in Christ,
he is a new creature: old things are passed away;
behold all things are become new.
(2 Corinthians 5:17)

The writings of this book are based on my own life experiences and how I overcame them through the Blood of Jesus. There are some of you who will read this book and become afraid; let me assure you, there is no need to be afraid. For those who come from an African background, you may not find this testimony strange or out of the ordinary, as you might be familiar with some of the scenarios mentioned here. Even though you may not have experienced them firsthand, you will be able to bear witness that these facts are real.

MY TESTIMONY

This is the story of my life and I testify to the power of God through the name and the Blood of Jesus Christ, and His power and ability to set even the worse captives free. I was born into a family of witch doctors in Nigeria, a country in West Africa. I grew up in a community

> There are people who attend church yet they are willfully active in the occult. serving Satan.

where the fetish priest or the witch doctors were recognized as the respected elders of the community.

My particular community was known to produce some of the most powerful witch doctors in the town; therefore, it wasn't anything extraordinary or unusual for me to be initiated and endowed with uncommon fetish powers at a very young and tender age. My family took pride in the fact that my grandfather was the most powerful witch doctor in the community; the mere mention of his name would cause fear and terror everywhere and in everyone.

To be honored in the community as a powerful personality among the celebrated fetish priests requires membership in several cults. When you belong to just one cult, people in the community do not fear or respect you as much as the person who belongs to two, three, or more cults. Then you will be terribly feared and respected because of the numerous dark powers you are assumed to possess.

My grandfather was a member of so many cults that no one knew exactly how many he had joined; because of this, he had become such a phenomenon as far as cult membership and the possession of dark powers are concerned, that he was an embodiment of fetish powers.

My father's role model was his father (my grandfather) and he strove to become dreaded by the entire community just like his father. He took over the leadership role and became a powerful witch doctor when his older brother died. He was initiated and became a leader with a membership in over sixteen cults. This was probably the highest number of cults anyone could belong to at a given time in our community. He became a witch doctor of great repute in Nigeria, not just within the local community.

My entire family got to the pinnacle of idol worship and associating with witchcraft, to the extent that we had a resident relic (a physical representative of the devil) at the back of our family house. This shrine was dedicated to Satan *(Esu)*.

My family's involvement in the occult world however did not disturb our membership and dedication to the Church. We attended all church services regularly; even my father was actively involved in many religious activities in the Church.

INVOLVEMENT IN OCCULT ACTIVITIES

It was a thing of pride at the time for me to be involved in all these occult activities with my family. I believed I was carrying a proud heritage. My chief duty at this time was to carry the dreaded (demonic) oracle bag that no ordinary person could carry unless you had been embodied with demonic protection and power. I would always stand behind my grandfather, cautiously walking a step behind him whenever he went to worship his demonic powers.

OCCULT PRACTICES

Witch doctors and fetish priests control the emotions of people by introducing fear into their hearts, thereby keeping them tied down in bondage and terror. Witch doctors are believed to be so strong that they have the ability to communicate with the spirits of the departed ancestors and demons. These witch doctors are also believed to be powerful human beings who regularly bathe in human blood; put on amulets that are extremely powerful; and possess awesome, demonic powers that could make anything happen.

Witch doctors are believed to have the power to expel witchcraft, perform something that looks like healing, and provide (demonic) money through the powers of these demons. Lots of rituals are performed by witch doctors to appease the demons – keep them happy and calm. The witch doctors themselves live in fear

> **Demonic rituals, initiations, hexes and verbal curses can all be broken through the blood of Jesus.**

of these demons because they believe that if they do not serve and worship the demons according to the *"demonic instructions or guide of worship,"* the anger of the demons could kill or destroy them and their entire families. As a result, a lot of weird and unprintable things were done by the witch doctors.

The fact that I was born into such a powerful family of fetish priests brought me and my family uncommon privileges, and we earned the deep respect of everyone in the community. Men and women of substance from all over the country came to consult with us in order to seek solutions to their complicated problems.

As I was growing up, I enjoyed the respect I received from my playmates; people around envied my background. It was later, after coming to know Christ that I realized that those who are raised in the homes of fetish priests are under satanic bondage and demonic covenants.

AN AFRICAN EXPERIENCE

It is common knowledge that every African has idolatry rooted either in their immediate past or their distant past. I have also discovered that many other cultures have occultism rooted in their background and in some cases, not too distant past. In Africa, powerful fetish priests are known to drink human blood, keep a number of human skulls in their shrines, and are able to summon powerful spirits to manifest themselves physically whenever a particular ritual is to be done.

Some witch doctors use their powers to achieve unimaginable acts of wickedness; for example, some witch doctors have used their powers to cause many women to remain pregnant for up to 24 months as a form of punishment to the woman or her family. Many people consult with witch doctors for their own evil purposes, such as desiring some wicked act to be performed on someone who has wronged them. It could even be a simple case of greed, coveting the possession of others or envying the progress or achievement of others. Many people have been driven to insanity or death as a result of such evil services.

Here is another common example: two people are involved in a conflict over a plot of land. One of them would consult a witch doctor saying, "***I need you to get rid of this other man so that this property of land will be mine.***" The witch doctor will then proceed to give *'his client'* a charm (some physical form of voodoo) that will be used to send the client's opponent to an early grave.

MY FAMILY FOUNDATION

As I mentioned earlier, my father was a first-class witch doctor. All the fetish priests in the city would rise in honor of my father at any event or gathering. He occupied one of the highest-ranking offices in the kingdom of darkness. His appellation ***"Baba"*** (meaning Father) meant he was a father figure to all witch doctors in the land.

It is characteristic of most witch doctors to marry several wives. Some of these unfortunate wives were women who had initially come in search of spiritual protection, conception, or some form of help, but ended up having their will captivated in spiritual bondage. Somehow, they found themselves married to their ***"consulting witch doctor,"*** even though many of these women were already married women living with their husbands prior to their visit to the witch doctor. In those days, whoever dared challenged a fetish priest or witch doctor was asking for trouble – big time! The wickedness of an average witch doctor was so great in those days that no one attempted to challenge them.

My father's power was beyond that of a witch doctor; he also had the power to kill at will. He had been known to reduce a person in his right mind to a state of insanity with just a wink of his eye. My father was so feared that no one was bold enough to look him straight in his eyeballs.

The two toughest masquerades in my town never staged an outing without first consulting with my father and his brother. Out of ignorance, I took a lot of pride in having such a dreaded fetish priest as my father.

My father, who was respected by all, had occultic business connections with many demonic houses in the city. He also occupied one of the highest-ranking offices in the kingdom of darkness. In spite of all these and contrary to the usual pattern or custom amongst his kind, he had only one wife – my mother – whom he forcefully took from her rightful husband. Due to my father's known and feared personality, my mother's lawful husband could not openly protest the unfair loss of his wife.

Shortly after the wrongful abduction of my mother, she became pregnant and gave birth to a boy who died not long after he was born. Many people secretly rejoiced, viewing my father's misfortune as poetic justice.

Right there and then, my father, furious and humiliated, purposed in his mind that this would never happen to him again. He would show his adverse critics that he was a strong man who could protect his own. Therefore, when his wife became pregnant again, he performed all kinds of demonic rituals to ensure that the child lived.

I was told that the pregnancy through which I was born was dedicated to many idols and cults for protection. On many occasions, my father would recite incantations over my mother's protruding stomach. For the sake of the baby, my mother was initiated into several cults throughout the period of the pregnancy. As a result, I was subjected to demonic initiations and covenants right from my mother's womb. This was the very faulty foundation on which I was born.

Immediately after I was born, I was made to undergo several initiations to ensure my survival: I was bathed in different rivers, and taken to the shrines of idols and various occult houses. Many incisions were made on my body and I was given diverse things to eat. I also had to drink several mixtures of strange concoctions.

When I was about six or seven years old, my grandfather took me for a walk in a thick forest, taking the path that headed toward a river. It was around one o'clock (1:00 a.m.) in the morning. On my head, I carried a satanic concoction covered in a bowl. My grandfather was walking behind me and chanting incantations. I was instructed not to look back or else I would die. I was told that an evil spirit was waiting for me at the other side of the river to receive the concoction I was carrying on my head. On getting to our destination, somehow, I handed the bowl over to the spirit that I could not see and I was immediately translated to our house.

As the first child of my father, I was brought up to worship and serve idols. I was to follow in his footsteps. I remember being fascinated at the fact that the food given to us as gifts for our services was always in surplus amounts in our home. Each day, we would receive fowls (chickens or hens), goats, snails and parrots, along with other things. I have no recollection of my father or mother ever buying most of our food items because people needing the evil services of my father would bring them to us in large quantities as requirements for the worship of our idols to accomplish their demands. So of course, we profited in that area.

Right from my early teenage years, my first duty in the morning was to appease *Esu* (Satan) by pouring palm oil on the idol in the shrine placed at the backyard. I was very faithful in doing this because of the honor, fame, and recognition I received from other priests in the dark kingdom.

However, there was a strange practice within our family. At the time, we did not consider it strange, and this was that in spite of all these evil works, we were strong and active religious Christians. My father lived a religious Christian life and never missed any church service or function. This was both hypocritical and amazing to me, despite all of my father's juju (voodoo) and occult activities. 'Baba' was a dedicated church member par excellence, a renowned, ceremonial "Christian."

He ensured that all members of his family were always present at every service in the local Orthodox Church, and that all prayers and creeds were religiously memorized and recited whenever necessary. However, immediately after the Sunday service, we would head for a nearby prominent fetish market, to buy the fetish materials needed for the demonic worship of idols. Every morning as a ritual, my father would first worship Satan, and then he would pray like a Christian with all his children.

INHERITING EVIL POWERS

My experiences as a child made me crave for and desire my father's envied position, though within me, I felt something was wrong somewhere; I felt that this demonic worship and lifestyle was all wrong. As my father grew old, I started preparing myself to take over the mantle from him, since I had the coveted position of being the rightful heir to my father. Enquiries were made from all the oracles in the town by other witch doctors to find out who would succeed my aged father, as this was the custom of the cult.

After a long wait, the idols were consulted on this *"all important"* issue. There was great anxiety within my family as well as in the town to know whom the idols had chosen. As mentioned earlier, in most cases, the firstborn of the incumbent is usually chosen, so it was no surprise that the mantle fell on me. I was filled with pride and a sense of achievement; my joy knew no bounds since I knew that at my father's death, I would step into his *"exalted"* position in the society. In preparation for this, I was initiated into higher demonic cults.

After my initiation, I became an 'apprentice' witch doctor (also known as *Kekere Awo*). 'Baba' and I were the only ones who knew how much havoc and problems we caused or created in the lives of people who came to us for help. Many who sincerely poured out their hearts to us, looking for solutions to their problems, went home with additional problems without even knowing it.

Some wicked people, after pre-arrangement with my father, would bring their friends for consultation under the pretence of helping them. Alas, with our help, such ignorant people would go back home with added demons that would destroy their businesses, homes, families, or whatever the case may be. We were engaged in diverse acts of wickedness, which included using a woman's placenta and the hair of a newborn baby for money-making rituals. Of course, materials for making some of these charms were usually obtained from children brought to us for one form of treatment or the other.

DOUBTING THE EVIL POWERS

Even though I kept on "advancing" in the practice of wickedness, I felt empty and unfulfilled in life. This was about the same period my mother died. As a young boy, I started getting curious and having serious doubts about the idols. In confusion, I asked, "If the idols were as powerful as we believed them to be, why couldn't they protect my mother from dying at a young age?" After much thought, I felt I needed a change of scenery, so I decided to go with a friend of mine and relocate to Lagos – the then business and commercial capital of Nigeria (West Africa).

Having made my decision, I quietly began to make the necessary preparations to leave, knowing that my father would not want to release me seeing that I was very useful to him and his idols. He called me one day to warn and inform me that the oracle had decreed that no one within the family was to travel within the next seven days, so as to avoid eminent danger. Meanwhile, I had already planned to leave for Lagos the next day without informing him. Although I was afraid, somehow, I found the courage to disobey the instruction from one of our powerful gods.

> **There is fulfillment and contentment only in Jesus. I had all the powers I wanted, but I was still empty.**

My friend and I left very early the next morning. As God would have it, we arrived at Lagos safely without any accident or eminent danger, as prophesied. From then, I began to lose faith in the powers of idols: were they true deities? Were they authentic or just charlatans and deceivers? How come nothing terrible happened to me on the way to Lagos, in spite of the feared threat from the demonic idols?

At this time, I had already completed my high school education and was hoping to go further. So in Lagos, while I was working, I enrolled in a correspondence school called "Exam Success" where I obtained a Higher National Diploma in Business Administration. I worked with different government establishments such as the

Federal Ministry of Works and Housing, Federal Palace Hotel, as well as some companies in the private sector.

Still I realized that though I had good jobs and was well paid, I was not fulfilled in life nor was I at peace. I seemed to be searching for something. As a young man, I was quite successful; my house was furnished to my taste and I lived in wealth. While working at the Federal Ministry of Works and Housing, I was posted to work in the northern part of Nigeria, a place where in addition to one's regular salary; one could make easy money on the side. After some years, the Federal Government cancelled the contract I had gone to supervise, and I subsequently left their employment.

As time went by, I noticed one thing: I was not able to hold on to a good job for a long period of time before losing it. After the Federal Ministry of Works and Housing, I finally got a good paying job with the Federal Palace Hotel, which at the time was the number one hotel in Nigeria (like a present day 5-Star hotel). Now I had money, but I was not married, and by this time I was close to forty years of age. I became worried that things in my life were being unnecessarily delayed.

MY CONVERSION

During one of my annual vacation periods, about thirteen years after I had left my town and my father, I decided to go back to my hometown to spend my vacation with the rest of my family. At this time when I got to my hometown, I refused to stay with my father. Instead, I stayed with one of my younger brothers who at the time happened to be a born again believer. While at home, I was persuaded by my younger brother to accompany him to Church for a special service. I must confess here that I only consented to going to the Church because of my brother's incessant pleadings. However, the decision to go to Church with him became the best decision I ever made in my life because it was at that church service ***I met with the Lord Jesus Christ Who transformed my life.***

We got to the fellowship early that day, and I was fascinated by the people who were offering intercessory prayers; the service had not yet started. So I took the position of an on-looker, taking in everything that was happening around me. All of a sudden, I heard an audible voice urging me to bow my head and join in the prayers. I resisted, but the voice spoke again, a little stronger. I felt it must be God because everyone else was busy praying and when I looked around, nobody was talking to me, so I bowed my head and closed my eyes. I found myself weeping and confessing my sins, asking God to forgive me and promising to serve Him for the rest of my life. At that time, I was about 25 years of age.

And that was how I gave my life to Jesus. I became born again at about 7:00 p.m. on August 1, 1978 in my hometown. Subsequently, I burnt my entire collection of juju (voodoo) charms and forsook all my former demonic practices. The peace of God which passes all understanding came upon me from the very first day of my salvation. Glory be to God! Without delay, I joined a gospel Church; I became a member of a Church that preached holiness and laid emphasis on the purity of heart. Although I had become a bona fide child of God, yet to my surprise, I began to grapple with failure in just about everything – again!

At the time of my conversion I continued to work as an employee at the Federal Palace Hotel. When I realized that my Christian growth would be jeopardized if I continued working there, I resigned. After years of working at the hotel, I had no savings. Many of my colleagues had several cars; some of them had even built houses. I began to feel that I did not possess the ability to achieve anything in life; whatever I laid my hands on turned negative.

I thought that being born again, things (my life) would begin to improve, but the contrary was the case. After gaining employment with a notable private company as an Assistant Administrative Manager, I was still very much under attack of the presence of some forces of darkness lurking and operating in my life. I sensed that the spirits in charge of poverty, ill-luck, and failure were attacking me. I seriously lacked the knowledge on how to deal with them.

Many terrible dreams and nightmares assailed me; I saw many horrible demons and terrifying men in my dreams. While sleeping, I often felt peculiar sensations of literally being pressed down physically, even though there was nobody else in the room. At other times, I felt like I was being gagged at the mouth – unable to utter a word – by unseen forces.

These experiences were a constant source of worry and anxiety to me. In the midst of all my trials, the devil kept suggesting that I turn my back on Jesus Christ and return to the idols to seek for solutions. I continually resisted the devil and kept on reciting the Word of God:

"Therefore if any man be in Christ, he is a new creature: old things are passed away: behold all things are become new." **(2 Corinthians 5:17)**

During this period, I did not know anything about deliverance; I was just a young covert manifesting my zeal for the Lord. And though my problems were weighing me down, I was determined not to return to idol worship or occult practices.

Being "born again" does not stop demonic afflictions and attacks. Every yoke must be broken.

MY CALL TO MINISTRY

I heard the Lord calling me into ministry work, so I took steps to answer the call of God upon my life. The call was to serve in the ministry on a full-time basis, so I resigned from my job and enrolled in a Bible School. Upon graduation, I was employed by a Church and worked as the Western State District head for the ministry in Nigeria. The work and its growth were quite challenging. Unfortunately, the Church closed down and the members went to other churches.

Later, the Holy Spirit began to impress upon my heart the need for me to be free from demonic powers. I did not quite understand or know how to handle this, as the Church to which I belonged at the time did not have or teach any revelation concerning deliverance. We were taught that once:

"Christ hath redeemed us from the curse of the law…."
(Galatians 3:13)

We are no longer under any bondage. So at the time, I believed this teaching and, therefore, thought I was free; not knowing that there were some demonic covenants in my life that needed to be broken; as well as several curses which had been placed upon me before and after my birth that I needed to be delivered from. I had concluded that since I was now born again, all was well. I was wrong!

One day, God, in His infinite mercy, opened my understanding to His Word and the following Scriptures came alive to me:

"Thou shalt have no other gods before me.

Thou shalt not make unto thee any graven image, or any likeness of anything that is in heaven above, or that is in the earth beneath, or that is in the water under the earth.

Thou shalt not bow down thyself unto them, nor serve them: for I the Lord thy God am a jealous God, visiting the iniquity of the fathers upon the children unto the third and fourth generation of them that hate me..." (Exodus 20:3-5)

"I beseech you therefore, brethren, by the mercies of God, that ye present your bodies a living sacrifice, holy, acceptable unto God, which is your reasonable service.

And be not conformed to this world, but be ye transformed by the renewing of your mind, that ye may prove what is that good, and acceptable, and perfect will of God." (Romans 12:1-2)

"Because ye have said, "We have made a covenant with death, and with hell are we at agreement; when the overflowing scourge shall pass through, it shall not come unto us: for we have made lies our refuge, and under falsehood have we hid ourselves:"

Therefore thus saith the Lord God, "Behold, I lay in Zion for a foundation a stone, a tried stone, a precious corner stone, a sure foundation: he that believeth shall not make haste.

Judgment also will I lay to the line, and righteousness to the plummet: and the hail shall sweep away the refuge of lies, and the waters shall overflow the hiding place.
And your covenant with death shall be disannulled, and your agreement with hell shall not stand; when the overflowing scourge shall pass through, then ye shall be trodden down by it." **(Isaiah 28:15-18)**

MY DELIVERANCE

I prayed and fasted for years, going from one *"Prayer Mountain"* to another, so I could be alone with God. As at this time, I knew I was dealing with demons and that they were the source of my problems; I just did not know how to get rid of them. When my last venture failed in June 1986, I wanted to run away from Nigeria and start a new life abroad, with the hope that I would have a better life. Again, all my efforts toward that direction failed woefully.

EXPLOITS THROUGH PRAYERS

I had the good fortune early in life of imbibing the culture or habit of going to the mountains for prayer and meditation. In my country of Nigeria, there are a number of plateaus and mountains that have become noted as prayer resorts or retreat centers. Some of these prayer mountains were established by some notable African Pentecostal fathers. When I heard of how some of these African church fathers spent time on the mountain, praying and fasting continually for days, I got challenged; challenged to pray like no one ever did. I was in my late 30's when I began to seclude myself on the mountain to pray. The thought of marriage was far from my mind at this time, even though my immediate younger brother was already married with two children. The evil spirit that was assigned to me from the satanic kingdom did not allow me the time or peace of mind to focus on or make plans on achieving success in my life.

UNCOMMON ZEAL

I subsequently cultivated the habit of going to the Prayer Mountains. When I was in the kingdom of darkness, we did nothing in half measures. We were so committed to keeping all the laws and avoiding all the taboos. As such, I came into the Christian faith with the same kind of zeal with which I practiced voodoo.

People, who have lived in the western world all through their lives, have only a faint idea of what voodoo or occult worship is all about. Some people believe that voodoo represents the worship of ancestors, rocks, rivers, and other elements of nature. Most voodoo practices center on the use of charms. Voodoo practices are prominent in countries like the Republic of Benin, Togo, Nigeria, Angola, Central Africa, Brazil, Cameroun, Haiti, South America, Congo, etc.

> **God created everything on earth; however when evil incantations are spoken into them, they become demonic.**

Christian converts that come from a background of idolatry, naturally handle Christianity with a fervency and seriousness than those who were born and/or bred in Christian homes. So bearing this in mind, it was natural for me to seek God's face in an aggressive manner. I had started going to the prayer mountains to fast and pray, before I even discovered that our Lord Jesus often went to the mountains for prayers and personal retreat. The Bible passages below also compelled me to follow in the footsteps of Jesus Christ regarding this principle:

> *"And when He had sent the multitudes away, He went up into a mountain apart to pray: and when the evening was come, He was there alone."* **(Matthew 14:23)**

> *"And it came to pass in those days, that He went out into a mountain to pray, and continued all night in prayer to God."* **(Luke 6:12)**

***"And when He had sent them away, He departed into a mountain to pray."* (Mark 6:46)**

I meditated deeply on the above passages and realized that anyone with my kind of background would have to go the whole nine yards in order to make it. I decided that if there were anything or any place called the highest point in the ministry of prayers, I would get there. And so that was how I started going from one prayer mountain to the other, denying myself of food and water, in search of the knowledge and power of God.

> **May God open your spiritual eyes and understanding like he did mine, to see the truth. Amen.**

Three times I stayed on a mountain (a prayer resort center) for 40 days, and then on another mountain for four months (without coming down). Both Ikoyi and Ede mountains were popular prayer retreats in Nigeria – at the time – so I spent the whole of 1987 going from one mountain to the other. It was while on one of such mountains that the Lord finally spoke to me and told me of the evil deeds committed by my father, while in the process of marrying my mother. I learnt that it was these evil deeds that had exposed me to many demons that had affected my life adversely.

God opened my eyes to see what truly happens when charms are made. Before incantations are pronounced on them, the charms are harmless, but after the incantations have been made, particular demons inhabit the charms. These charms are then rubbed on the body or put in water or some other form of liquid for drinking. Some of these charms are used for cooking while some are worn around the body as amulets. And so in my case, so many charms were made for me and/or on my behalf at different stages of my life.

God told me that these charms represented covenants between me and the devil. He (God) reminded me of how I was initiated into all manner of cults when I was young, and also that I had some binding blood covenants with the demons attached to them. This was the reason why those demons had access to visit me even though I was a born again believer. God further revealed to me that all the dogs, parrots, and goats that were killed for me or on my behalf for the worship of idols, represented blood covenants between me and the idols. He said that the demons would not leave even though I prayed, because I had not broken the covenants that bound us together. God led me to this Scripture:

***"If the foundations be destroyed, what can the righteous do?"* (Psalm 11:3)**

God gave me the revelation or knowledge of my faulty foundations. He illustrated this with the story of Prophet Elisha and how he had to heal the waters of Jericho from bitterness and deliver the land from barrenness.

Thereafter, I renounced the covenants I made with the idols, including those made on my behalf by my parents and others through prayers in the name of Jesus. I broke all forms of inherited family curses operating in my life, applied the Blood of Jesus on myself and then was prayed for by a man of God.

To the glory of God, I received total deliverance. It took me nine years of prayers after my salvation before I finally received my deliverance because there was no deliverance ministry that I knew of at that time.

CHAPTER 2

FAULTY FOUNDATIONS

*If the foundations be destroyed,
What can the righteous do?*
Psalm 11:3

In the Sermon on the Mount, Jesus Christ likened the one who builds his house on the sand to *"a foolish man."* And of such a house, the Lord said:

"And the rain descended, and the floods came, and the winds blew, and beat upon that house; and it fell: and great was the fall of it." **(Matthew 7:27)**

What the Lord Jesus propounds here is a universal truth. Those involved in the building industry such as: civil engineers, architects, bricklayers, etc., will readily tell you that without a solid foundation, a building cannot stand. A weak or faulty foundation will most certainly cause a standing building to collapse in the face of the mildest storm. This same principle applies to the human life. Your future depends on your spiritual foundation. If your life is built on the platform of a very bad spiritual beginning, it will produce a bad future. Hence, the type of foundation laid is very important.

Many of us with roots in Africa have very faulty beginnings. Often times, the problems we encounter in life originate from our birth, the very foundation of our lives. The ignorance of our parents and the wickedness of men, conspire together to give us a crooked spiritual beginning. As we grow up and build upon this foundation, instead of standing firmly, we collapse like a pile of cards. Everything we do to improve the quality of our lives falls flat. Instead of success, we achieve failure. In the land of riches, we are surrounded by poverty. All the bad luck of this world gathers together and hangs over our heads.

I was in such a despicable state when the Lord spoke to me during my retreat on the mountain. He led me to the following Scripture:

> **"If the foundations be destroyed, what can the righteous do?" (Psalm 11:3)**

I meditated on this for a while, before God opened my eyes. I realized then, that the source of my predicament was my faulty foundation; which had been destroyed by the wickedness of my ancestors. The fact that I was righteous through the Blood of Jesus could not save my physical life from collapsing. God required that I go back to my foundation and amend it, only then would I begin to enjoy His blessings.

There are many children of God who simply find it difficult to *"be successful,"* no matter how hard they try. They have fasted, prayed, bound, loosed, participated in innumerable night vigils, yet things keep getting worse. Some of them have even entered the phase where they have concluded that God is no longer in the business of answering prayers. To such people, I say:

> **"Jesus Christ is the same yesterday, and today and forever." (Hebrews 13:8)**

Examine your foundation; your problems may be located there.

> **"If the foundations be destroyed, what can the righteous do?" (Psalm 11:3)**

This was the profound revelation that changed my life and turned me from failure to success. This was the central message that God gave me, which changed the lives of many for good. Unfortunately, many Christians whom God has ministered this same message to, have yet understood the revelation. Some Christians have assumed that perhaps some grievous or besetting sin is responsible for all their problems.

They continue to ask God for forgiveness of the sins which He has already forgiven. Such people are applying the wrong medication to their sickness. To discover the solution to any problem, we must first know what the problem is. Since a lot of people do not know what their problems are, they pray amiss, and since God will not answer such prayers, they continue in their problems.

Due to the cultural and traditional religious practices, it is very rare for people not to suffer the consequences of an idolatrous foundation. Many people who have fallen into this particular problem have what is called *"a faulty foundation."* Foundational problems come in different garbs and also from different sources.

HUMAN AGENTS

As a former junior witch doctor *(Kekere Awo)* and an apprentice to a renowned fetish priest, I learnt a few tricks of how the devil uses human agents to destroy the future of young lives (i.e., the lives of infants and/or young children). Under the guise of ministering to them, they change the glory that God has given to these young ones through diabolical means. They destroy their foundations.

Back in the day, in rural communities, there were women who were specially assigned or commissioned to bathe newborn babies traditionally. Whenever a birth was announced, one of such women would go to the family of the newborn, singing traditional songs and dancing to welcome the baby. She would then carry the baby and sing soothing lullabies before performing the traditional bath. It was such a grand gesture that people would think that the woman genuinely loved the child. With my exposure in the kingdom of darkness, I must truthfully say here that most of these women are witches who are actually out to corrupt the life and foundation of these children that they have access to.

One of such women confessed openly during one of our crusades that while performing this traditional assignment, she had bathed more than 500 babies, and that the fate of these babies were sealed. She disclosed that none of those children would ever make a headway in life. According to her, whenever she was invited to bathe a child, she would pull out a strand of demonic hair from her own head, place it neatly on her palm and dance her way to the house where her service was needed. Immediately her hair touched the hair of the newborn baby, two things would happen:

i. The baby would automatically be initiated into the witchcraft cult from that day.
ii. The destiny of such a baby became a matter to be tabled at the witchcraft coven. The plan of God for that baby would be tampered with.

As witch doctors, we tampered with the foundations of many people, and those who operate in that evil realm still exist and continue in such evil work today. As stated earlier, the 'placenta' was a priceless item amongst fetish priests. The hair of an eight-day old baby is valued like gold; we were always eager to buy it at any price. The hair is particularly vital in money-making rituals, and it

Have you ever wondered what hospitals do with a baby's placenta? Do you really know how the placentas are being disposed of?

was easy to obtain especially from *"Alfas" (Muslim Clerics)*. The Islamic child naming ceremony requires cutting the hair of an eight-day old baby. The Alfas sold this for quick money, which made it easy for the witch doctors to have a constant flow of this resource for their evil deeds.

It was also easy to secure placentas for our rituals. Unscrupulous nurses and doctors were always ready to supply them to us at a price. Traditional midwives were another source. We would look at the star of a child through the placenta to determine how the baby whose placenta we had secured would fare in life. **Poor parents!** If only they knew what their ignorance was costing them!

Note: Always ask for your baby's placenta so as to bury it yourself or ask the doctors what they do with it. Have you ever wondered what the hospitals or disposing contractors do with them?

These are some of the spiritual reasons why some people live their lives weighed down by problems, poverty, bad luck, bad health, etc. Their glory had been stolen while they were babies.

Many children of God are miserable in life even though as Christians we are righteous through the Blood of Jesus; from the moment we become born again believers, we should start living a life of freedom in Christ Jesus. Unfortunately, long before many become Christians, their foundations had already been tampered with and unless such foundations are repaired, these believers cannot enjoy the abundant life that Christ has provided.

FOUNDATIONAL PROBLEMS OF A CITY

In some instances, it is the foundational problems of a city or village that affect the future of its citizens. In 2nd Kings the people of the city of Jericho went to Elisha when they were perplexed by the problems facing the city. According to them, it was a pleasant city in most respects, but there was a major problem:

> *"And the men of the city said unto Elisha, Behold, I pray thee, the situation of this city is pleasant, as my lord seeth: but the water is naught, and the ground barren."* **(2 Kings 2:19)**

These were serious problems for any society. No water means no land to farm and no crop to harvest; the very existence of the people was being threatened. They had probably fasted and prayed so that relief would come to their land; obviously, nothing happened. They continued to suffer lack of water. Jericho's land remained barren – meaning that hunger, poverty, and lack were constant features in their lives.

Jericho was a cursed city. Its foundations were destroyed when Joshua cursed it, long before these men were born. Yet, they were suffering the consequences of that curse. Many people wallow in the mud of poverty today because of the particular village, city, or town they come from or reside in. The effect of these long standing curses and other foundational problems manifest in their lives that nothing they lay their hands on ever succeeds. Some people were born in a particular town, nurtured with the water from its rivers and fed with fruits from its grounds, thereby partaking in the curse on that town and/or city and its land and water. They are definitely bound to share in its foundational problems, i.e., the curses or evil covenants.

I have been invited to minister in lots of villages, towns, and cities, and I noticed that many of them were still suffering from foundational problems that were ingrained in the land. The curses have affected the lives of the residents and their children.

Some of these people who moved from their hometowns carried these faulty foundations with them; yet, these curses and covenant bondage are still manifested in the new locations to which they moved.

In the course of my ministrations, I have encountered children of African origin living in abject poverty in the United States, United Kingdom, Europe, and Japan, etc. They live unfulfilled and unprogressive lives, even after studying and acquiring good education, they keep on experiencing terrible setbacks in their endeavors. Such people need to examine their foundations, just as the men of the city of Jericho did when they met Elisha. The men of Jericho were in a terrible state. Elisha came on the

Many people today are suffering because of the place they come from; much wickedness done by the first land owners passed on to their children.

scene and proffered a solution. Thank God for the Spirit of God in the life of Prophet Elisha. He was led to the very source of these problems – the spring or the fountain, the very foundation of the water. In our different churches today, many ministers of the gospel are being frustrated for their inability to help. The Bible says:

> *"And he said, Bring me a new cruse, and put salt therein. And they brought it to him.*
> *And he went forth unto the spring of the waters, and cast the salt in there, and said, Thus saith the LORD, I have healed these waters; there shall not be from thence any more death or barren land.*
> *So the waters were healed unto this day, according to the saying of Elisha which he spake."* **(2 Kings 2:20-22)**

If the root of the problem had not been attacked, the people of Jericho would never have had a permanent solution. If they had applied temporary measures, they most certainly would have continued to experience the same recurrent problems. At best, with the simple prayers of faith, they might enjoy some temporary relief. If they had not attacked their problems at the very foundation, they would still have continued to record failure in their lives.

Let me illustrate further with a pathetic but true story of a young woman who could not get married. She was a paragon of beauty, a true child of God, well behaved and prayerful. She prayed hard asking God to give her the husband of her dream; unfortunately, all of her testimonies were sad stories. Six times she had tried to get married, and six times she encountered disappointments. A suitor would come, woo her, and at the point of planning the wedding, something would go wrong. Every time, the young man would turn cold and dump her like a filthy, smelly rag. And this happened six, horrible times!

She didn't know what the problem was, but she knew there was a problem. Then one day, she attended one of our crusades where it was revealed that at birth, witches had tampered with her life. At the time a man showed interest in her, at night, the witches would go to her and replace her head with that of a wrinkled, ugly old woman, to scare away any man who proposes marriage to her!

I actually saw her rightful head being exchanged with a demonic one. The demonic head stood in the way of her success in life. While that condition remained, her success potential (especially in the area of marriage) was zero. However, she was set free through the mercy of God during a deliverance session.

The prayer of deliverance is what many people need today. Many Christian families fast and pray for long periods of time over particular problems without getting results; I will still encourage them not to relent in their efforts. The problem of faulty foundations calls for strategic revelation and concerted prayer and fasting. The problems that were introduced into your foundation will continue to torment you until you separate yourself from them through deliverance prayers. This is fundamental for just about every believer.

> **If your foundation has been tampered with, it may be the explanation for what you are going through; even after you have fasted and prayed hard.**

There was a young African who traveled overseas in search of the *"Golden Fleece."* After successfully obtaining university degrees in three different disciplines, he returned home to Nigeria and settled down in the commercial city of Lagos. The time came for him to get a good job and with his excellent qualifications that should have been an easy task, but he met with brick walls wherever he went. He could not secure any employment. He spent several years searching for a job, but could not locate one. He searched everywhere: the federal, state, and government organizations; private establishments; and so on. He even moved from the south of the country (Lagos) up north to try his luck in another city. All he encountered were brick walls. While his friends were establishing themselves in all works of life, he was suffering severe deprivation and poverty. He couldn't understand why his plight was so frustrating and unproductive.

One day, he was invited to a 3-day deliverance program. He attended this program because he was at a point in his life where he was ready to try anything. On the last day of the event, he had a revelation while he was sleeping at home. He saw a baby that had just been born. A woman came, rejoiced with the new mother and performed the traditional bath of the baby. Unknown to anybody, the woman who had also offered to help bury the placenta, secretly wrapped it up and took it to a fetish priest; this was the normal practice in that locality. The fetish priest then threw the placenta into a burning fire where he added other fetish items. The baby began to cry in anguish.

As the story unfolded, the jobless man who was dreaming suddenly realized that he was that suffering baby. At that point, he started crying. Suddenly, something miraculous happened. In the dream, an invisible hand started coming down from heaven. The hand reached down and put the fire out. It took the placenta and gave it back to the baby. The baby stopped crying, grabbed the placenta, shrieked happily and started laughing. That was the end of the dream and the brother woke up.

The Holy Spirit told him that he had just witnessed the story of his life. He was over forty years of age and he didn't know that he had a foundational problem, but God was ready to set him free.

From that day, things changed for him; the Lord opened many doors for him and he began to prosper. At the first office he visited after that night (seeking employment), he was given a contract worth $35,000.00. The Lord had opened the brother's eyes to see that things were terribly wrong with his foundation. The problem started from birth, but after prayers of deliverance were made, he was fully delivered and set free. His faulty foundation was rebuilt.

Remember:

"If the foundations be destroyed, what can the righteous do?" (Psalm 11:3)

The righteous can do nothing; it is God Who can do something. The righteous should seek deliverance and God will deliver them and help them rebuild their faulty foundation.

Fetish priests and other agents of the devil know that the best time to steal the glory of an individual is at birth. If you have fallen prey to them and you have been struggling on earth, it is most likely due to a problem that was created at the very foundation of your life, and it must be dealt with. Then you will begin to succeed and prosper.

God in His infinite mercy will set you free. Amen!

CHAPTER 3

DEMONIC COVENANTS AND POSSESSION

S in is the source of suffering in man. Right from the time Adam disobeyed God and ate the forbidden fruit in the Garden of Eden, sin entered into the world, and every man born of a woman inherited the nature of sin. The presence of God left man because God cannot behold sin. The prince of darkness (the devil) took over and sent his messengers (the demons) to move in and reign supreme over the life of man. Sin therefore is the primary cause of demonic possession.

We can safely say that anybody who lives in sin is a slave of the devil. But God Who is so kind and merciful, out of love sent His only begotten Son (Jesus Christ) to die for the sins of mankind. Jesus is the only One Who can save us from the consequences of our sins:

"Neither is there salvation in any other: for there is none other name under heaven given among men, whereby we must be saved.' (Acts 4:12)

When we believe in Jesus Christ and accept Him as our Lord and Savior, the devil stops being our father and God adopts us as His sons:

"...To redeem them that were under the law, that we might receive the adoption of sons.' (Galatians 4:5)

We become born again; we also become new creatures.

Ordinarily, one will expect that a born again Christian will be free from demons and their activities, but as you have seen from the story of my life so far, a true child of God can be under demonic affliction, oppression, and obsession. And as long as he (the Christian) stays in that position, he can never make any progress in life.

This truth has confounded many. It is commonly thought that since old things have passed away, we should not have to suffer anything from the past.

"Therefore if any man be in Christ, he is a new creature: old things are passed away; behold, all things are become new." (2 Corinthians 5:17)

If **'all things are become new,'** why then should a Christian continue to suffer setbacks, poverty, and frustrations that were inflicted on them by demons? We need to understand some fundamental truths concerning this.

Man consists of spirit, soul, and body. When we become born again, only our spirit is renewed or becomes regenerated; only the spirit becomes a new man. It comes alive. It replaces the nature of sin with the nature of God and becomes the dwelling place of the Holy Spirit.

"Jesus answered and said unto him, "If a man loves Me, he will keep My words: and My Father will love him, and We will come unto him, and make Our abode with him." (John 14:23)

When the spirit of man becomes the abode of God, demons or evil spirits cannot have access to that part of a Christian. God is righteous; demons are unrighteous. God is light while demons are the opposite.

> *"Be ye not unequally yoked together with unbelievers: for what fellowship hath righteousness with unrighteousness? And what communion hath light with darkness?"*
> **(2 Corinthians 6:14)**

The soul, on the other hand, is not saved at the new birth, or the body. And because of this, they are both still open to demonic attacks and afflictions.

Concerning the soul:

> *"Wherefore lay apart all filthiness and superfluity of naughtiness, and receive with meekness the engrafted word, which is able to save your souls.*
> *But be ye doers of the word, and nor hearers only, deceiving your own selves."* **(James 1:21-22)**

The soul consists of the mind, will, and emotions. It takes time and obedience to the Word of God for the soul to be saved. The body can remain oppressed by the devil. This is why it is still possible for Christians to suffer physical ailments and disabilities. During the ministry of our Lord Jesus Christ here on earth, He had to deliver many from demonic oppressions of the body and soul. An example of this is given below:

> *"And, behold, there was a woman which had a spirit of infirmity eighteen years, and was bowed together, and could in no wise lift up herself.*
> *And when Jesus saw her, he called her to Him, and said unto her, "Woman, thou art loosed from thine infirmity."*
> *And He laid His hands on her: and immediately she was made straight, and glorified God."* **(Luke 13:11-13)**

It is written that God delivered many who suffered all manner of diseases by the Apostle Paul's hands. These diseases were caused by demons.

"...So that from his body were brought unto the sick handkerchiefs or aprons, and the diseases from them, and the evil spirits went out of them." **(Acts 19:12)**

God is a powerful God. All power has been given to our Lord Jesus Christ, and the Bible says:

"That at the name of Jesus every knee should bow, of things in heaven, and things in earth, and things under the earth;
And that every tongue should confess that Jesus Christ is Lord, to the glory of God the Father." **(Philippians 2:10-11)**

Why then should God allow His children to suffer under Satan's yoke? At this point, we must stress a few facts: God allows this because He is a just God. He does only what is right. The devil has no power outside of what God allows him. God is not a wicked God Who wishes to unleash undue punishment on His children. If God permits the devil to torment His children, there must be a good reason for it.

As the Lord continued to open my eyes, I could see very clearly that many Christians suffer seriously from the hands of the devil because of the evil covenants and curses embedded in their lives or in their families. God respects covenants: human or spiritual, good or evil. He does not violate them and He does not interfere in other people's covenants, because He is a righteous Judge.

Covenants are formal agreements that are legally binding, whether in heaven or earth, be it spiritual or physical. Any form of infringement or violation of such covenants always attracts one form of punishment or another, especially regarding curses. These covenants and curses stay in force from one generation to another in the families of those concerned.

HOW DO THESE COVENANTS AND CURSES COME INTO OUR LIVES?

(1) Through Parents' Religious Activities

The story of my life shows that demonic covenants and possession enter into the lives of many largely through the ignorant activities of their parents and forefathers. In their search for power, protection, and the material things of life, such parents dabbled into the kingdom of darkness. Unknown to them, dining with the devil will have grave consequences and repercussions on their families for generations to come.

My father thought he was protecting me when, even before I was born, he initiated me into several cults. He thought he was incubating and protecting me with power by using all those concoctions he forced down my throat as a baby. When he rubbed the incisions he made on my body with powerful potions and charmed powdery substances, he thought he was securing the future of his firstborn son. But at each instance, he was actually selling me to the devil! While growing up, I didn't know the implication of all these things that were done. This is also the plight of many believers.

Satan, *"the deceiver,"* has played on this lack of knowledge from time immemorial. In his subtle way, he lured our parents into making a series of covenants with the kingdom of darkness.

> ***"Because ye have said, We have made a covenant with death, and with hell are we at agreement; when the overflowing scourge shall pass through, it shall not come unto us: for we have made lies our refuge, and under falsehood have we hid ourselves:"*** (Isaiah 28:15)

When our fathers were told to offer animals, such as dogs, poultry, goats, etc., as sacrifices to their small gods, little did they know that they were either making blood covenants with the devil or upholding the covenants already made by their own fathers. This is also the case when fetish priests, under the guise of giving them power, healing or protection, ask them to make incisions on their bodies and rub some demonic powder on the cuts. To them, these were innocent rituals and herbal remedies, but God explicitly warns:

"Ye shall not make any cuttings in your flesh for the dead, nor print any marks upon you: I am the LORD." **(Leviticus 19:28)**

There are many other rituals that have kept people under demonic covenants. As stated earlier, these covenants do carry promises and curses with them. When the terms of these covenants are violated, when the promises are broken, the curses attached to them come into effect in a negative way.

Some women who have had problems with child bearing, barrenness, miscarriages, and still births — in their search for children — have consulted with some river spirits with promises that if their prayers were answered, they would offer certain sacrifices to the spirits, either weekly, monthly or annually. Inadvertently, they have dedicated these children to the river spirits or the demonic powers controlling them.

This is known as *"marine initiation."* Such children are invariably surrounded by bad luck, lack of faithfulness, poverty, and 'anti-success' spirits, sexual perversions, etc., if they do not serve these spirits from where they were covenanted. This is just an example; it is also applicable to all demonic covenants.

"Thou shalt have no other gods before Me." (Exodus 20:3)

The Lord's injunction is that we should have nothing to do with other gods, but our parents had a lot to do with idols. Whether they were aware of this holy order or not, their ignorance did not absolve them from the consequences of this disobedience; now the curse of their disobedience has come to haunt and affect the lives of their children. Most demonic covenants that operate in our lives were not directly contracted by us, but by our parents or by our ancestors through false religious activities.

God has made all the necessary provision to forgive our sins and have our spirit man renewed. However, God will not have anything to do with our demonic covenants. We have to come to a decision concerning the covenants in our lives, a choice or decision in which we will decide if we want to continue in such unholy alliances or not.

(2) Through The Womb

On many occasions, demons enter into a child while yet unborn or at birth. Demons can easily possess the fetus where there is shock arising from fear or trauma on the part of the mother; particularly where there is a disagreement between the parents over the pregnancy – for example. Think about a baby (or fetus) who grew in a demonic womb of a witch (mother); such a child has been under an evil covenant before birth.

> **Spirits can enter into people at any age, but they have been known to come especially at the time of birth or during childhood.**

Spirits of rejection or abortion often enter during pregnancy, in cases where the mother's spirit rejects the child or the mother has feelings of personal rejection. This is particularly true if the mother desires to abort the pregnancy. These spirits can enter in the baby before birth and remain there throughout its life. Once the spirit of rejection has entered, it could bring with it many other spirits. When the spirit of fear is allowed to enter into a marriage, the demons of fear can easily enter into the children produced by such a marriage. This type of demonic possession can bring about physical afflictions, such as asthma.

These spirits may lie dormant for many years before they finally begin to manifest. In today's society, considering the major breakdown of marriages, the rate of unmarried men and women sleeping together, getting pregnant, and having children under acrimonious circumstances, we should expect a great outpouring of demonic activities among young people. A case in point: remember the wickedness that surrounded my parent's marriage and the consequences on my life.

(3) Parental Disobedience

Where parents, particularly fathers, do not walk in the ways of the Lord, the home is open to demonic attacks, and the children usually grow up in rebellion. If there is no teaching of the Word of God in the home, there are no absolute values for the children to subscribe to. As the children grow up, there is nothing to prevent them from engaging in all kinds of sexual immorality and other sinful practices, which in turn bring about demonic possession.

For instance, parents who encourage or are neutral to their children's habit of smoking and drinking will see them become addicted to these habits. These habits are sinful, and Satan uses them as an avenue to enter into these young lives. They ultimately become possessed and afflicted.

(4) Occult Involvement

Before some people became born again believers, they had been involved in some form of association or group with occult connections. In some cases, it could be their parents or ancestors who were involved in cults, like the Ogboni Society, the Ubiquitous AMORC (Ancient Mystic Order Rosae Crucis), the Rosicrucian Order, and so on. These linking associations (whatever the involvement) paved the way for demonic activities in the lives of such people.

(5) Material Possessions

Sometimes we harbor occultic or demonic books or objects in our homes, and these are an abomination in the eyes of God.

"Neither shalt thou bring an abomination into thine house, lest thou be a cursed thing like it: but thou shalt utterly detest it, and thou shalt utterly abhor it; for it is a cursed thing." **(Deuteronomy 7:26)**

We should particularly be aware of any images or carvings with any occult significance, e.g., zodiac pendants, rings and posters, special regalia, Halloween condors, etc. If you keep demonic properties in your home, you can rest assure that demons will reside with you.

(6) Divination

(Joshua 13:22; 1 Samuel 6:2, 28:8; 2 Kings 17:17; Isaiah 3:2, 44:25; Jeremiah 27:9, 29:8; Ezekiel 13:6, 9, 23; 21:21, 23, 29; 22:28; Micah 3:6-7, 11; Zechariah 10:2)

Divination is the act of giving false prophecy or seeking the will of the gods through the spiritual realm by examining and interpreting omens or manipulating people by depicting the past and trying to foretell the future by demonic powers. A definition of 'divination' states: **'it is the practice of attempting to foretell future events or discover hidden knowledge by occult or supernatural means'** (http://dictionary.reference.com). A lot of false pastors and prophets use the spirit of divination. Many people believe that the only way to be *"led"* is through visions, but God does not give visions all the time to His servants and prophets. My late father would guide many through the spirit of divination; his clientele included many **"men and women of God"** who sought for power at all costs.

Many believers, who are always searching for prophets and seers on every issue and decision of their lives, should also realize that it is possible to be led astray. Divine prophecy will bring out a definite answer to the situation instead of leading to confusion or depression. However, there are some pastors and prophets who operate ignorantly under these influences of familiar spirits or witchcraft. They might not know that their ability to see is actually from an evil source. Stop seeking directions from star readers, etc.

The Lord has warned us seriously:

> *"There shall not be found among you any one that maketh his son or daughter to pass through the fire, or that useth divination, or an observer of times, or an enchanter, or a witch."* **(Deuteronomy 18:10)**

Divination is a serious offence that will not go unpunished.

> *"Ye shall not eat anything with the blood: neither shall ye use enchantment, nor observe times."* **(Leviticus 19:26)**

> *"And he made his son pass through the fire, and observed the times, and used enchantments, and dealt with familiar spirits and wizards: he wrought much wickedness in the sight of the LORD, to provoke him to anger."* **(2 Kings 21:6)**

(7) Relating To The Dead

(Deuteronomy 12:31, 14:1-2, 18:10; 2 Kings 17:17)

> *"Ye are the children of the LORD your GOD: ye shall not cut yourselves, nor make any baldness between your eyes for the dead. For thou art an holy people unto the LORD thy God, and the LORD hath chosen thee to be a peculiar people unto Himself, above all the nations that are upon the earth."* **(Deuteronomy 14:1-2)**

God is a jealous God. He demands loyalty and obedience from His children. Therefore, He warns us to avoid any practice that is abominable in His sight. In some tribes, it is customary and mandatory for people to shave their hair upon the death of a family member. Such practice is nothing but the renewal of a covenant with demonic forces made by one's ancestors.

(8) Sorcery

(Deuteronomy 18:10, 14; Leviticus 19:26; 2 Kings 21:6; Isaiah 2:6; Micah 5:12)

Sorcery is an attempt to control and manipulate circumstances or people through the power given by demons or evil spirits. There are two types of manipulators:

i. **Aggressive Manipulators**
   These are those who are under witchcraft manipulation that have accepted evil suggestions forced on them, whether they want it or not. They cannot control their manifestations no matter how hard they try.

ii. **Soft Manipulators**
   This type of manipulation is not aggressive. Soft manipulators bring their suggestions to their victims once in a while and very subtly. However, they will not allow their victim any rest until they succeed in making that individual do that which was suggested to them without making it look like it was forced on them.

Aggressive and soft manipulators are witches and wizards who use their powers as remote control devices to destroy the destinies of their victims.

(9) Transference From Other People

There are several ways through which demons can be transferred from one person to another.

(i) **Sex**
For instance, in the act of sexual intercourse outside of marriage, demonic activities can occur readily as demons are transferred from one person to another. In the case of a Christian marriage, this should not happen if both parties are fully committed to Jesus Christ. Where one party is not committed, the other party needs to know how to apply the sanctifying power of the Blood of Jesus, in order to stay free from demons. One can enter into demonic covenants through wrongful acts of sex.

(ii) **Wrong Association**
In any occult organization or group, or in a church where the leaders are not born again, a dominating personality *(anyone who serves as an authoritative role model)* can transfer spirits to other people either in ignorance or by choice. In a secular organization or in the Church, admiring, doting, or adoring members can be moved by the charisma of the authoritative individual, so much that they begin to replicate or imitate all of his habits, personality, character, and appearance. This can take the form of having the same haircut, wearing the same type of clothes, having the same manner of speech, etc. This opens up such people to the transference of spirits from those they are copying.

(iii) **Through Deliverance**
When we, as men of God, minister deliverance to others, we need to hold firmly to the authority of Jesus Christ; otherwise, the demons expelled from those we minster to may seek to attack us. If they do attack us, then we need to know how to resist them through the Blood of Jesus. In particular, this means maintaining a wholesome mind when ministering to persons of the opposite sex. In such a case, we should always ensure that there is another person of the opposite sex present with us. A man should never minister to a woman alone, or vice versa.

(iv) Soul Ties

A man or woman may be subject to a matriarchal spirit from a controlling mother, or a dominating and controlling patriarchal spirit from the father. An unhealthy domination by either parent over the child will cause a dominating spirit to be easily transferred into the child. As a result, one may observe that the kind of lives our parents and ancestors lived, and the choices they made, could determine the course or our lives now and in the distant future.

(v) Demonic Laying On Of Hands

Not everyone should be allowed to lay hands on believers (or on anybody else for that matter). Only anointed men of God under God's true leading, should be allowed to do this. As a believer, you must be very cautious and careful as to whom you allow lay hands on you; otherwise, there might be an unhealthy transference of unclean forces. One of the most powerful methods used by my father in destroying destinies was to lay hands on his victims.

SECTION B

Ancestral Yokes

"And it shall come to pass in that day, that his burden shall be taken away from off thy shoulder, and his yoke from off thy neck, and the yoke shall be destroyed because of the anointing."
(Isaiah 10:27)

"And they shall no more offer sacrifices unto devils, after whom they have gone a whoring. This shall be a statute for ever unto them throughout their generations."
(Leviticus 17:7)

CHAPTER 4

INHERITED FAMILY CURSES

A lot of people stumble through life without being able to fully tap into the various blessings that God has prepared for them. They stagger from one serious problem to another, from one major disaster to another, and they never achieve their full potentials. If such people were to be factories or manufacturing companies, their capacity utilization would never go above 20 or 30 percent at any point in their lifetime.

In almost all of these cases, the cause of bondage is usually not their fault; the source of their problems can be traced to curses inherited and passed down the family line from their ancestors or forefathers. Even more painful is the fact that most people or families struggling under such curses are often ignorant of the source of their troubles.

COMMON PATTERNS

You can easily see a clear pattern in families that suffer from inherited curses: certain peculiar problems occur from generation to generation. For instance, poverty could be an endemic in the family. From generation to generation, the family turns out lines of paupers, people who are so poor they just manage to survive from one day to the next. In some other cases, it could be that the members of the family always get married very late in life, or that members of the family tend to die at a young age – they don't live beyond 45 years of age.

If your family falls within a particular category and, upon deep scrutiny of your life and progress, you may be shocked to find that you are heading for a similar end. For example, if you are mature in age yet are still unmarried, you are well on your way to confirming the recurring pattern of late marriages within the family. In that case, it is likely that you have inherited a family curse.

I came across a woman who discovered a particular truth about her family before it was too late for her. She came to me for counseling and prayers; according to her story, every first male child born into her family dies around the age of forty. If the firstborn was a female, at about that same age, she would go insane. Without a doubt, this was an inherited family curse and I told her so. The truth helped her. We knew how and where to direct our prayers of deliverance. God rolled the curse away from her life. She is now over fifty years old; she is alive and healthy.

There are different examples of how inherited family curses wreak havoc in the lives of many unsuspecting Christians. Sometimes, it takes a thorough examination of one's life, situation, and family to know that there is a problem. Occurrences that you think are not important may turn out to be very pivotal to your progress. For example, if your father found it difficult to live with one wife, even if you are married to a queen, the same fate is likely to befall you unless you break it.

If you are a woman and your mother was the type that went from one man to another, and was never really able to settle down — even if your husband gives you the whole world — the evil spirits operating in your family lineage will drive you out of wedlock, unless the power of the Lord breaks their grip.

In some families, nobody becomes successful in life, despite all the money invested to obtain the best form of education available. In other families, every old person loses their sight at a certain age – if you are at that age in your family, you need to examine yourself. You are certain to have that same problem even if you are a born again Christian!

If an inherited curse is at work, you are bound to suffer its consequences, except you pray the prayer of deliverance to break this curse. Unfortunately, many people who suffer these predicaments pray incorrectly because they are ignorant of the sort of battle with which they are confronted.

THE ROOT CAUSE OF INHERITED FAMILY CURSES

(1) Idol Worship

The main cause of family curses is the sin of idol worship. Concerning this, God explicitly warns:

> *"Thou shalt have no other gods before Me.*
> *Thou shalt not make unto thee any graven image, or any likeness of any thing that is in heaven above, or that is in the earth beneath, or that is in the water under the earth. Thou shalt not bow down thyself to them, nor serve them: for I the LORD thy GOD am a jealous God, visiting the iniquity of the fathers upon the children unto the third and fourth generation of them that hate me.'* **(Exodus 20:3-5)**

The warning is clear, unequivocal, and unambiguous. God said we should neither worship nor serve idols. He says if we do, He will visit the iniquities on succeeding generations. It is immaterial whether you are ignorant of the consequences of your actions or not; that is not God's problem. When God says something, He means it and He does it; He keeps to His Word.

Note therefore, that every time you secretly visit the fetish priest, star readers, and astrologers, or participate in some false religion, you are bringing curses on the lives of your children. And these curses will pass from generation to generation for four hundred years. The curses could attract poverty, sickness, diseases, or marital problems. Whatever the case, these curses will last for four generations.

My own life aptly illustrates this fact. My father was an idol worshipper, and my life was miserable until 1987 when God delivered me. The vicious cycle of trials and tribulations that I underwent is the usual fate that awaits the children of witch doctors, Alfas (Muslim Clerics), traditional warriors and rulers, cult members, and those who worship idols in whatever form including the practice of Halloween. Offspring who achieve some measure of success in life will be brought down at one point or the other, because God is a jealous God *"visiting the iniquity of the fathers upon the children."*

It doesn't matter if your father, the idol worshipper, gave his life to Christ and became born again two days or two years before his death; the curse will keep rolling down the line unless it is purposely broken. God is just; He keeps His Word and stands by the law.

The gravity of the problem of inherited family curses for anyone with faulty foundations and for people of every culture of this world (not just of African origin), cannot be overemphasized. Thanks be to God, idol worship will be a thing of the past, and the gospel is here to take over.

Interestingly, apart from Jesus, Who was a 'super deliverance Minister,' there were two other powerful deliverance ministers in the Bible: Moses in the Old Testament and Paul in the New Testament. Perhaps if they had not been deliverance ministers, they would not have been successful in their missions.

Paul was a missionary to the Gentiles who were principally idol worshippers. He had to be a deliverance minister; otherwise, he would not have been able to achieve much in his ministry. Moses, for his part, was born in Egypt, here in Africa where idol worship was the norm.

These two great men of God had revealing and insightful things to say in the Bible about demons, witchcraft, and other such phenomena. For instance, the practice of cutting marks or making incisions on the face and/or other parts of the body was (and to an extent still is) rampant in Africa, and now has become a fashionable art form in America and all over the world (popularly known as **Tattoos**). However, there is a clear warning in the law of God concerning this:

> *"Ye are the children of the LORD your GOD: ye shall not cut yourselves, nor make any baldness between your eyes for the dead."* **(Deuteronomy 14:1)**

Moses was always talking about evil spirits and wizards, and Paul made it clear that:

> *"For we wrestle not against flesh and blood, but against principalities, against powers, against the rulers of the darkness of this world, against spiritual wickedness in high places."* **(Ephesians 6:12)**

Idol worshippers are not children of God; they are clearly in league with the very forces that Paul says we war against. God hates idol worship with a sincere hatred. And the measure of His contempt for this act is evident in the book of Jeremiah, where He exposes the powerlessness of idols and the folly of their worshippers:

> *"For the customs of the people are vain: for one cutteth a tree out of the forest, the work of the hands of the workman, with the axe.*
> *They deck it with silver and with gold; they fasten it with nails and with hammers, that it move not.*
> *They are upright as the palm tree, but speak not: they must needs be borne, because they cannot go. Be not afraid of them; for they cannot do evil, neither also is it in them to do good."* **(Jeremiah 10:3-5)**

This apt description mirrors a peculiar form of idolatry I have seen practiced among some tribes in Africa (specifically the Yoruba tribe of Western Nigeria), namely, the worship of twins! Whenever twins are born in this particular tribe, the children are automatically named: ***"Taiwo"*** (meaning ***"the first of the two to taste the world"***) and ***"Kehinde"*** (meaning ***"the one bringing up the rear"***). In the event that one of them dies, the family makes a wooden carving called ***"Orisa Ibeji"*** (***twin idol***) to represent the dead twin. This lifeless piece of wood then becomes an object of worship, and the family would relate to it as though it were the living sibling to the surviving twin.

Sometime ago, I was blessed with a set of twins. Just like my father who got married when he was close to fifty years of age, I also got married somewhat late in life. Since we were late starters – in marriage, my wife and I prayed to God to take us through an express route so that we could have all the children we wanted before age and other natural obstacles set in. To the glory of God, He answered our prayers and gave us two boys (my twin sons).

The events that were to follow cast further light on the dangerous practice of the idol worship of twins among the Yoruba tribe of Western Nigeria. Immediately after the birth of my twins was announced, traditional dancers descended on my home, singing the praises of these little tots, and calling them "Orisa Meji" (meaning "two idols"). But I put my foot down and said, "Not in my house!" I chased them away and cancelled their declarations.

Since it was customary to hail (or praise) twins, the family members who were among the rejoicing crowd were not happy with me. They believed that what I did was a taboo, and that I was breaking our local tradition. Of course, they believed that my boys would not live long as a result of my not performing the rituals. But I stood my ground!

God gave me two sons, David and Joseph, not two idols. To the glory of God, my sons are alive and well today. If you want real twins, go to God in prayer. A lot of people get into trouble because in their desperate search for children, they abandon God and go to consult with evil spirits to seek the face of idols.

There is a tendency on the part of some people to think that it is only when they lie prostrate before a carved object, offering sacrifices in a shrine, that a sin or transgression has been committed. Let me point out here that there are many other seemingly innocuous acts that we engage in, all in the name of tradition or custom that are expressions of idol worship.

(2) Demonic Names

Some family curses also come from the demonic names that these families adopt; names derived from family idols. This is also common in many cultures. In America, for example, we do not attach any importance to names and their meanings; as a result, we answer to any name, good or evil. In Africa, those who worship certain rivers adopt the names of such rivers; for example, in the Yoruba tribe of Western Nigeria, we have: "Oshun," "Osa," "Okun," and so on. They use such names as prefixes to their family and first names. Other names begin with some other idols such as: "Sango," "Ogun," "Oya," "Egun," "Orisa," "Awo," and so on.

Others believe in their family's familiar spirits, i.e., spirits that operate within the family. As a result, any child born into such a family and is perceived to resemble a dead relative (maybe grandmother or grandfather), has a special name (or prefix) attached to his or her name. This is so because the child is seen as a reincarnated being (of that dead relative); he or she becomes venerated – an object of worship. When looking at a typical Yoruba family, it is rare not to find someone with the name: "Babatunde" (meaning "Father is back"), "Babajide" (meaning "Father has risen"), "Iyabo" or "Yetunde" (meaning "Mother has come"), "Yewande" ("Mother has sought me out"), and so on.

> **The knowledge you possess in God will give you power to overcome and stand against cultural and traditional idolatry in any form.**

(3) Curses Pronounced On The Family

Back in the day, there were lots of disagreements, arguments, and quarrellings between families: these disagreements stemmed from bitter land disputes, wife snatching, broken marriages, and other diverse marital issues, disputes over chieftaincy titles and all kinds of acrimonious rivalries. In the course of these quarrels, many unwholesome steps were taken by different families. Among other things, they pronounced curses on each other. Unfortunately, some of those curses have affected many lives and have continued to operate within those families. Long after the original parties in the dispute had died and the dispute has been forgotten, children born into such families continue to suffer the consequences of the curses pronounced on their ancestors.

When my father snatched my mother from her rightful husband, the man's family was not happy about it. Curses were exchanged between his family and my father's family. Although at this time I was not yet born, I suffered the consequences of those curses that my father brought upon the family. Every one of his children did.

Perhaps one of the most vivid examples of how an inherited family curse can wreak havoc in the life of an innocent person is seen in one of Abraham's experiences. His story also offers us another confirmation that the Word of God will stand, no matter who you are.

> **There are many who name their children without knowing the meaning of the name; this is dangerous. You could be pronouncing curses on them through their name.**

Abraham was a friend of God, yet he was barren well into his old age. He was not a sinner as he conversed with God on a regular basis. However, Abraham was ignorant of the source of his problems; he had inherited a curse but was not aware of it – just like you and I. In the Bible, we see a clear pattern that confirms that Abraham's problem was inherited. His father "Terah" was an idol worshipper. The generations before his father had a record of giving birth to their first child quite early in life – between the ages of 29 and 35. It was Terah who broke that cycle:

vs. 12 – And Arphaxad lived <u>five and thirty years</u>, and begat Salah...
vs. 14 – And Salah lived <u>thirty years</u>, and begat Eber...
vs. 16 – And Eber lived <u>four and thirty years</u>, and begat Peleg...
vs. 18 – And Peleg lived <u>thirty years</u>, and begat Reu...
vs. 20 – And Reu lived <u>two and thirty years</u>, and begat Serug...

vs. 22 – And Serug lived <u>thirty years</u>, and begat Nahor...
vs. 24 – And Nahor lived <u>nine and twenty years</u>, and begat Terah...
vs. 26 – And Terah lived <u>seventy years</u>, and begat Abram, Nahor, and Haran.
(Genesis 11:12-26)

Terah, an idol worshipper, was 70 years old when he had Abraham – meaning that he was barren for at least 35 years.

> *"And Joshua said unto all the people, Thus saith the Lord God of Israel, Your fathers dwelt on the other side of the flood in the old time, even Terah, the father of Abraham and the father of Nahor: and they served other gods."*
> *(Joshua 24:2)*

The curse therefore started from Terah and lasted for four generations: Isaac inherited this curse and so did Jacob his son. Abraham who was not a party to his father's offence, suffered for whatever it was Terah had done. And even though Abraham was so close to God, that any request He made to God was answered, this physical need of his (a child) was a problem that went unanswered. Of course God was merciful to him and subsequently answered his prayer for a child.

Note also that the length of the period of barrenness reduced with every generation:

- Terah was barren for 35 years
- Abraham was barren for 25 years
- Isaac was barren for 20 years
- Jacob was barren for 7 years.

For more clarification, read the following passages:

Terah	– Genesis 11:26
Abraham	– Genesis 21:5 (He was called when he was 75 years old)
Abraham & Sarah	– Genesis 12:4-5
Isaac	– Genesis 25:20, 21, 26
Jacob	– Genesis 30:1

(4) Curse Of Lying

It was not only the curse of barrenness that was upon Abraham's family; there was also the curse of lying and marital problems inherited directly from Abraham's bloodline. With little or no prompting, Abraham lied concerning Sarah his wife:

> *"And Abraham said of Sarah his wife, she is my sister…"(Genesis 20:2)*

Isaac also inherited this "lying spirit":

> *"And the men of the place asked him of his wife; and he said, she is my sister…"(Genesis 26:7)*

Lying was second nature to Jacob, Isaac's son. He lied to his old blind father so as to fraudulently obtain his brother Esau's blessings.

> *"And he came unto his father and said, My father: and he said, Here am I: who art thou, my son?*
> *And Jacob said unto his father, I am Esau thy firstborn; I have done according as thou badest me: arise, I pray thee, sit and eat of my venison, that thy soul may bless me." (Genesis 27:18, 19)*

Of course, Jacob's children told him cruel lies too, when they sold their brother Joseph into slavery and made Jacob believe he was dead. This completed the cycle of four generations of liars within Abraham's family.

(5) Traditional Marriage Rites

For some people, diverse curses enter into their lives on the day of their traditional or cultural wedding ceremonies. In certain parts of Africa, these ceremonies usually involve the presentation of such items as kolanuts, honey, bitter kolanuts, salt, etc. In most cases, the presentation of these items has deep demonic covenants attached to them.

Although the guests consume some of these items after the ceremony, family representatives would send portions of the items to their hometown or villages, to be offered to some family idol or juju. In most cases, the newlyweds are not aware of this. The bride and groom then proceed to the Church to carry out the Christian wedding ceremony, unaware of the covenant that has been made on their marriage.

Naturally as Christians, the couples move on with their lives, expecting to be blessed by the same God Who violently detests any contact with the idols that they have unknowingly made a pact with! Straight from church, some couples are paraded before people chanting their *"Praise names"* (***Oriki***). Among the Yoruba tribe of Western Nigeria, this is a lengthy poem singing praises of a person and his ancestral lineage, going back several generations. Unfortunately, none of these "Oriki" give praises to God or to Jesus, just to idols and demons.

As the man's ego becomes boosted by this relentless infusion of flattery and praise singing, what is actually happening is that the demons ruling the family have already possessed him, already having begun to manifest themselves in his body. As you receive the praise, you also activate the curses that run your family; which have now been empowered to operate in your life. This is one of the methods by which people transfer and renew curses in their families.

(6) Through The Womb

Another avenue for inheriting family curses is through the womb, where most of us stayed for nine months before we were born. While in the womb, an object called the 'umbilical cord' links fetus with a small placenta, through which the food taken in by the mother gets to the fetus. God cleanses this food for us. Also through this route curses and evil spirits can be transferred to the child being formed.

When you have identified a pattern of problems which points to the likelihood of an inherited family curse at work in your life, the next thing to do is to present yourself for deliverance prayers under the guidance of an anointed man of God. After fervent prayers, there will be reactions and solutions.

Sometimes the more you pray, the more the problems appear to be unmovable. Some people fast and pray, and sometimes join the prayer band or team, but the more they pray, the more they see themselves eating in their dreams (a manifestation of demonic oppression). The more they pray, the more they dream of men or women fondling and seducing them. This simply means that the demons are fighting back, initiating their victims all over again. You want to evict these demons, but they chain you down because they have discovered a covenant or a curse standing against you in their records.

When you continue to experience terrible dreams, especially in the midst of fervent prayer, it is the demons' saying to you, "We are here; we have not gone yet." Do not let physical or spiritual pride hinder you from seeking your freedom. Self-deliverance does not apply in all cases. God will give you freedom, in Jesus' name. However, you must take the right steps.

CHAPTER 5

DEMONIC INITIATIONS AND DEDICATIONS

Initiation is the process or ritual by which an individual is admitted into a covenant binding society.

Demonic dedication is the process or ritual of consecration or setting something or somebody apart for an unholy or evil purpose or an evil deity. Initiation can also be defined as Satan's method of evangelism. He (Satan) does not come openly, but he employs deceitful ploys and tricks. Anyone who has at one time or the other been involved in some form of cult, false religion, voodoo, palm reading, Halloween, or star reading needs deliverance.

There are different types of satanic initiations and dedications. Some initiations are easy to recognize while others need special illumination and spiritual revelation from God in order to be exposed. Some initiations are done openly, while others are disguised. Whatever the case, an initiation is binding, no matter the process. There is no such thing as a big or small initiation; all initiations are deadly.

> *"When thou art come into the land which the LORD thy God giveth thee, thou shalt not learn to do after the abominations of those nations. There shall not be found among you anyone that maketh his son or his daughter*

to pass through the fire, or that useth divination, or an observer of times, or an enchanter, or a witch. Or a charmer, or a consulter with familiar spirits, or a wizard, or a necromancer. For all that do these things are an abomination unto the LORD: and because of these abominations the LORD thy God doth drive them out from before thee." **(Deuteronomy 18:9-12)**

The above Scripture reveals some examples of those who need deliverance. People practicing or visiting those who practice divination, necromancy, palm readers, false religion, etc., need immediate deliverance, for they have been automatically initiated into the satanic kingdom. There are a variety of other examples that are not quoted in the above passage.

MAJOR SATANIC INITIATIONS AND DEDICATIONS

(1) Initiation Through Food Blessed By Satan Or His Agents

There was a certain woman in Nigeria who used to own a restaurant. She was very successful and had lots of customers, but the secret of her success was that she made an agreement with Satan. She was giving up babies as an offering in the spirit realm. One day, two believing brothers came in to eat. As the waitress was serving the food, the Holy Spirit opened the eyes of one of the brothers, and he saw a baby crying by the entrance, all covered in blood. He immediately told his friend and they decided to leave. Before leaving, they bound all the demonic strongholds of that restaurant; after that day, the woman's business went bankrupt.

Beware of Halloween goodies (candy, cookies, and so on) given to children. Halloween is witchcraft. In America, we eat all kinds of food without blessing or praying over it, even as Christians. Remember to bless your food before you eat.

(2) Initiation Through Dresses And Jewelry: Anything Dedicated To Satan

There was a born again sister who had a friend. One day, they both decided to go to the market to buy some jewelry. She did not know that her friend was a witch who was looking for a way to get her initiated. Her "witch" friend took her to another witch who was selling jewelry. The witch friend encouraged the born again sister to choose a necklace that was bewitched. On that night in her dream, the sister found herself in a meeting of witches. It took months of intensive prayers to break the covenant. Jewelry made to look like the cross (crucifix) with a circle on top of it is a satanic cross used in the church of Satan.

Be careful of what you wear. Jewelry or clothing designed with the images of cursed animals, such as snakes, will be a place of habitation for snake spirits that destroy and wreck lives spiritually.

Another way witchcraft agents recruit and initiate people is by taking one of the belongings of their victim. The victim will simply notice that a particular belonging or item of clothing is missing; this missing item may not be found or it may eventually be found in a strange place.

(3) Initiation Through Reading Books Inspired By Satan

Just as God inspired the Bible, evil forces have inspired some books. Just as a book written by an anointed man of God can bring refreshment, healing, or restoration, a book written by satanic agents can affect the reader negatively. Moreover, the eyes are also a point of contact for initiation. Initiation can take place through the eyes when you read books, watch pornographic movies, demonic horror movies, and questionable television programs that are all inspired by demons.

(4) Initiation Through SEX

This is one of the easiest ways through which people get contaminated and initiated. Such demonic people invade the Church looking for fresh prey to destroy. Once a sexual act has been committed, initiation has taken place, and the victim starts doing things that are out of tune. A man was once involved in a relationship with a certain lady. One night in his dream, he found himself on top of the sea with the lady. The lady informed him that she was going to show him her real house. The next second, they were at the bottom of the sea. Behold, there was a beautiful city in the sea. The lady took the man around and showed him a particular place where men's sperm were stored. She said it was the place where they destroyed destinies, especially those that were divinely programmed by God to succeed. The man said that there was a propelling force that hindered him from running away.

> Seek deliverance from proven and anointed Ministers. Do not let spiritual pride hold you back from getting your release.

The lady took him to another place that was filled with skeletons. She said it was the place where they stored the bones of all the people they had eaten. They then take the bones and remodel them. For example, they make them into children, and they give to all barren women who come to them in their quest for children. After showing him round the city, they got married underneath the sea, and there was a great celebration.

When the man woke up, he suffered a terrible headache. He began a desperate search for a church, because he knew that a link had been established between him and the lady, and he no longer wanted to have anything to do with her.

(5) Initiation Through Sex With Witches

As believers, we should realize the importance of territorial laws. For example, having sex with witches knowingly or unknowingly is a violation of territorial laws, and it results in initiation or dedication into witchcraft. There are many similar laws that should not be violated in the spiritual realm, lest one becomes a victim of demonic attacks. Wearing clothes that are charmed by witches is another territorial violation. The result is witchcraft assault.

(6) Initiation Through Demonic Child Naming Ceremonies And Dedications

Somebody once narrated how each time a baby was named in their family, a piece of white cloth would be spread over a calabash filled with concoctions. This is an example of how babies are dedicated (to the satanic kingdom); such covenants become very hard to break even at the age of forty. Satan is wicked, he does not joke with covenants. He will ensure that the stipulations of the covenants are executed.

(7) Initiation Through Demonic Ordinations

Occult preachers have ordained some; such people need deliverance. How many priests and ministers of God have sold their souls to the devil?

(8) Other Major Initiations:

1. Visiting Spiritualists **(Micah 1:7; Romans 1:24, 26, 27; 1 Corinthians 10:7-8; Revelation 2:14, 20-22)**
2. Witchcraft marks printed on the body (incisions, tattoos, etc.)
3. Consulting the dead
4. Consulting star readers (Astrology, horoscope, etc.)
5. Consulting palm readers
6. Demonic hair attachments
7. Partaking in demonic communion

8. Involvement in false religion (Rosicrucian Fraternity, Christian Science, Eckankar, etc.)
9. Practicing human sacrifice **(Leviticus 18:21; 20:2-5; Deuteronomy 12:31)**

CHAPTER 6

WITCHCRAFT AND SPIRITUAL MANIPULATORS

(Exodus 22:18; Leviticus 19:31; 1 Samuel 28:7-23)

Witchcraft is commonly defined as the use of magical powers to influence, control, or manipulate people or events. It is commonly known as sorcery, and has been an integral part of the folklore of many societies for centuries.

It is absolute foolishness to think that witchcraft or initiation into witchcraft is only found in the remote parts of Africa or India. Truth be told, there is witchcraft in America, England, and especially in the Church; they conveniently refer to this as Halloween or any other ceremony. A few years ago, two American ladies from New York came to see me just after I had ministered at a conference. They said this is the first time they had come to understand this topic, and that the teaching has helped them to finally fathom what was wrong with them. They confessed that while they were very young, their mother took them out late at night and made them walk through some specific streets, while instructing them to make some signs with their hands. According to the ladies, nothing has worked well for them since then, and they always felt some unknown thing biting them all over their bodies. Medical doctors could not find a scientific cause or explanation for their condition.

Like these two ladies, many people do not know how they were initiated into the satanic kingdom. Still many do not even know that they have already been initiated, yet they know something is wrong somewhere. We all know that ignorance of the law is no excuse. In America, driving ignorantly at 80 miles per hour in a speed zone of 35 miles per hour will not stop the police officer from issuing you a ticket. The same principle applies to the spiritual world.

There are five classes of witches

Three of these five classes consist of people (or victims) who do not know they are witches. Such people always find themselves attending mysterious meetings or eating raw food in their dreams. Such "blind witches" were contaminated or initiated into witchcraft through some of the means discussed earlier in this book.

Witchcraft is similar to sorcery. It attempts to control and manipulate. For this reason, witches and wizards use incantations. Believers should be very cautious of this fact and protect their belongings with extra care. It is very easy to be contaminated by the spirit of witchcraft; as a matter of fact, it is the easiest spirit to receive. Take for example the beauty salon; some beauticians are hired by evil forces to recruit and contaminate their customers, and in exchange, they get more customers. They use the customer's hair for evil practices, and the customers become unconsciously initiated into witchcraft.

> **It is possible to have been initiated into a cult and not know it. Witches seek converts through every mode. Pray to check your life for such initiations.**

Believers should always pray while visiting a beautician. Our head is the spiritual doorway to our lives; that is why the enemy is interested in contaminating our head. The doorway on our heads is designed to receive healing, anointing, and godly spiritual power.

There are so many examples of witchcraft in the Church. I was invited to preach in a Church one day and just as I was about to start the ministration, the Lord opened my eyes to see that of the twenty-six members of the choir, eighteen of them were operating with the witchcraft spirit. Sure enough at the end of the service, one of the ladies came to see me to confess and repent. According to her, the pastor had been contaminated.

There is another example of a Christian couple that had been married for twenty-three years. The Lord revealed to members of the prayer team that the man's wife was a witch. When the lady was confronted, she said it was true. Now think about the harm she must have done to the husband and the family in their twenty-three years of marriage. Amazingly, they both got married in the Church as believers.

A certain woman who was a witch, in the spirit realm, turned her husband into a horse that she would use to ride to her witchcraft meetings. In other words, she would ride the horse (her husband) whenever she attended her witchcraft meetings. Each time her husband woke up, he would complain of backache. He heard about a gospel crusade and planned to attend. During the crusade, he decided to give his life to Christ. Through the word of knowledge, the preacher prayed for his backache. Suddenly, the man felt something come out of his back, and he was healed instantaneously. The following night, the wife got up as usual to go to her witchcraft coven, but she could not find her horse. All she could see in the spirit realm was a very bright light. After trying all she could to find her horse (her husband), she finally decided to run into the bright light. The light struck her and she became spiritually and physically blind.

The man woke up the next day feeling very well, but his wife had gone blind. He decided to take his wife to the crusade where he gave his life to Jesus and was healed. She reluctantly agreed to go. That very day, she also gave her life to Christ and was healed. She decided to publicly confess all that she had done as a former witch so as to be totally free from the bondage of the kingdom of darkness.

If you have been affected or contaminated by witchcraft forces, the siege is over today, in the name of Jesus! The Holy Spirit will deal with any form of witchcraft manipulation in your life!

Some people have never given thought to the fact that witchcraft attacks might actually be the reason why they cannot keep a stable relationship. Such attacks can also bring financial instability and poverty.

Other witchcraft activities or operations include accidents and death. Witches mark their victims and order their appointed time of death, which is in fact the day that they are being offered as sacrifice. In the physical realm, the victim just dies on that day from some flimsy reason (usually accidents of any kind).

Again, I say to you: *"The siege is over in your life, in the name of Jesus!"*

Some people believe that there are good witches. These are the kind of witches that use witchcraft to obtain a man's love (love charm), live long, enjoy prosperity, and so on. All the same, it is the work of witchcraft and it is an abomination to the Lord. There is nothing like "good witchcraft or witches." White witchcraft or good witchcraft is all satanic.

The Lord will destroy every spirit of "good witchcraft" in the name of Jesus!

Halloween is a disguising program of satanic witchcraft. **BEWARE!**

Some people who are tormented by witchcraft spirits tend to go to other demonic powers to look for freedom. Be ye not deceived, true freedom can only come from God through our Lord Jesus Christ.

"Thou shalt not suffer a witch to live." **(Exodus 22:18)**

I agree with the Word of God.

Every operation of witchcraft in your life will cease, in the name of Jesus!

Every manipulation of witches and wizards against your life will cease, in the name of Jesus!

The Blood of the Lamb will erase the marks of witchcraft upon your life, in the name of Jesus!

> *"And ye shall be holy unto me: for I the LORD am holy, and have severed you from other people, that ye should be mine. A man also or woman that hath a familiar spirit, or that is a wizard, shall surely be put to death: they shall stone them with stones: their blood shall be upon them.* (Leviticus 20:26-27)

CHAPTER 7

DEMONIC DIARIES

As a born again Christian, you may have to deal with this nagging contradiction: you have given your life to Christ and you are living holy, and by right, you expect a turn-around in your circumstances, considering the fact that the Bible tells us that old things have passed away and all things have become new. But instead of having a new lease on life, you are faced with the same old frustrations and difficulties.

Aside from covenants and inherited family curses, you may be a victim of manipulations of the kingdom of darkness that targets even the holiest of saints, especially when they are not vigilant.

An incident in the life of Apostle Peter is very instructive. On the night He was betrayed, Jesus gave Peter a startling revelation:

> ***"And the Lord said, Simon, Simon, behold, Satan hath desired to have you, that he may sift you as wheat…"*** **(Luke 22:31)**

This statement caused Peter to vigorously reaffirm his loyalty to the Lord. Of course, we all know that before dawn, he had denied Jesus Christ three times – just as the Lord had predicted.

Here was Peter, a disciple and follower of Jesus, who had sacrificed his secular profession in order to diligently serve the Lord. Along with the other disciples, he was always by the Lord's side. But in spite of his closeness and devotion to the Lord, he was ignorant of the evil plans that the devil had for him. He didn't know that while he was busy serving the Lord, the devil was equally busy hatching a plan to snatch him.

To the glory of God, our heavenly Father sees into every plan or design of the devil. The Lord saw Satan's plans and warned Peter. However, Peter vehemently disputed what the Lord had said. His refusal to accept the facts as foretold by the Lord was only to compound his problems. Jesus, after warning Peter of Satan's designs, said:

"But I have prayed for thee, that thy faith fail not: and when thou art converted, strengthen thy brethren." **(Luke 22:32)**

Since Peter refused to believe, Jesus had to allow a partial fulfillment of the revelation, in spite of having prayed for him, in order to convince him. Many believers today are like Peter. They argue because they cannot see beyond the physical realm.

We all have wonderful plans that we hope to implement sooner or later. However, many of us forget that there is a kingdom of darkness out there that does not wish us well. If you are one of those floating from day to day in blissful ignorance, I have news for you: just as you have made beautiful plans for your life, the devil too has mapped out his own plans for your life. He has drawn up a diary or calendar for your destruction. He has a list of items to implement every day, every week, every month, and every year.

I call this the **Demonic Diary** because this is where the forces of darkness list all the havoc they intend to commit in the life of every Christian. They keep these evil plans secret, and begin to implement them one after another. Sometimes, the pattern of a believer's life may simply mirror the implementation of the devil's diary.

In such a case, you must remember that the kingdom of darkness has its blueprints on how each individual runs his life; in real life, the same individual will unconsciously begin to operate within the limits of that blueprint, thereby deviating from the will of God. This is why it is important for all believers to grasp this revelation concerning the devil's diary. You cannot afford to be complacent. You must learn to cancel the devil's diary.

In the book of **Revelation, chapter 12**, the Bible tells us about the war that took place in heaven. The devil had a diary of evil plans to cancel the divine order of things and he wanted to implement them.

God stopped the satanic move. He sent Angel Michael to put a stop to Satan's foolish ambition. What if God didn't know about the devil's diary? Suppose He was like us – mere mortal – who, most of the time, do not understand what the kingdom of darkness is planning?

> **Commit thy way unto the LORD; trust also in Him; and He shall bring it to pass.**
> (Psalm 37:5)

I thank God for His omniscience and omnipotence. The devil's plans were scuttled.

In one of our programs, we were ministering to a girl of about sixteen years. As we were praying for her, the devil spoke out through her:

"Leave us alone! Why do you want to send us away? We have planned her life and we cannot go back. At twenty-two, she will commit her first abortion. At twenty-six, she will get married. At twenty-eight, she will have her first miscarriage..."

The implication of this was that between marriage at twenty-six and having a miscarriage at twenty-eight, there would be a period of barrenness. That was not all. The devil had further plans for the unsuspecting girl.

> **"Devise your strategy, but it will be thwarted; propose your plan, but it will not stand, for God is with us."**
> Isaiah 8:10 (NIV)

"At thirty-two," the voice continued, "she will have an accident and break a rib. And at thirty-four she will die. Why are you troubling us anyway? We have numbered her days. She is ours!"

The devil was speaking through the mouth of the girl, while she was not conscious of what she was saying. If it were not for the fact that the devil spoke out, she would have found her life following the same pattern that the forces of darkness had mapped out.

You need to pray that every demonic diary that the devil keeps (in order to dictate the direction of your life) be destroyed.

When God gave me that revelation, I began to understand why many ministers of God have fallen. Sometimes, the devil marks out a man of God who is on fire and is busy moving all over the place. The devil's plot is such that at a certain point in his life and ministry, the pastor will commit adultery. At some other point, he will have an accident, and still at another point, he will be killed.

If such a pastor had been aware of this revelation, he would have prayed against the devil's demonic diary, saying:

"Lord, whatever the kingdom of darkness has written against my ministry, I cancel it. Every item in the diary which they want to implement, I reject!"

These evil plans would not come to pass. If, as ministers, we had been praying such prayers, we would have cancelled and voided a lot of problems and ugly situations we are being confronted with. When I received this revelation, I said to my wife, **"This is our weapon!"**

I have also discovered, in the course of deliverance ministrations, that the devil sometimes reveals some yet to be implemented evil schemes from his diaries. For instance, we were ministering deliverance to the barren wife of an outstanding minister of God. The demons cried out, *"No, no, no...you can't cast us out of this place. You can't!"* In reply, I said, **"We have the right."** The devil, speaking through the mouth of the woman, said, *"I know. But this one is mine. I entered into her when she was thirteen. This is my home. You can't just cast me out."*

We insisted that he had to go. Then he (the devil) said, *"Ooh...I made her barren and killed her mother."* A few minutes later, he added, *"We are about to kill her husband. We've perfected the plan. Her husband will soon die."* In such cases, the forces of darkness often reveal the contents of their diaries. So it is now left for the deliverance minister to nullify the entries in these diaries.

We must realize that the kingdom of darkness tries to implement every agenda written in its diaries. In the book of Revelation, we see how they sought to implement what they had written against the Almighty God; in the book of Genesis, they wrote all sorts of things against Joseph.

I often tell people that Joseph's sufferings were not part of God's plans for his life. When God gave him the revelation of greatness, there was no mention of him being imprisoned. God told him that he would be the head, and that he would rule over his family, and his brothers would bow down to him. God did not say, "You will go to prison." **(Genesis 37:3-10)**

The devil saw all this, wrote his own counter blueprint and instigated the brothers to frustrate God's revelation and plans by selling Joseph to Egypt **(Genesis 37:18-36)**. But because God is Almighty, He made sure that what He revealed to Joseph came to pass **(Genesis 42:6 and 43:28)**.

In the same vein, when God wanted to send His Son, Jesus, to the world, His design in heaven was to bring Him to the earth through the womb of a woman. As arrangements were being made in heaven, the forces of darkness were also perfecting their own devices to scuttle God's original plan and to kill the child Jesus.

Revelation 12 tells the story of how the great red dragon with seven heads, ten horns, and seven crowns on its heads, stood waiting to kill both mother and child. This prophecy came long before the birth of Jesus Christ was to be carried out at an appointed time, as seen in **Matthew 2**, when Jesus was born in Bethlehem.

What was foretold was unfolding in the physical. The red dragon mentioned in **Revelation 12:3** refers to the devil. The dragon, whose primary desire was to devour the child, set his scheme in motion by recruiting agents – demons as well as human agents. Herod, who was the king at the time, suddenly became Jesus' archenemy. Following the inquiries of the wise men concerning the King of the Jews who had just been born, and whose star they had seen in the East, Herod ordered the killing of all young boys under the age of two, who had been born in Bethlehem, and in the surrounding towns and villages **(Matthew 2)**. He was determined to eliminate Jesus!

Now, note that Herod had become the human agent whom the dragon was using. He was not the dragon, but the spirit of the dragon had possessed him. The dragon's agents (demons) cannot carry out their deeds in the physical without human agents.

Herod, in trying to kill the child Jesus, sought to destroy His star. But God, Who is wiser than men, knew all their evil plans.

In **Revelation 12**, we are told that the woman faced with the devilish intentions of the dragon, fled into the wilderness where God had prepared a place for her to dwell safely for one thousand, two hundred and sixty (1,260) days. This is confirmed in **Matthew 2** when God told Joseph to go to Egypt with the mother and child, and not to return until the appointed time.

The question now is this: if the dragon could brazenly dare to derail God's divine plans for Jesus, the King of kings, will he not try to hinder God's plan for your own life? The answer is obvious: Yes, he will. Every time you are pregnant with a vision, there is always a dragon waiting to mess it up. There are evil forces waiting with eagerness to wreck every good thing you are planning.

As I pointed out earlier, the dragon operates through human agents. And these agents can be found everywhere, especially in your family. Indeed, there may be spiritual dragons in your family waiting to destroy your vision. These dragons can be anybody: stepmother, brother, neighbor, colleague at school, co-worker, pastor, etc. The dragons in Joseph's life were his own blood brothers. After he told them his vision of greatness and promotion, they resented him and plotted to destroy the vision.

An example of this phenomenon took place in a meeting we held in Abuja, the federal capital city of Nigeria. As the meeting got underway, we prayed fervently that God should reveal deep secrets and deal with the enemies of our stars. After the meeting, we all dispersed. I was visited by a very distraught brother who had attended the meeting. And he had every reason to be upset.

Apparently, while going home from the meeting, he received a phone call informing him that his mother had just died. The brother was shocked because until her sudden demise, his mother has been in good health – without any trace of illness. If her death was not caused by ill health, then what could have been responsible? The brother rushed to me with the news as he was convinced that his mother died as a result of his prayers in the meeting.

On another occasion while in Church, we prayed that God would reveal the secrets behind our problems. We went through a period of protracted prayers, coupled with fasting. During that period, a male member of our congregation went home after a Sunday service, and met his sister trying to calm some people who were locked in a fierce dispute outside his house.

He walked up to his sister to inquire what the problem was. Immediately his sister laid eyes on him, a strange thing happened; it was as if something snapped inside her. Without warning, she made a staggering confession openly. As he walked toward her, she swiftly rounded up the parties whose dispute she had been trying to resolve and shouted at them, *"The two of you had better stop fighting before we ruin your lives the way we ruined my brother's life!"*

The brother was flabbergasted. He thought he had heard what his sister had just said incorrectly. And so he asked her again: *"Sister, what did you just say?"* Without a change of expression or apparent show of remorse, she replied, *"Yes, we were the ones who ruined your life. Do you remember when our elder brother and I came to visit you about eighteen years ago? At that time you had a big shop, where you received and welcomed us. When we were leaving, you gave us some money. That was the day we wrecked you. Our brother was carrying on him the evil charm (juju) that we used to destroy your business. He dropped it somewhere in your store, but you were unaware of it, and from that day (18 years ago), you began to suffer,"* she concluded. Needless to say at this point, that the brother was speechless and in shock. The parties that had been fighting, by now had abandoned their dispute – they were all attracted by a more engaging drama.

As we have seen from the foregoing examples, these spiritual dragons, whether operating from within or outside the family circle, are only out to achieve one purpose: to sow misery into unsuspecting lives. Time and again, we see how these forces attempt to subvert God's will in people's lives, albeit with varying degrees of success. Another area in which they are particularly active is in trying to frustrate people's plans for marriage, as the following examples will show.

I once met a thirty-seven year old woman in Lagos, Western Nigeria, who desperately wanted to get married. She had tried on several occasions, but her efforts proved abortive. Hers was not just a simple problem of incompatibility or not finding the right man. If anything, she was richly blessed; she was beautiful, had a good job, a nice car and a house. In spite of all these, she was miserable because she had a problem that was truly peculiar.

She told me that every now and then, she would hear a voice speaking to her clearly, saying, *"Don't waste your time, your husband is in the sea. You cannot get married to any physical husband. If you make any attempt, we are going to kill you or kill the man."* Being subjected to such a strange phenomenon is enough for anyone to consult a psychiatrist. But in the face of this spiritual attack, the sister remained undaunted in her desire to find a husband.

> **Every diary of the devil for your life must be cancelled and erased, in the name of Jesus!**

She made two attempts at getting married. Mysteriously, on both occasions, the men involved died! Then the strange voice would return to taunt and warn her, saying, *"Don't waste your time, your husband is in the sea. You cannot get married to any physical husband."*

This is a terrible example of how the kingdom of darkness can block marriage plans. This case had to do with the phenomenon of the spirit husband. The sister told me that she had even seen the spirit husband physically. Sometimes when she was on the road, she would see him and converse with him, but no other person could see him. On countless occasions, he had slept with her and sexually molested her in her sleep.

There is also another case of a sister who was warned by the spirit husband never to get married. She started attending our Church and soon got married. The spirit husband was enraged and said to her, *"You got married, didn't you? Have I not warned you?*

Who asked you to start attending that Church, anyway?" Then the spirit angrily said, *"You will be barren!"*

In spite of this strange prediction, she became pregnant. And that was when her troubles started. Unfortunately, her husband got transferred to another area and they left the Church. The forces of darkness attacked the woman when she was about two months into her pregnancy; she started bleeding. The spirit husband appeared to her and said, *"I told you not to get married to anybody. I also told you not to get pregnant. Let's now see the power of your Church do something. I am going to kill you in your pregnant state."*

It was at this point that the woman told her husband, "This is not a matter for the hospital. Take me back to that Church." They came back to the Church and as we were praying, the spirit husband came and took away the sister's purse containing all the money she had. He could not harm her; his aim was to destabilize her.

> **Spirit husbands and familiar spirits work to destroy marriages.**

After we had prayed and she was delivered, she wanted to go home but could not find her purse. We searched everywhere but could not find it. I told her not to worry, as she would find it by the grace of God. Just as she stepped outside the Church, the spirit husband appeared to her holding her purse and said, *"Can you see your purse? Until you come back to me, I will not let you have it back."*

When the sister got back home, she fell ill and started bleeding again. She was rushed to the hospital unconscious because her father did not believe in deliverance prayers. At the hospital, she had reached the point of death, when she suddenly regained consciousness and looked around at her surroundings. She immediately pulled out the drip (IV Solution) that was stuck in her vein saying, *"What is this? All of this cannot solve my problem. Can't you see the man sitting over there, calling me? Please take me back to the Church; that is the only place where I can maintain my deliverance."*

Meanwhile the spirit husband was sitting right there, visible to her only and no one else. The spirit husband said, *"I told you…*

you are not going to give birth to this child." When it was obvious that the sister was not responding to the treatment given at the hospital, she was brought back to the Church. To cut the story, we prayed for her and she became well, and later had her baby safe and sound.

There is another example I must mention. We were ministering to a lady when the Lord opened my eyes to see that she had the image of a man. She was covered completely with the image of a man and as a result, any man who saw her did not want to marry her! The spirit husband that she was yoked to prevented any other man from being attracted to her.

As we ministered to her, she fell down shouting and rolling violently on the floor. Five hefty male ushers could not hold her down. After a powerful ministration, the terrible forces that had been oppressing her left her. The woman was about 40 years old and three months after the ministration, she met her husband.

These are examples of how spirit husbands or dragons frustrate marriage plans. There are many today who are suffering under the yoke of these forces and do not know how to break free. Perhaps in your own life, you have had your marriage plans frustrated again and again; maybe you are well into the age of maturity but men just do not seem to be interested in you. It would be wise to present yourself for a deliverance check-up and ministration.

Spiritual dragons can also follow you anywhere and to any continent, because they have their agents everywhere – all over the place. This is the reason why when you travel out of your country, people whom you have never met may frustrate you and block your progress, leaving you to wonder how your enemies could have traced and found you in a distant or foreign land.

Let me illustrate this point with an incident that happened some years ago while I was ministering in the city of Providence, Rhode Island, in the United States. I was to minister at a Church in

Are you suffering from marital problems, spirit husband/wife, or are you just being frustrated all around and on every issue?

****

Seek Deliverance!

the evening, but that particular morning, the host minister and some others were with me in the church fellowshipping, when some people rushed in carrying a girl who originally hailed from Ogun State, which is in the Western part of Nigeria. When she was brought in, she was incoherent and violent. We held her down and prayed for her.

After about thirty minutes of deliverance prayers, she became conscious. The moment she opened her eyes and realized that she was inside a Church, she burst into tears and said, *"Lord, why? This was why I ran away from Nigeria. Still my enemies followed me here?"* I laughed and said to her, "Sister, wherever you go, these forces of darkness or spiritual dragons monitor your movements."

If you are in Africa and you run to a place like America or England, believing that you will be out of the reach of these wicked spirits, it is just as foolish as imagining that you do not live under the heavens.

So how do these forces monitor their victims? The kingdom of darkness has a worldwide network through which it keeps tabs on people. Within this network, you could have what are called **Familiar Spirits** (they are called *Familiar* because they are spirits that operate within your family). These are agents from your paternal or maternal sides of the family, as well as 'contractors' of sorts working for both sides. When my father was deeply involved in occult practices, he could contact these three sets of people to find out details on anybody's life.

These 'contractors' are the ones who get information from anywhere in the world. Sometimes they operate in the physical, but mostly they operate in the spiritual realm. The fact that you live in the United States does not hinder them from getting information about you.

I recall the case of a woman in a city in the Western part of Nigeria; her husband was transferred to work in Lagos – also in West Nigeria. While the husband relocated to Lagos, the wife stayed behind with the family. In his new office, another woman developed an interest in him. She was demon possessed and an agent operating with evil forces. She wanted to have an affair with the man, so she went to her coven to demand that the new man in her office be given to her. Her request was granted. Oblivious to what had transpired in the spirit realm, the man kept on being nice to her in the spirit of being a good neighbor, and in no time, got quite friendly with her.

The lady finally confronted the man and told him about her feelings. She demanded to have a relationship with him. The man however, turned her down on the grounds that he was already married, and as a born again Christian, he could neither have an affair nor two wives. He assured her that he loved his wife and that the Bible says that only death could separate him from his wife.

> **For the weapons of our warfare are not carnal, but mighty through God to the pulling down of strong holds.**
> (2 Corinthians 10:4)

Having received this information, she went back to her witchcraft coven to demand for more powers so she could visit the man's wife. This was a woman about whom she knew little, next to nothing. She did this in the spiritual realm. She didn't even have the address because the wife could easily be traced through their network.

The possessed lady was released to go on her evil assignment at about 1:00 a.m. – a time they assumed that the man's wife would be deeply asleep. But thank God, this born again sister did not sleep that night; God had spoken to her to observe an all-night prayer vigil. She started praying at about midnight and the witch appeared at about 1:00 a.m. She tried everything in her power to get into the house and kill the man's wife, but failed woefully and shamefully.

Unwittingly, the man had endangered the life of his wife by telling the woman that only death could separate him from her. And the innocent woman would have been killed if not for the mercy of God.

Clearly, we can see that while the dragon uses his human agents to torment you, he has prepared others to monitor you wherever you are, to ensure that your plans are frustrated. Remember that while Herod emerged as Jesus' archenemy, it was the wise men that brought news of the birth of Jesus to him, thereby flagging off a series of persecution and slaughter that was to follow **(Matthew 2)**.

I have good news for you. God will slay every spiritual dragon waging war against you. The dragons sought to derail God's plans for Jesus, Joseph, and Peter; Satan failed because they abhorred sin and trusted in God. Before the dragons can be destroyed, sin must die.

The choice is yours. You may go on sinning and allow these spiritual dragons free access to destroy God's plans for your life. Alternatively, you can stay away from sin and watch you star shine brightly as God has ordained it.

SECTION C

Secrets Of The Dark Kingdom

The heaven shall reveal his iniquity;
And the earth shall rise up against him.
Job 20:27

Can any hide himself in secret places that I shall
not see him? Saith the Lord.
Do not I fill heaven and earth? Saith the Lord.
Jeremiah 23:24

CHAPTER 8

RESURRECTING YOUR STAR

You have a star. Every human being does. Each of us has come into this world with our individual star. Some people come with stars that are bigger and brighter than others. But whatever the form or dimension of the star is, it is an inevitable and biblical fact: we are all born with our own personal stars.

When our Lord Jesus Christ came into this world in human form, He was no different. Like every human being, He was born with His own star.

> *"Now when Jesus was born in Bethlehem of Judea in the days of Herod the King, behold, there came wise men from the east to Jerusalem, Saying, Where is He that is born King of the Jews? For we have seen His star in the east, and are come to worship Him."* **(Matthew 2:1-2)**

I can also state from my involvement with the occult in the past, that all people have a star that represents them. Your star can reveal deep secrets about your life and the future to come. It is very tempting for one to want to know what the future holds. Some people engage in a search for these mysteries of the unknown through an array of star readers, astrologers, fortune tellers and so on – people who peddle their divination skills before innocent victims.

Let me quickly make an important point here. **I am using the "Star" here, as a symbol of your "destiny."** I am not focusing on stars as your destiny. Using your star for such purposes as reading your destiny is demonic. If you are one of those who religiously turn to fortunetellers or the horoscope pages of newspapers and magazines to learn what the "stars" may have in store for you, I insist that henceforth you desist from such activities. It is a demonic practice that God hates and abhors. God said:

"I make fools of fortune-tellers and frustrate the predictions of astrologers. The words of the wise I refute and show that their wisdom is foolishness."

It is clearly and distinctly stated in the Bible how God feels about such practices. Therefore, you have no excuse for enslaving yourself to palm readers, astrologers, horoscope experts, or diviners of any form or fashion. You must not try to search for what the future holds through any type of means that God disapproves of. If you are a child of God and you need to know any mysteries about anything, including yourself, ask your heavenly Father in prayer.

"Call unto me, and I will answer thee, and show thee great and mighty things, which thou knowest not." **(Jeremiah 33:3)**

Now, as it was in the case of Jesus, your star can reveal what you are to become and portray the heights you will attain in life. This information can be a potent weapon in the hands of the enemy to harm you. Then your star can become a source of grief for you!

In **Matthew 2:3**, we are told that Herod was greatly troubled by the news that a child had been born with a big and bright star, a child who was destined to be the king of the Jews. So what did the jealous King Herod do? Right there and then, his wicked mind made a plot to kill the newborn child. However, the Lord frustrated his plans when He warned the wise men in a dream not to cooperate with Herod's diabolical plans.

> *"And being warned of God in a dream that they should not return to Herod, they departed into their own country another way."* **(Matthew 2:12)**

The Word of God makes it clear to us that God is also working to disappoint the devices of our enemies just as He worked against Herod.

> *"He disappointeth the devices of the crafty, so that their hands cannot perform their enterprise."* **(Job 5:12)**

THE ENEMIES OF YOUR STAR

We all have those who hate our progress. It is an unfortunate fact that these people are found especially in our families. The enemy is the devil and he uses these people as the enemies of your star. These people can be categorized into two main groups: **"The Wise Men"** and **"The Herods."**

These two groups surround you everywhere you go.

A. The Wise Men

It is important for us to observe the role the wise men played in the chain of events surrounding the star of Jesus. They are referred to as *"the Magi"* which literally means *"Magicians."* But there is no question that they were also accomplished and professional star gazers. Due to this fact, they had the ability and the expertise to interpret what the bright star that they saw represented. They recognized that the child that was born was the King of kings; hence, they brought Him gifts meant for a mighty king. They were also skillful enough to track the star to the birthplace in Bethlehem, and also knew what the sex of the child was.

Today, such worldly "wise men" still abound, and they have similar abilities to those of the wise men involved in the biblical story of the birth of Jesus Christ. This is another way of saying that they have access to valuable information about us through our stars. These present day "wise men" are agents of the kingdom of darkness and possess the ability to get important information about us.

B. The Herods

The second group is referred to as "the Herods." The "Herods" are usually heads of families (male or female) whom we confide in and with whom we share every detail of our plans and aspirations.

These two sets of enemies are united by one common goal: the desire to ensure that you do not succeed in life or that no one supersedes their achievements within the family. King Herod could not stand the thought that someone had been born in his domain with a brighter star. If the "Herod" of your family is an engineer, he will ensure that no other engineer emerges within that family. If he is a professor, he would oppose the rise of another potential professor. And if he were poor, he would wish that you all remain poor or poorer.

> **Be careful of every word that you speak, so as not to ensnare yourself and others.**

These enemies of your star are especially dangerous because their hostility or hatred toward your star is always concealed. If anything, they will always feign to have deep love for you. As you confide in them about your dreams and plans, they counsel you and pretend to point you in the right direction. In reality, however, their intention is to use the information they have gathered (from you) against you, working to make you fail.

When King Herod secretly called the wise men to get information about the star of the newborn Jesus, he said:

> *"...Go and search diligently for the young child; and when ye have found him, bring me word again, that I may come and worship him also".* **(Matthew 2:8)**

What dubious pretence! This was Herod's true intentions:

> *"And when they were departed, behold, the angel of the Lord appeareth to Joseph in a dream, saying, Arise, and take the young child and his mother, and flee to Egypt, and be thou there until I bring thee word: for Herod will seek the young child to destroy him."* **(Matthew 2:13)**

Herod's intention to kill Jesus was confirmed by the ferocity of his anger and determination when he discovered that the wise men had tricked him.

> *"Then Herod, when he saw that he was mocked of the wise men, was exceeding wroth, and sent forth, and slew all the children that were in Bethlehem, and in all the coasts thereof, from two years old and under, according to the time which he had diligently inquired of the wise men."* **(Matthew 2:16)**

There is certain information about our lives that are vital, such as our date of birth, mother's name, where one's placenta was buried, etc. Can anyone truly know how many people within his or her family have access to these types of information? It is not possible.

In the hands of agents of the kingdom of darkness, such information is like dynamite. For instance, they could have seen from the day of your birth that you are destined to become a great man or woman. Due to the fact that they do not want you to amount to anything in life, they would do everything (using the data they have on you) to abort what your star has foretold. They may have seen the glory on your head, but they will fight to ensure that you do not shine forth. There are four major things the enemies can do to someone's star:

(a) They can try to kill the star
(b) They can bury the star
(c) They can sell the star
(d) They can transfer the star.

(A) ATTEMPTS TO KILL YOUR STAR

If your star has been tampered with in an attempt to kill it, you will discover that nothing ever works right in your life. Whether you are in school, employed by someone or own your business, you will always fail. Even when you deeply desire to improve yourself, your best efforts will not get you the results you desire.

My star was tampered with from birth in an effort to kill it and it remained that way until 1987. Until then, I was unable to make some headway in life. Acquiring an education was a struggle. I told God I wanted to have a very good education and become a professor – that was my aspiration in life.

I wanted to achieve what my father could not achieve. Unfortunately, my mother who had promised to pay my school fees, died. When I started working, I made no progress until 1987 when God spoke to me about rebuilding my faulty foundation. Part of the problem with my foundation is that it rested on a start whose brilliance was almost dead. Shortly after the Lord rebuilt my foundation, my star received a new energy and began to slowly shine again; people began to relate to me with favor and my life changed for the better. When the forces of darkness succeed in killing your star, you are dead! Ill-luck will be the only companion of those who operate on a daily basis with dying stars; they will struggle endlessly without succeeding.

I know of a young man with an interesting story. He was once my driver (chauffeur). When I first met him at my auto repair workshop in Nigeria, he was about 25 years old. He was not an auto mechanic; he was just an errand boy. Part of his job description was to assist the automobile technicians in picking up and carrying the necessary tools needed while repairing broken down vehicles. One day, I took a look at the young man and had the urge to interrogate him. I asked him if he was training to become an automobile technician, and he said, "No."

"What are you doing here, then?" I asked. He explained that he ran errands for the technicians to earn a little money for his upkeep. "At least, I can eat," he said. As for shelter, he disclosed that he was squatting with one of the technicians.

When I probed into his family background, he told me that his father was a chartered accountant in the employment of a university in Nigeria and his mother lived in London. I found this quite strange; how could the son of an accountant whose mother lives abroad, live like a destitute?

"So what on earth are you doing here, running errands?" I asked aloud. "I don't know," he replied. "I just found myself here."

I felt compassion for him. At that point in time, I needed a driver. So I asked him if he could drive and he said he could. So I gave him my car and he became my driver. In the car, we began talking and I asked him why didn't he go back to his parents. He said it was a long story.

According to him, his parents had done so much for him, but all he ever gave them in return was trouble. He told me how his father sent him to high school, but later tried in vain to get him into a university.

Sadly, he said that when his father saw that he wasn't too bright academically, he tried to get him to learn a trade. He started with printing, but it didn't work out. His father opened a bakery for him; that failed also. He said there was nothing his parents didn't do to make him a success; he failed them woefully all the way. So I asked him why he did the things he did. He replied that he did not know why. All he knew was that within him, he desperately wanted to succeed, but the harder he tried, the more he failed.

When I later suggested that we should visit his father, this young man protested vehemently, "Oh no, Sir!" he exclaimed. He was so sure that his father would never want to set his eyes on him again. But I stood my ground. If I was going to take this young man under my wings, it was only right that I met with a member of his family. And his father seemed to be the most appropriate person to see.

One day, we went to see his father in the quiet confines of his home, and to my pleasant surprise, this gentleman was a devout Christian! In spite of the irresponsible acts of his son, he welcomed me with open arms, and as we settled down, he began to tell me his side of the story about his son's life.

His story corroborated with his son's story. This was his first son indeed, and everything a father should do for his child, he had done to the best of his ability. But the son was just a total misfit! With him, nothing worked. To compound matters and make things worse, he said the son broke into his home on several occasions, stole and sold his properties. This was a harrowing tale from an agonizing father and a desperate son! God opened my eyes to discover that what was happening to the young man was not an ordinary thing. His star had either been tampered with to kill it or it had been buried. I knew then that he really needed help.

When his father ended the story, I said to him, "Sir, can you formally hand this boy over to me? God will use him for His purpose." The father was obviously relieved that I hadn't come "dump this burden" on him. He said, "Ha! He is all yours! You cannot leave him here. You have to take with you as you leave. Maybe God will use you to train him; this is fine with me."

We left and from then on the young man drove me wherever I went. I soon noticed one thing about him. He did not conduct himself the way most drivers (in Nigeria) would. He enthusiastically partook in every deliverance event I was conducting; he would be the first to raise his voice to God on any prayer point that was raised. He prayed to God mightily and the God that answers prayers looked down on him with mercy. He had been my driver for a brief span of about four months, when the Lord resurrected his star.

"And ye shall seek me, and find me, when ye shall search for me with all your heart." (Jeremiah 29:13)

This young man was determined to change his destiny. He sought God in truth and indeed he found God. His mother who had long forgotten about him (as everyone else had) suddenly remembered him! She sent papers to help him regularize his travel documents so that he could go to live with her abroad. Today, this young man had settled down to a good life in London, and he is now married with children. **Praise God!**

(B) THE BURIED STAR

There is a world of difference between a star that is being killed and a star that has been buried. If you originally had a big, shining star that had been buried by the enemy, it is possible that the radiating glory of that star may still shine out to some extent. Although you may not be utilizing the maximum potential of your star, the radiance is such that it can still be felt. There is still some evidence that something is there.

There are many people who have minor successes and triumphs, and are satisfied with it. They are ignorant of the fact that they are not tapping into the full glory of their God-given potentials. Such people really need to pray for the resurrection of their stars.

(C) THE SOLD STAR

When your star has been sold, the consequences can be just as devastating as if it were killed. I recall that back in the day, my father who was a witch doctor used to go to some Muslim clerics (*Alfas*) who usually named babies born into Muslim homes, to purchase human hair. Muslims give names to their newborn babies on the eighth day (after birth), and before the naming ceremony takes place, they shave off the baby's hair. Some unscrupulous clerics would secretly sell the hair that would then be used by witch doctors (like my father) for money-making charms.

This type of charm can come in the form of a bar of soap, which is sold to those in search of quick wealth; the more the individual who paid for the soap uses it, the more the child's life (the one whose hair was shaven) would be rendered useless. This is one way of selling out someone's star to another person.

The biblical story of Joseph is a classic illustration of a life whose star was sold. Here was a young man whose star had foretold a great future. In the book of **Genesis 37**, we see that Joseph's brothers did not really hate the boy; however, they hated the fact that he obviously had a brighter star and future. When the opportunity arose, they ganged up and plotted to kill him.

> *"Come now therefore, and let us slay him, and cast him into some pit, and we will say, Some evil beast hath devoured him: and we shall see what will become of his dreams."* **(Genesis 37:20)**

They actually wanted to kill his star, but quickly thought about it and decided to bury him in a dry well instead. Finally, they sold him to some Midianite traders who were on their way to Egypt.

> *"And Judah said unto his brethren, What profit is it if we slay our brother, and conceal his blood? Come, let not our hand be upon him; for he is our brother and our flesh. And his brethren were content. Then there passed by Midianites merchantmen; and they drew and lifted up Joseph out of the pit, and sold Joseph to the Ishmeelites for twenty pieces of silver: and they brought Joseph into Egypt."* **(Genesis 37:26-28)**

The first set of people who bought Joseph did not know the contents of "their package"; and because of their ignorance, they soon sold him to Potiphar, one of the king's officers and captain of the palace guard. From the moment Potiphar made Joseph overseer of his house and over all he had, the Lord blessed the Egyptian for Joseph's sake. Potiphar had no covenant of blessing with the Lord, but God prospered him on account of Joseph's destiny.

> *"And it came to pass from the time that he had made him overseer in his house, and over all that he had, that the Lord blessed the Egyptian's house for Joseph's sake; and*

the blessing of the Lord was upon all that he had in the house, and in the field." **(Genesis 39:5)**

This is a prime example of how some people steal the stars of others and prosper, while the original owners live a life of severe lack and suffering. In some cases, the person using your star may give you handouts, money and material things from time to time to make you happy and keep you under him perpetually. If only you knew that the person was luxuriating in the glory that should have been yours, you would not have allowed things to go that way.

(D) THE TRANSFERRED STAR

As a deliverance minister, I have discovered that there are so many methods which wicked people employ to steal the brighter stars of others. I was ministering in one of the northern states of Nigeria, when the Lord revealed to me that there was a woman in the congregation whose life had been ruined by her stepmother. Somehow, the stepmother managed to switch the bright star of this sister to that of her own daughter. Her daughter, who was in Lagos, started prospering while this sister suffered.

> **When the forces of darkness succeed in killing your star, you are dead!**

THE CHARMED SCARF

The Lord revealed to me how it all happened. When the sister was about seven years old, the stepmother put a black magical ring on a scarf and gave it to her to tie on her head. After the sister had put it on, the stepmother took back the scarf and the ring and gave them to a fetish priest. The fetish priest used the ring to make some charms for the stepmother's own daughter. From that day, the sister's star was transferred to her half sister in Lagos. There and then, the Lord ministered to me as I prayed for her; He would turn her situation around. This sister was fortunate enough that God had mercy on her and retrieved her star that was stolen by the simple act of putting on a scarf given to her by her own stepmother. Many of us receive things and gifts in such a manner without paying attention to a deeper spiritual significance that may accompany such exchanges. We have to be careful about the gifts we receive.

THE DEMONIC MIRROR

Some gifts, especially those presented to us during weddings, could potentially be dangerous. A Christian sister who was given a mirror as a wedding gift, was barren for sixteen years as a result. As long as she looked in that particular mirror, the barrenness persisted. This was her condition until the Lord revealed that the gift was a demonic one.

Please, don't misunderstand me. I am not saying people should not receive gifts. After all, it is the traditional custom in most parts of the world, that during certain ceremonies (weddings, birthdays, etc.), people bring gifts as a sign of solidarity. I, as a minister of God, receive gifts all the time. What I advise is that whenever a gift is given to you, especially wedding gifts, first put them aside, pray over them and cancel every spell from the kingdom of darkness. Plead the blood of Jesus over them before opening even a single wrapping. Once you have done that, you are free.

OBEDIENCE AND YOUR STAR

Sometimes the fate of our stars is determined by our ability to listen to God and follow His leading in every circumstance. In whatever we do, we must never move without knowing the mind of God.

In **Matthew 2:13** God told Joseph to flee to Egypt with the baby Jesus and not to return until God said so, because Herod sought to destroy the child. Joseph obeyed and fled into exile; by so doing,

Jesus escaped Herod's wrath. He did not return until an angel of the Lord appeared to tell him that Herod – the archenemy of Jesus' star – was dead.

> *"But when Herod was dead, behold, an angel of the Lord appeareth in a dream to Joseph in Egypt, saying, Arise and take the young child and his mother, and go into the land of Israel: for they are dead which sought the young child's life."* **(Matthew 2:19-20)**

The same fate that befell Herod will befall all who have vowed that you will not prosper or be happy as long as they live. The same fate also awaits all those who have tampered with your star.

Whether your star has been sold, buried, transferred, or killed, you can be rest assured that Jesus Christ, Who is the Resurrection and the life, can and will resurrect it. As long as you repent of your sins and stay on the Lord's side, your star will be tamper-proof.

CHAPTER 9

DREAMS AND DEMONIC MANIPULATIONS

So far we have seen various ways through which demonic activities are introduced and sustained in many lives. But perhaps one of the most significant avenues that we have not addressed is our dreams.

Dreams are important and are a natural phenomenon that is common to virtually every human being. The dream phenomenon is so commonplace that most of us do not take them seriously; neither do we make any effort to analyze or evaluate them in order to find out what they are all about. In fact, some people dismiss any serious attempt at analyzing dreams and regard them as superstitious exercises. Yet, dreaming is scriptural. The Bible tells us that God speaks to us through dreams. So can the devil too!

Whether we believe it or not, whether we accept it or not, when we sleep, there are things that happen in our dreams that affect us in the physical.

> *"...The kingdom of heaven is likened unto a man which sowed good seed in his field: But while men slept, his enemy came and sowed tares among the wheat, and went his way."* **(Matthew 13:24-25)**

There is no ambiguity here. When the enemy comes, he does not come to play or sow blessings; he comes to sow bad things into your life. And this is the authoritative Word from Jesus, the Master and Supreme Teacher. He says that there are certain things that witches, demons, and the kingdom of darkness in all its ramifications, can do to you in your sleep in order to contaminate your destiny. Jesus is not warning sinners or unbelievers; He is talking to children of the Kingdom.

> *"The field is the life of a man; the good seed is the pre-ordained purpose or vision of God for the man in the kingdom; but the tares are those things that will destroy the vision, such as wicked spirits and contamination in world pleasures."* **(Matthew 13:38)**

The witchcraft spirit, the familiar spirit, the spirit wives and husbands and so on, are the children of the devil that come out at night to sow tares among the wheat. Is it any wonder, therefore, that many Christians are being harassed and still suffer all manner of manipulations in their dreams?

THE DIVERSE NATURE OF MANIPULATIONS

Demonic manipulations in dreams occur in various ways:

(1) Forgetting Your Dreams

One very common form is when someone dreams and upon waking up, he or she cannot recollect any detail of that dream. If you fall into this category all the time, then know that it is time for prayer. What you are experiencing is a typical witchcraft manipulation. This can affect you in two ways:

   (a) If you are unable to recollect or remember your dreams, you cannot know if God is passing a message across to you;

neither will you know if the devil is wreaking havoc in your life. How then will you know whether to reject what you saw in your dream or claim it? The desire of the kingdom of darkness is for you to have no recollection of your dreams, so that you will not be able to pray or do anything about it. The result is that whatever evil thing has been planted into your life, will ultimately become a reality.

(b) The phenomenon of people not recollecting their dreams is a very dangerous one because those who are affected may be operating as blind occult members without knowing it. They are not allowed to know or remember what they do in the occult gatherings. They will participate in all sorts of wicked activities – like eating their ritual meat, visiting the river, and so on, without having the slightest clue of what they are doing, because their memory has been darkened or covered.

So if you do not remember your dreams, the thing to do is pray that the Holy Spirit will cause you to remember your dreams and that God will enlighten your spiritual understanding.

(2) Not Dreaming At All

This is yet another form of manipulation. People who do not dream at all, or those who think they do not dream are living a dangerous life, just like those mentioned in the earlier example. True, it is not compulsory that one should dream every night or all the time, but not to dream at all is unnatural. Even people born blind have dreams. I have interviewed blind people who confirmed that they do have dreams and very vivid ones too! Now if you do not dream at all, then you need to pray. It may be that the kingdom of darkness has sealed up your spiritual memory.

(3) Using Deceptive Covers

Another variant of witchcraft manipulations in dreams shows how devious the enemy can be. While demons are attacking you or contaminating your life in your dreams, they assume the faces of people close to you, thereby diverting your attention from the real source of your troubles. Understandably, most people will jump to the conclusion that the faces they see attacking them in their dreams are the architects of their day-to-day woes. Such dreams always lead to hatred toward those faces they see in their dreams. The truth may shock us: those we have identified as our enemies may be innocent victims of demonic manipulations in dreams. Demonic manipulations in dreams come in numerous forms; many manifest in diverse forms other than those that have been treated here. However, throughout the course of my counseling, I have come to identify some of these as common examples.

> **Not dreaming at all or forgetting your dreams? You need to pray! That is a dangerous place to be!**

In a lot of cases, these manipulations occur in the lives of Christians. Indeed, there are Christians who are frustrated because the more they pray, the more they are held subject to these evil manipulations. The question which naturally arises is: how is it possible for the kingdom of darkness to gain access or entrance into our lives to manipulate our dreams, when the Bible tells us that as children of God, we are surrounded by a wall of fire? There are clear reasons for this.

WHY DEMONS MANIPULATE OUR DREAMS

(1) Unbroken Covenant

Demons and other forces of darkness are able to distort and twist our dreams as a result of some unbroken covenants in our lives.

This is why as a born-again Christian it is possible that the more you bind and cast out these demons, the more they visit you in your sleep to torment you.

We are often tied to these covenants through mistakes made by our parents in their desperate search for children, or by our observance of what we regard as **"simple"** traditional ceremonies and rites. We may also open the gateway by our own unwholesome religious or spiritual practices. And sometimes, these covenants and initiations are renewed by what we eat or drink in our dreams.

In all of these, one thing is obviously true: somewhere along the line, the Word of God has been breached. When we go to offer sacrifices to idols we have created for ourselves (by ourselves), we offend God and attract to ourselves very grave consequences. The Bible in **2 Kings** reminds us of how such an act of deviation incensed God:

"But he walked in the way of the kings of Israel, yea, and made his son to pass through the fire, according to the abominations of the heathen, whom the LORD cast out from before the children of Israel. And he sacrificed and burnt incense in the high places, and on the hills, and under every green tree." **(2 Kings 16:3-4)**

"And they left all the commandments of the LORD their God, and made them molten images, even two calves, and made a grove, and worshipped all the host of heaven and served Baal. And they caused their sons and daughters to pass through the fire, and used divination and enchantments, and sold themselves to do evil in the sight of the LORD, to provoke him to anger." **(2 Kings 17:16-17)**

"And he made his son pass through the fire, and observed the times, and used enchantments, and dealt with familiar spirits and wizards: he wrought much wickedness in the sight of the LORD, to provoke him to anger." **(2 Kings 21:6)**

(2) Parental, Pre-natal, and Ante-natal Activities

Right from birth, most of us have been marked down and dedicated to particular idols in our families, villages, places where we live or have lived. For some of us, this was done even before we were born. And this is just one of the primary ways by which the enemy gains access into our lives.

In their search for children, some parents have dined with the devil. Out of sheer desperation, many parents have led their unborn babies into trouble. Some people want a child at any cost, and would go to any length to obtain one. Some are perhaps blessed with a number of girls and would do anything to have the elusive yet desirable baby boy or vice versa.

In their search, such parents visit shrines and sacred rivers and consult with water and familiar spirits, indeed all types of evil spirits. They are made to drink all manner of concoctions, buy all kinds of ritual items and participate in all kinds of rituals.

For others, the problem is that their babies are delivered stillborn. In order to prevent a reoccurrence, ritual items are demanded by the fetish priests to appease their gods. In addition, when such babies are born alive, they are inflicted with marks and incisions and sometimes have to wear amulets around their legs for "protection."

All these marks, incisions and ritual objects automatically link these babies to demonic covenants.

(3) Traditional Naming Ceremony

The traditional naming ceremony takes different forms in different areas of Nigeria and Africa, but one thing that is common to them all is the offering of ritual items like sugar-cane, sugar, honey, alligator pepper, dried fish, kola-nut, a local clay pot, dried rat and dried lizard, among other things. The question people fail to ask is, "What do these items have to do with naming a child?"

In reality, these items are offered as sacrifice to the evil spirit or the familiar spirit controlling a family, and every family has one! You may not know this. Naively, people assume that they are just performing some harmless and arcane traditional rites.

Now, for any new child to belong to the community, a sacrifice of ritual objects has to be made. After you have paid the price, the witchcraft spirit or any other spirit active in that family, enters the child. And from that moment on, a relationship has been established. Having paid in full what may be considered as your *"membership fees,"* it is now easy for the evil forces to attack you, should the need arise. All they have to do is go to the shrine at which you were dedicated, and communicate with the resident idol. And because you have fully paid up your dues, your spirit, soul, and body will respond whenever they wish to make contact. You are now linked to their network and they will keep monitoring your life.

> **If possible, avoid every tradition that you cannot explain or be in control of.**

(4) Traditional Marriage Ceremony

Just as the case with the traditional child naming ceremony, the traditional marriage ceremony requires participants to present similar ritual items like the ones earlier mentioned – including alcoholic drinks.

There are Christians who object to this ceremony, but in most cases, they are not firm with their objection. Sooner or later they succumb to the pressure and accept compromises that attract the same divine disapproval and punishment as they would have received if they had gone through the actual rites.

The compromise may take the form of the bride and groom paying for or providing the required ritual items without presenting themselves to receive any incantations or prayers offered to idols.

However, have you ever stopped to ask, *"What happens to these items? Where are they taken? What is their final destination? To what gods are they being offered?"*

The truth is that portions of these items are taken to the villages and offered in sacrifice to ancestral and family idols, thereby establishing and reinforcing covenants with them. In cases where they are not taken to the village, some over-zealous relations would end up invoking the "spirit of the ancestors" and some other family gods. In either case, demonic spirits are released to follow and monitor the couple wherever they go.

Always make a habit of asking questions and seeking answers. Seek and you will find!

(5) Demonic Religious/Spiritual Literature

Not long after I became a Christian, I found myself reading a dangerous book in search of knowledge – ***"The Sixth and Seventh Book of Moses."*** Luckily, God ministered to me to stop reading the book, and to burn it so that I would not open the gate for evil spirits to come into my life. There are Christians who are still reading and experimenting with such books. Moses (in the Bible) never wrote any sixth or seventh book.

For those with a Nigerian or African background, membership of and participation in the religious activities of the "white garment" or syncretic churches (they are called "white garment churches" because members are required to be uniformly dressed in flowing white soutanes) exposes you to all kinds of demonic spirits – especially water or marine spirits.

As those who have passed through these churches will confirm, people seeking solutions to spiritual problems are often subjected to unscriptural baths in streams, rivers, and at road junctions, with all manners of strange invocations. This is ultimately a gateway for demons, if ever there was one!

SOME COMMON DREAM PATTERNS

Let me state from the onset that I do not interpret dreams. It is only God Who has the divine key for interpreting dreams. I would like to advise those who write books claiming to interpret dreams, to be careful of their interpretations. In just about every case, the same dream doesn't usually have the same meaning in the Bible. Signs and symbols in a dream can be very relative and personal.

Having said this, I should point out that whatever explanations I give here regarding dreams have been informed by my personal experience and confirmation through the process of counseling. In the course of counseling people over the years, I have heard them relate certain kinds of dreams over and over again, and the manifestations in their physical lives have been remarkably similar.

For example, there are people whose dreams always come true. Others have dreams which present one picture, only for the opposite to manifest in the physical. What do these patterns indicate?

(1) Dreams That Always Come True

If you are a believer and your dreams often come to pass, then God may be showing you things that are about to happen. And the reason God reveals such things is so that you can pray about them. It is not only believers who have dreams that come to pass. There are unbelievers who have similar experiences. The question is whether such dreams come from the Spirit of God.

(2) Dreams That Manifest The Opposite

If your dreams always turn out to be the opposite of what you dreamt about, then there is the need to pray that God should show what exactly is going on. The fact that you are seeing negative things in your dreams does not automatically mean that terrible things are about to happen in the physical. Sometimes when you dream and God presents you with a negative picture, you end up having something positive manifest.

For example, Joseph dreamt that his elders would bow to him, the youngest. In the part of the world where I come from, it is unheard of and an abomination, for an elder to bow to a younger person. For someone with my background and origin, such a dream would be regarded as a bad dream, and would certainly not be seen as a sign or move of God.

A key point to note, however, is that the regularity of a particular kind of dream, irrespective of whether a dream is good or bad, indicates that either God or the kingdom of darkness is passing a message on to us. This is the case as long as it is a regular dream.

I should also point out that it is not every dream that is of the devil. This is why we need divine guidance to interpret our dreams. Sometimes, our dreams are a product of our inflamed imagination.

> **Many have eaten demonic contaminations in their dreams and have woken up doing nothing about it. There is neutralizing power in the blood of Jesus!**

If you are sufficiently burdened by a matter before falling asleep, do not be surprised to find yourself having lurid dreams about the same matter in your sleep.

There are some demonic dreams of which we shall provide some insights in the light of the Bible and practical experience in the field of deliverance.

(3) Having Babies, Getting Married, or Being Pregnant In Dreams

If you regularly have dreams in which you find yourself getting pregnant, married or carrying babies, chances are that you are already married to a spirit wife or husband in the spirit realm. Again, this can be traced to the covenants made by some of our parents in their desperate search for children.

Now because you are already married to these demons in the spirit realm, they will make sure that your family life (if you are married in the physical) is hell. You will find yourself staggering from one matrimonial crisis to another.

If you are not yet married, these forces will chase away any man or woman showing interest in you. The reason is simple: the moment you get married in the physical, you will devote yourself to your real living wife or husband, and the spirit spouse does not like that.

It may well be that you are in search of a child, but you regularly have dreams where a strange man makes love to you. The result would be that while in the spirit realm you give birth to babies, in the physical, you have miscarriages, stillbirths, and babies who die shortly after birth. As you are well aware, both men and women have God-given reproductive eggs. When these demons have sex with you in your dreams, they contaminate these physical eggs, thereby ensuring that by the time they are released, they are already dead.

Sometimes, an expectant mother may constantly see blood in her dreams. This should be an indication to her that her inability to carry her pregnancy to full term and have a successful delivery is not just a medical problem, but also one that needs to be handled spiritually also.

(4) Eating And Drinking In Dreams

Again, it is not every time you eat or drink in your dreams that it signifies something evil. It is probably demonic if it becomes a regular and/or reoccurring phenomenon. The consequences or implications of eating in a dream vary, but two examples you are about to read should illustrate the dangers.

A Christian sister once told me a story of how she found herself in a dream with her close friend (who was also a Christian) eating a local Nigerian delicacy – roasted plantain (popularly called *'boli'*). Suddenly, one of them realized that they did not sanctify the food before they started eating it. Despite the fact that they had worked their way though half of the meal, they still prayed and blessed it.

As soon as they finished praying and opened their eyes (the sister was still dreaming), the leftover food in their hands was transformed into the mutilated remains of a baby's hand, still dripping with fresh blood!

Clearly, this shows that some of the foods we eat in our dreams are not what they appear to be on the surface. These foods may be offered to initiate us into covenants or cults. It is possible to that the meat in this dream is their share from the occult rituals of an occult group.

If these Christians sisters now find themselves initiated into this cult – flying or attending meetings in their dreams with strange people – they would be shocked and surprised. Through their carelessness, they allowed the devil to gain entry in their lives in the dream.

Every dream is unique to the individual. Seek God for diviine interpretations.

Sometimes, diseases are deposited into our lives through the things we eat in our dreams. A few years back, I was called to pray for a lady living in a town in Nigeria, who was ill. When I used to know this lady, there was nothing wrong with her hands, legs, or any part of her body. By the time I got to her after receiving the call, her hands and legs were grotesquely twisted and curled.

I asked what had happened and she told me that in her sleep (dream), she ate something and woke up to find her hands and legs shaking. Later both hands and legs got swollen and slowly became twisted. As I began to pray for her, the Lord revealed to me what had happened to her. There are many other cases like hers. People eat in their dreams and find cancer tumors or other deadly diseases in their bodies.

Eating in the dream could also lead to the weakening of one's spiritual life. People have reported the loss of the urge to pray or study the Bible after eating in their dreams.

(5) Flying In The Dream

If you fly around in your dreams, chances are that you are engaged in occult practices, or have partaken in the rituals performed for the protection of family members, such as witchcraft, Halloween, etc.

Some other people, who have experienced this phenomenon, also fly when there is a threat to their lives in their dreams. For instance, someone may be about to kill them and they suddenly take flight.

Some Christians who still fly in their dreams think that it is the Holy Spirit propelling them! This is not so. Flying around with your arms and legs spread wide, and your tie dangling downward, is certainly not the manner children of God are expected to travel to heaven. If the Holy Spirit is at work, we must be lifted up the same way Jesus Christ was lifted.

(6) Travelling In The Dream

From experience while counseling, I have observed that people who keep having dreams about traveling or trekking but never arriving at a destination are often locked in day-to-day struggles (in life) with little or nothing to show for their efforts.

(7) Being Pressed Down Physically

This is an experience many people have had. You just have this feeling of being pressed down by some weighty, formless, and invisible object. You want to push out from under the weight, but you can't. You feel like shouting, but cannot get your tongue to form the words.

This is a typical witchcraft operation, with the forces of darkness attempting to deposit some evil things in you. If you have been subjected to this terrifying experience, then you need to present yourself for a deliverance check-up, because the mark of these forces of darkness is already upon you.

(8) Being Chased By Wild Men, Animals, etc.

This often suggests that some form of attack is underway and one has to be prayerful to ward it off.

(9) Associating With The Dead In Dreams

It is certainly not a good development when you regularly find yourself associating, chatting, and eating with dead people in your dreams. In some cases it could lead to death. It is generally indicative of the spirit of necromancy at work.

(10) Associating With Old Acquaintances, School Mates, etc.

Again, regularity is the key. If you keep finding yourself in the company of associates whom you have left behind for years, or you keep seeing yourself in (the poor setting) your village, hometown, or old neighborhood which you have not visited for years, then there is a battle on the way. You have to pray against setbacks, retrogression, and demonic associations.

(11) Marks And Incisions

People sometimes wake up in the morning to discover strange marks and incisions on their bodies. This indicates some form of initiation or the renewal of some former initiation. Invariably, proper investigation will show that there is something demonic in the victims' origin or past.

The cases touched upon here are by no means exhaustive. And again, I repeat that it is only God Who has the divine keys for interpreting dreams.

This exercise enables us to see that what happens to us in our dreams should not be trifled with. We are spirit beings: our lives in the physical are often determined by events that have taken place in the spirit realm. That is why we have to be alert and scrutinize our dreams when they occur.

SECTION D

Believers And Satanic Attacks

*"And the LORD said unto Satan,
The LORD rebuke thee, O Satan;
even the LORD that hath chosen Jerusalem rebuke thee:
is not this a brand plucked out of the fire?"*
(Zechariah 3:2)

*"And the God of peace shall bruise Satan
under your feet shortly.
The grace of our Lord Jesus Christ be with you.
Amen."*
(Romans 16:20)

CHAPTER 10

WHY SOME CHRISTIANS DIE YOUNG

In the course of ministering deliverance to people over the years, I have discovered that many Christians live under the constant fear of death. They live from day to day assailed by anxiety and the expectation that death is waiting for them around the corner. They go through a tremendous amount of emotional trauma on account of this fear, that even their spiritual lives and growth are adversely affected. This should not be so.

Dying young is not the portion of a Christian. The Word of God is clear on this. God has made this promise to all those who belong to Him:

> *"There shall nothing cast their young, nor be barren, in thy land: the number of thy days I will fulfil."* **(Exodus 23:26)**

> *"Thou shalt come to thy grave in a full age, like a shock of grain cometh in its season."* **(Job 5:26)**

If we clearly understand what God has said about His children in these instances and in so many other passages of the Bible, we will see that the message is clear and unambiguous: **We shall not die young!** God gives all believers the assurance that they will live long and fulfilled lives. This is His perfect will for us.

Those of us who understand God's faithfulness and the immutability of His Word are often puzzled and disturbed when a young man or woman dies in the Church. *"Is this not contrary to God's promises?"* they wonder.

To begin with, we need to understand that not everybody who dies in the Church is a genuine child of God. Some are counterfeit Christians and as such are open to the attacks of the devil. Many who claim to be Christians do not understand "Christianity." They have made themselves believe that Christianity is all about going to church, speaking in tongues, singing in the choir, and going to the house of God for service or fellowship. Yet they are not genuinely born again. Outside the Church, they continue to live a perverse and unholy life, committing sin with impunity.

We must remain secure and unafraid until the appointed time when God calls us home. We should be glad to go home!

When evil befalls them, because we do not know who they really are in their closets, we mourn them. When sudden death comes upon them, we grumble that God has been unkind. We grieve that "children of God" have suffered premature deaths, whereas in reality, their father, the devil, has just claimed their souls. Under normal circumstances, a genuine Christian cannot be an easy prey for the devil because with all his wiles, he has no audacity to touch the life of a Christian. Why? As a Christian,

"...and your life is hid with Christ in God." **(Colossians 3:3b)**

"When Christ, who is our life..." **(Colossians 3:4)**

For the devil to have access to the life of a Christian, he has to first take the lives of God, his Creator and then that of Christ, his Conqueror. Of course, we all know that this is an impossible task; the devil cannot even contemplate such a feat. In Christ therefore, we remain secure until the appointed time when God has planned for our exit from this earth.

This, however, does not mean that a true Christian cannot die young; they die every day through the tricks of the devil.

I once knew a young medical doctor who was fervent for the Lord. His wife had a baby girl and one day this little girl fell ill with fever. So my friend the doctor, decided to take her to the hospital. On the way, he too suddenly fell ill. In spite of all the prayers of the brethren, the young man died within three days – leaving behind his wife and baby.

Another young fellow, a teacher and a hardworking Christian, both at home and in the Church; suddenly started feeling weak and tired. He called his wife and told her to prepare some food for him. But alas! Before the food was ready, he was already a dead man! Why does God allow things like this to occur after He has promised to keep those who belong to Him till old age?

WHY DO SOME CHRISTIANS DIE YOUNG?

It is the perfect will of God for Christians to live long, however, the devil is perfecting his own plans to ensure that careless Christians do not achieve this. I have since discovered, with the help of the Holy Spirit, some of the major doorways through which Satan sends many believers to an early grave.

(1) Door Of Fear

Fear is an awesome weapon in the hand of the devil: the fear of death, fear of poverty, fear of accidents, and the fear of anything at all. The devil uses this weapon at will against the believers. As the Lord opened my eyes, I found that in spite of God's promises, it is possible for a Christian to die young if he entertains fear in his heart. This has been the reason behind the deaths of many Christians.

Satan knows that if he manages to keep someone under the bondage of fear, that person's life is open to any evil attack or affliction.

Fear is a destructive emotion. It is engineered by the devil, and not by God. It is because of its potency in the hands of the devil that, consistently in the Bible, the Lord exhorts His children not to give room to fear. He assures us that with Him on our side, there is nothing to be afraid of, no situation, no sickness, and no battle. There is absolutely nothing to fear.

> *"And he answered, Fear not: for they that be with us are more than they that be with them."* **(2 Kings 6:16)**

> *"Thou shalt not be afraid for the terror by night; nor for the arrow that flieth by day."* **(Psalm 91:5)**

What is there to be afraid of anyway when we have the unflinching protection of the One Who is the Almighty?

> *"...Fear not: for I have redeemed thee, I have called thee by thy name; thou art mine. When thou passest through the waters, I will be with thee; and through the rivers, they shall not overflow thee: when thou walkest through the fire, thou shalt not be burned; neither shall the flame kindle upon thee... Since thou was precious in my sight, thou hast been honourable, and I have loved thee: therefore will I give men for thee, and people for thy life."* **(Isaiah 43:1, 2, 4)**

What a wonderful assurance! And the Bible is full of them!!! What more do we need to encourage us to stand firm and bold against the tricks of the devil? Yet, many Christians today allow fear to rule their lives. I hope that by the time you finish reading this book, you would have learned to hate "fear based on emotions." I hope that you would have acquired boldness in the face of every fear you face. That is what the Lord expects of His children.

> *"For God hath not given us the spirit of fear; but of power, and of love, and of a sound mind."* **(2 Timothy 1:7)**

Through faith, we can claim God's promises, but fear is the opposite of faith. The devil is a cunning enemy. He understands more than most Christians do, that fear and faith do not go together; one has to give way to other. The devil destroys many Christians through fear because they lack this pertinent knowledge.

Satan understands that fear weakens the faith of a believer in the Word of God; and once that happens, the believer becomes weak spiritually; then like lightning, the devil strikes him at the point of his weakness. Fear provides an entrance for evil powers to enter into the life of a believer. Fear is not of God; it is of the devil.

As a Christian, if you allow fear to dominate your life, you have opened yourself up to the attacks of the devil. It means that you trust the devil more than you trust your God; you do not trust God's injunctions (not to fear) and His assurances (that He is watching over you). Believe it or not, that which you fear will certainly come upon you. For instance, a Christian living in the perpetual fear of witches, familiar spirits, and death, is under the danger of dying, whether he is young or old.

Fear was the undoing of Job in the Bible. Job was a righteous man, even God, Who cannot behold sin, testified that his life was holy and pleasing to Him. But the devil was able to use fear as a tool to attack him. Every day of his life, fear consumed Job; he had no peace of mind because he was always afraid of one evil or the other befalling him. What he feared eventually caught up with him, in spite of his righteousness.

> **Death is also a spirit. Stand up and rebuke it. If it is not your appointed time, death is an illegal errand.**
>
> *****
>
> **God did not send him (death)! Take your life back from its grip!**

"For the thing which I greatly feared is come upon me, and that which I was afraid of is come unto me. I was not in safety, neither had I rest, neither was I quiet; yet trouble came." **(Job 3:25-26)**

Job accepted the devil's offer and paid dearly for it. He lost everything he was afraid of losing. His fears were not even hidden to those around him. When problems invariably came upon him, one of his friends was quick to remind him:

> *"Is not this thy FEAR...?"* **(Job 4:6)**

This was, indeed, his fear. The devil gained entrance into Job's life by creating fear in him concerning his children, his property, and his health. Every day of his life, he would wonder, "Suppose I lose my children." "What if I became poor?" "What if I fall sick?" "What if....?" "What if...?" Well, all his fears eventually became a reality, as the Bible states:

> *"For as he (a man) thinketh in his heart, so is he..."*
> **(Proverbs 23:7)**

If you had a dream that you were killed, and instead of rejecting the dream and focusing on God's promises that say you will not die young, you allow the fear of death to creep into your heart, then you are likely to die. If you met a prophet who claimed that he foresaw your death. If you accept that prophecy, the fear of death will likely kill you before the actual death comes knocking. When a believer harbors the fear that a particular sickness may kill him, it will happen in spite of God's promise of good health and a long life span. God said, "Fear not..." Who then should you believe: Your Savior or Satan, your enemy?

> *"The thief cometh not, but for to steal, and to kill, and to destroy: I am come that they might have life, and that they might have it more abundantly."* **(John 10:10)**

It is also written that part of the ministry of Jesus, through His life and death here on earth, was to destroy him (Satan) who had the power of death.

> *"Forasmuch then as the children are partakers of flesh and blood, he also himself likewise took part of the same; that*

> *through death he might destroy him that had the power of death, that is, the devil; And deliver them who through fear of death were all their lifetime subject to bondage."* **(Hebrews 2:14-15)**

Having won the victory over Satan on the cross, Jesus said:

> *"And when I saw him, I fell at his feet as dead. And he laid his right upon me, saying unto me, Fear not; I am the first and the last: I am he that liveth, and was dead; and behold, I am alive for evermore, Amen; and have the keys of hell and of death."* **(Revelation 1:17-18)**

It is the devil, the liar, who creates an atmosphere of fear and death. Any Christian, young or old, who does not know how to trust God more than the devil, and does not know how to reject the spirit of fear, and replace it with that of boldness, may find himself or herself going to an untimely grave.

(2) Door Of Sin

Nothing kills a Christian faster than sin; if there is anyone who knows this to be true, it is the devil. He therefore works relentlessly, putting all kinds of temptations in the paths of believers to ensure their spiritual and physical death. Unfortunately, a lot of Christians commit sin habitually without weighing the consequences. Let such Christians be aware that the devil is just around the corner, waiting to pounce on you.

> *"Be sober, be vigilant; because your adversary the devil, as a roaring lion, walketh about, seeking whom he may devour."* **(1 Peter 5:8)**

As a child of God, if you commit a sin, you should get on your knees immediately and ask for forgiveness. Any delay could be deadly. For your information, the devil has plans (laid out) for destroying your life. The only thing has been shielding you from those demonic plans is the wonderful grace of God.

The only time your life is safe from the devil's attack is when you are in fellowship with God. When you are living in sin, you are out of fellowship with the Only One Who can shield you.

"He that diggeth a pit shall fall into it; and whoso breaketh an hedge, a serpent shall bite him." (Ecclesiastes 10:8)

When you commit sin, you break the hedge or the fence that the Almighty God has built around you to shield you from evil. Once that fence is broken, you are in trouble, because the devil is always looking for such opportunities, to creep in, attack and kill. He knows it's the only way he can get to you.

For instance, imagine a young and upright man who makes a virtue of living holy. One day, the devil tempts him and he falls into sexual sin. If he doesn't check himself and go back to God, through this act of sexual immorality, he may become inflicted (or infected) with the deadly AIDS (Acquired Immune Deficiency Syndrome) virus, and eventually die. That would be the consequence of sin or disobedience to God.

The promises of God concerning our length of days here on earth are conditional. God calls for complete obedience to him before we can enjoy long life. He says:

"And if thou wilt walk in my ways, to keep my statutes and my commandments, as thy father David did walk, then I will lengthen thy days." (1 Kings 3:14)

In **Psalm 91**, God assures those who love Him, long life; just because they love Him.

"Because he hath set his love upon me, therefore will I deliver him: I will set him on high, because he hath known my name...With long life will I satisfy him, and shew him my salvation." (Psalm 91: 14, 16)

How can you show your love to God? By Staying away from sin and obeying His commandments.

> *"If ye keep my commandments, ye shall abide in my love; even as I have kept my Father's commandments, and abide in his love."* **(John 15:10)**

As long as we abide in God's love, nothing can harm us. God calls for complete obedience to His Word. Anything short of that may lead to an untimely death.

(3) Door Of Ignorance

Many Christians die young because they do not know the God they serve. They lack the knowledge of His power, His promises, and His do's and don'ts. The devil now turns this ignorance to his advantage.

There are many believers today who, due to the fact that they do not give themselves to the studying of the Bible, do not know their rights as children of God. They do not know the kind of promises God has for them; neither do they know their God-given authority over death, Satan, sickness, troubles, sorrow and other life-threatening issues. Due to their ignorance, the devil sends his messenger of death to capture them.

> **Believe in God's Word and it would prove powerful!**
>
> *******
>
> **God is faithful even when you are not!**

The Bible is full of beautiful promises from God; take time to study it. Claim the promises and stand upon them. If you trust God and believe in His Word, His promises will come alive in your life. However, if you do not know these promises, how can you claim them and make them work in your situation? If you die young as a result of your lack of knowledge, it will be your fault (ignorance is no excuse). God's promises concerning your life are sure and certain:

"And they shall build houses, and inhabit them; and they shall plant vineyards, and eat the fruit of them. They shall not build, and another inhabit; they shall not plant, and another eat: for as the days of a tree are the days of my people, and mine elect shall long enjoy the work of their hands." **(Isaiah 65:21-22)**

If God has promised that you will live long enough to enjoy the fruits of your labor here on earth (if you stay away from sin and fear), then nothing can stop you from receiving this promise. If the devil attacks you with a deadly sickness and you know what God's Word says and you put your trust in the Word for healing, you will be able to stand up and confidently say, *"Devil, you are a liar! I reject your sickness. I will not die but live because according to my God:*

"I shall live long to enjoy the work of my hands" **(Isaiah 65:22)**

"I shall not die, but live, and declare the works of the LORD." (Psalm 118:7)"

Believe it or not, the devil recognizes the authority of the Word of God; he will flee from you. If you don't know the Scriptures to use to counter the devil at your time of need, then you are doomed. Many young Christians in the past have been doomed to unwarranted and untimely deaths.

God respects His promises (and His Word) even more than His name. He expects you to know them. He expects you to remind Him of these promises when you are in trouble. That is the only time He will arise and confront the trouble on your behalf. Many fail to do that and die young as a result.

In **Isaiah 38:1-8**, you will find an inspiring story of a man who knew his God. His name was Hezekiah and he as the king of Israel at that time. One day, he became ill and was at the point of death. Isaiah, the prophet, went to him and said, *"King, you are going to die. The Lord says you should write your will, set your house in*

order, say goodbye to your beautiful palace and your loves ones, because you will not recover from this illness." Hezekiah was a man of faith, who knew the promises of God for him, concerning long life. He faced the wall in his closet and cried to the Lord: ***"Excuse me, Lord! You have to remember Your promise, that I will not die young. I have served You faithfully, with all my heart. I have not allowed sin to distract me from Your presence and I have always done what is good and right in Your sight. Oh Lord, remember!"***

The ever-faithful God replied him: ***"Yes, my son, you are right. I have heard your prayer; I have seen your tears. You will no longer die. I will add fifteen more years to your life."***

Hezekiah lived because he pleaded his case with God; he was bold enough to claim the promises of God. So God arose on his behalf and revoked the death sentence. It's like being in a worldly court of law. A lawyer has to learn the laws of the land and know how and when to use them. He has to know how to quote or cite these laws when he is pleading the case of his client. Mere head knowledge is not enough. He has to apply the right arguments, laws, and decrees that are appropriate enough to win high cases. If he uses the wrong ones, he loses his case.

The laws and decrees for a victorious lifestyle are contained in the Bible; these are the words of God. Learn them and use them to confront the situations that arise in your life. They are the weapons you have against the devil when he confronts you with fear, untimely death and other evils. God's promises never fail. You must know how and when to use them. Always remember: **God honors His Word!**

A young man was warned by two different prophets not to travel at a certain point in time, because they foresaw an accident and subsequent death on his way. Not only did the young man not accept the warning, he dared the hand of death to come and take him away.

To begin with, he had run out of money so he needed to go back home to his parents; there was no way he was going to avoid traveling. He eventually decided to travel home. Predictably, the devil tried to attack him with fear, but as a Christian, he knew his rights. He said to Satan, "Devil you are a liar. The God that I serve has promised that I will not die young. I believe Him and not you."

Quoting passages from the Bible, he reminded Satan that he had nothing to be afraid of, since Jesus had already conquered death on his behalf. He went on to express his confidence in God. There are so many confessions of confidence in the Bible that you can apply to your situation, if only you will study to find them and keep them in your heart:

"Be not afraid of sudden fear, neither of the desolation of the wicked, when it cometh. For the LORD shall be thy confidence, and shall keep thy foot from being taken." **(Proverbs 3:25-26)**

"Behold, God is my salvation; I will trust, and not be afraid: for the LORD JEHOVAH is my strength and my song; he also is become my salvation." **(Isaiah 12:2)**

Having the knowledge of the Word of God and applying it appropriately, the young man scared the devil away and broke the bondage of fear, and if the devil had indeed planned to kill him on that journey, he failed woefully. He went on his journey and God kept him from having an accident and from death.

Here's another testimony. Some sort of misunderstanding arose between a young Christian and a witchdoctor. The witchdoctor tried to show off his evil power by pronouncing a death sentence on the young man. In fact, he "decreed" that the brother would die within seven days. The brother, however, knew his rights in Christ Jesus. He threw all fear away and issued his own decrees to counter that of the witchdoctor.

To everyone's amazement, the first son of the witchdoctor died on the seventh day! As if that was not enough, the second son died seven days after the death of the first son! The witchdoctor had to surrender. He came to the brother begging for forgiveness.

I believe, just like King Hezekiah, that God cannot go back on His Word – to care for you, to stand by you, and to shield you from untimely death – but if due to your carelessness and ignorance of

His Word, you allow the devil to kill you, well, that's just too bad. Many Christians have died young for the same reason.

What I have been saying in essence is: do your part to stay alive, and our Lord Jesus Christ will do His part to keep you alive. Stay away from sin, and live in total obedience to God; reject fear in its entirety (except the fear of God), and gain awareness of the promises of God in your life (by studying the Bible).

If after doing all these things, a Christian still dies young, then only God in His infinite wisdom knows why. Nobody can explain the mysteries behind God's works – no, not one! Why? The Lord gives us this answer...

> *"For my thoughts are not your thoughts, neither are your ways my ways, saith the LORD. For as the heavens are higher than the earth, so are my ways higher than your ways, and my thoughts than your thoughts."* **(Isaiah 55:8-9)**

Let me share the testimony of a fellow Christian to illustrate this. He was a young man ready for marriage, so he prayed to God to send him a partner. An answer came in the form of a comely sister and shortly after they got married. Like any young African couple, they were eager to start a family right away; so their joy knew no bounds when it was confirmed that a baby was on the way. Joyfully, they watched the pregnancy grow.

In the ninth month, a strange thing happened. Signs that would normally expel from the private part of a woman in labor started manifesting from her mouth. Water and blood were flowing freely from the mouth of the sister. The perplexed husband rushed his wife to a Church and rallied some ministers of God around her to pray. As they prayed, the Holy Spirit opened the eyes of one of them to see what was happening in the spirit realm.

"Forces of darkness are surrounding your wife, and they are set to take her away!" he warned. Of course, the brother did not believe this. He exclaimed, "Darkness?" How could forces of darkness surround his beloved? She was a child of God, or so he thought.

He simply couldn't accept that. He immediately decided to withdraw his wife and take her back to the hospital. He had no time for that kind of talk. Unfortunately, she died on the way; the baby too couldn't be saved. This marked a turning point in the life of the young man.

He was very angry with God. He had no wife and no baby. He couldn't understand how God could possibly be *"so wicked."* He was sorrowful and wept like a baby as he fell on his bed back at home. **"Why? Oh God, why did this happen?"** He was still pondering on this *"injustice"* when he fell into a deep sleep out of exhaustion.

He got an answer right away. In a dream, the Lord appeared to him in the form of an old man who had a young companion with him – a boy. In the dream, the old man reached out and took the boy's hand. Then he said to the man (the one dreaming), "Boy, you want to know how God works? Come; let me and my son show you how." He joined the man and the boy and they embarked on a journey.

After traveling for a while, they approached a beautiful house they saw in the vicinity and knocked at the door. *"Yes,"* he heard a reluctant voice answer. The man stepped out of the door to face him. Without a doubt, he was the rich owner of the house. *"What do you want?"* he asked in an unfriendly manner.

The old man explained that he and his companions were weary and needed a place to sleep, and asked if he could possibly help. *"No. I don't welcome strangers in my house. I don't know you. Go away,"* he said bluntly. The old man had to beg and cajole him before he finally agreed to allow them to sleep over but not inside the house; they had to sleep in the rough basement of the house.

In the morning when they were about to depart, the old man called the rich landlord and gave him a huge sum of money. The young man in the dream didn't understand this. He said to the old man, *"This doesn't make sense, Old man. Why are you giving so much money away to someone who was so nasty to us and who wouldn't even give us a good place to sleep in his house?"* The young man wasn't happy about this at all, but the old man replied with a smile, *"Don't worry about that. You want to know how God works, so just follow me."*

They continued on their journey and soon, it was getting late and it was time to rest again. This time, the only house they saw was an old building without windows, which was owned by a very poor man. They approached the man and before they could ask, he welcomed them into his home, offering them the only mat he had – which was the one he slept on. That night, he slept on the bare floor.

In the morning, the old man invited this poor fellow outside the house. He then took some flammable gasoline, poured it all over the house and burned it down. Then he departed with his entourage, leaving the poor man as he wept and shouted, *"My house! Oh, my house…!"*

The young man dreaming wanted to run away, but the old man firmly said to him, *"No! You must not run away."* The brother became frightened. As far as he was concerned, it took a wicked person, a sadist, to do what the old man had just done. *"The man who wasn't nice to you and who is already rich, you gave money. The one who is poor, who needs money, you burnt down the only property he had!"* At this point, the brother started thinking that this must be the devil.

> **Always remember that on earth and in heaven, nothing happens without a reason.**

They continued on their journey all the same. After a while, they came across a woman and her only child, a girl of about eighteen years old. The old man approached the mother and said, *"My dear woman, we have been journeying for a while, looking for a particular place."* After explaining his problems, he pleaded, *"We have not been able to trace this place. Please, could you allow your daughter to take us there?"*

At first the woman was reluctant. The girl was her only companion and ran all her errands; moreover, she didn't want to take any risk with her only child. But the old man was very persuasive. Finally, the woman released her daughter for the assignment.

As they went on their way, they came to the foot of a bridge built over a mighty river. They were to cross the bridge, but what did the old man do? He pushed the girl – the only child of her mother – into the river below. The girl drowned and died!

"What wickedness," the brother exclaimed in shock. *"I've been traveling with the devil."* He decided to escape from the old man before it was too late; after all, he could be the next victim. He took

to his heels. *"Stop there!"* the old man ordered in a thunderous voice that tolerated no nonsense. As the brother stopped and turned at the command, the old man had transformed into God. The little boy with Him had become Jesus Christ. The brother was paralyzed by such an awesome presence. God continued to speak.

"...You wanted to know how We work, and that is what My Son and I have shown you. Now I will explain:

The rich man wasn't nice to us, yet I gave him more money. He is a godless rascal and he cannot go to heaven. The world is the only place where he can enjoy himself, so I let him have more money to do just that (enjoy himself). His eternity is ensured in hell..."

"As for the poor man, We had to help him get rid of his poverty. He doesn't know it, but that wretched house of his was the source of his poverty. He inherited that house from his father when he was a little boy. When his father was building that house, he buried a great treasure in the ground for his little son to find and inherit some day. Bu the son grew up in poverty, ignorant of what lay right underneath.

Now, because he has no shelter, he will be forced to rebuild that house, and while he's digging the ground to lay a new foundation, he will discover his hidden treasure and he will never be poor again. So you see, we didn't do anything without a purpose."

"But God...did you have to push the young girl into the river? She was a nice girl; her mother was good to us," the young man asked. "That too, I will explain," God replied. "The young girl was a hindrance to her mother, but the poor woman didn't know it. Inside her womb is a doctor, a lawyer, and many great achievers. But as long as that girl lives, these other children will never be born. So now you know how We work."

Suddenly, the bereaved young man who had been dreaming, woke up, and a great understanding came over him: God had been speaking to him. God had been trying to tell why he allowed his wife and unborn child to die. It was because God had a purpose, and that purpose was for his own good. It was difficult to understand... but he understood.

That is part of the mysteries of God.

CHAPTER 11

CAUSES AND CURE OF BACKSLIDING

Many Christians who seek deliverance focus their attention on the obvious areas of demonic oppression, such as sickness, poverty, family curses, retrogression, barrenness, marital problems, etc. Unfortunately, due to ignorance, they neglect to acknowledge the most important deliverance (needed) of all – DELIVERANCE FROM SIN.

Deliverance from sin is the number one thing that an oppressed Christian must seek; otherwise he or she will continue to wallow in misery. Without being free from sin, deliverance in any other area in a person's life cannot be permanent. I am not talking about the process of being born again; rather, I am looking at the pathetic life of a believer who is already born again, a Christian who constantly falls back in a life of sin. The Bible calls him "a backslider."

WHO IS A BACKSLIDER?

According to the dictionary, a backslider is someone who "falls back from good ways into his old bad ways of living." A definition of backsliding also from the dictionary is "relapsing into bad habits, sinful behavior or undesirable activities." However, in the biblical sense, a backslider is someone who turns away from following the Almighty God to serve other gods; someone who at one time in his life decided to be a follower of Jesus Christ, but later went back into a life of sin.

Exodus 32 describes the backsliding of the nation of Israel on their way to the Promised Land:

> *"And when the people saw that Moses delayed to come down out of the mount, the people gathered themselves together unto Aaron, and said unto him, Up, make us gods, which shall go before us; for as for this Moses, the man that brought us up out of the land of Egypt, we wot not what is become of him... And the LORD said unto Moses, Go, get thee down, for thy people, which thou broughtest out of the land of Egypt, have corrupted themselves: They have turned aside quickly out of the way which I commanded them: they have made them a molten calf, and have worshipped it, and have sacrificed thereunto, and said, These be thy gods, O Israel, which have brought thee up out of the land of Egypt."* **(Exodus 32:1, 7, 8)**

Here was Israel, a nation that God had chosen and nurtured for His glory. He had loved them, delivered them from their enemies and performed great miracles on their behalf. He even destroyed the glory of Egypt for the love of Israel. Yet, one day, the children of Israel turned against this same God, to serve a god they had molded with their own hands from the golden earrings of their wives and daughters.

Backsliding did not start with the nation of Israel. From the very beginning, it had been a terrible weapon in the hands of Satan, which he used to enslave the children of God. Sadly, many people keep falling prey without knowing that there is a cure for it. Deliverance is the cure. At this point, I need to provide some explanations about this.

The first man and woman were created in the image of God, an image of holiness and righteousness. They were God's friends, and in their abode of the Garden of Eden, they remained sinless in their service to their Creator. They even fellowshipped with God in the cool hour of the day. However, on one sad day, according to Genesis 3:1-13, Satan disrupted this camaraderie. He deceived them into disobeying God and obeying his own lies. This was an act of backsliding; Adam and Eve became rebels against God – the first set of backsliders in history.

A lot of Christians have this major misconception about backsliding. They think it takes a supreme act of no longer going to church, not fellowshipping with the brethren or not studying the Bible for one to be described as a backslider. These are not the real issues. Rather, these are only the fruits of backsliding. The act of backsliding begins from the heart; it begins from the moment you disobey God's Word, or from the very moment you commit a sin. It does not matter how small the sin is in your eyes; sin is disobedience. The principal word here is disobedience. There are many backsliders in the Church today.

It's easy to be a backslider. If you look at the story of Adam and Eve, you will see the principle behind their backsliding. They shifted their focus from God and concentrated on the serpent. Satan, the serpent, who was responsible for their great fall, encouraged them to turn their attention away from God's Word and focus on the forbidden fruit. Satan still uses the same principle today to draw Christians away from the path of righteousness into bondage.

When your attention is diverted from God to any other thing, you are more likely to backslide. That other thing could be money, your wife or husband, properties, relationships, beauty, certificates and other laurels. One success begins to take you out of fellowship with God and His people; you have to be very watchful. You may well be on your way to a backslidden state.

Backsliding starts from the heart – that's what the Bible says. Before a Christian decides that he no longer wants to participate in godly activities – like going to Church, working for God, preaching the Word, etc. – you can be sure that his heart has long since departed from God.

"The backslider in HEART shall be filled with his own ways..." **(Proverbs 14:14a)**

The Bible teaches that a believer, who is filled with his own ways in his heart, is backslidden. Someone who is backslidden in his heart could still preach the Word, lead or sing praise and worship songs, prophesy or do some other work for the Lord. At a point in time, during their years in captivity, God acknowledged that this was exactly what the children of Israel were doing: they were carrying on in the presence of God as if they had were not backslidden; however, they were full of sins.

"Cry aloud, spare not, lift up thy voice like a trumpet, and shew my people their transgression, and the house of Jacob their sins. Yet they seek me daily, and delight to know my ways, as a nation that did righteousness, and forsook not the ordinance of their God: they ask of me the ordinances of justice; they take delight in approaching to God." **(Isaiah 58:1-2)**

If a believer is not watchful, his heart might have departed from God for years before he actually begins to withdraw from God's service. Take for example, King Solomon:

"For it came to pass, when Solomon was old, that his wives turned away his heart after other gods: and his heart was not perfect with the LORD his God, as was the heart of David his father. **(1 Kings 11:4)**

At this time, nothing bad was said about Solomon's spiritual commitment in terms of the work he did for the Lord. However, God who only looks at the heart of man saw that Solomon's heart had turned away from Him. He was no longer focused on God, but rather on the heathen gods of the strange women he married.

Like He did in the case of Solomon, God announced the backsliding of Israel long before it came into physical manifestation. God said:

"And my people are bent to backsliding from me: though they called them to the most High, none at all would exalt him." (Hosea 11:7)

Those who are deceived into backsliding always replace God in their hearts with other idols. The Bible is full of example:

1. Solomon delighted in strange women and replaced God with cheap idols. **(1 Kings 11:1-9)**
2. Saul, the first king of Israel substituted God in his heart with his love for the spoils of war. **(1 Samuel 15:1-24)**
3. Samson shifted his heart from God to the Philistine beauty, Delilah. **(Judges 16:4-31)**
4. Peter walked on water yet he looked away from the miraculous power of the Lord and relied on his own strength. **(Matthew 14:22-32)**
5. Judas Iscariot counted thirty pieces of silver, and he put greater value on them than he did on the Son of God. **(John 18:1-5)**
6. Jeshurun saw prosperity and looked away from God.

"But Jeshurun waxed fat, and kicked: thou art waxen fat, thou art grown thick, thou are covered with fatness; then he forsook God which made him, and lightly esteemed the Rock of his salvation. (Deuteronomy 32:15)

All of these people saw something else that caught their attention and they looked away from the Lord. These distractions consumed their hearts and they backslid. No matter what you focus on, if it is not on God, you will fall into a backslidden state. You have to decide, either to give up the other thing you are so focused on or lose your salvation.

God looks at the heart and if your heart is enticed by satanic devices, then it is time to cry out to the Lord. Don't pretend or cover up using Church and religious activities. **Remember this: Satan is the cause of backsliding!** His trick is to make you shift your mind and focus from God to some idol. When this happens, you will find yourself living a life of deceit before the Lord, the Church, and yourself. Consequently, you stand the risk of perpetual bondage.

WHY IS THE LIFE OF A BACKSLIDER SUCH A DIFFICULT ONE?

Generally, the life of an unstable Christian – one who keeps falling in and out of sin – is a pathetic one. Why? It is simply because he is on the wrong side of God. He is neither hot nor cold, and of such a person, the Lord says, *"I will spue (spit) thee out of my mouth"* **(Revelation 3:16).** He can never be set free from the oppression of the devil until he is delivered from the sins that plague his life – in other words, the sins which he finds difficult to get rid of.

(1) God Is Angry With The Backslider

When Israel, God's chosen race, forsook the Lord and turned to serve the golden calf, what was God's reaction? Anger and the readiness to destroy the people! God said to Moses:

"Now therefore let me alone, that my wrath may wax hot against them, and that I may consume them: and I will make of thee a great nation. **(Exodus 32:10)**

(2) The Lord Puts A Plague On The Backslider

As He did to the children of Israel, in spite of Moses' pleadings, the Lord said:

"...Nevertheless in the day when I visit I will visit their sin upon them." **(Exodus 32:34)**

The Bible records in the next verse that the Lord did that which He had promised:

"And the LORD plagued the people, because they made the calf, which Aaron made." **(Exodus 32:35)**

(3) God Distinguishes Between The Righteous And The Backslider.

"Now the just shall live by faith: but if any man draw back, my souls shall have no pleasure in him. **(Hebrews 10:38)**

(4) A Backslider Ends Up Being Enslaved By The Devil

Paul admonishes that backslidden is not a state to be in:

"But now, after that ye have known God, or rather are known of God, how turn ye again to the weak and beggarly elements, whereunto ye desire again to be in bondage?" **(Galatians 4:9)**

God says virtually the same thing here:

"Thus saith the LORD, Where is the bill of your mother's divorcement, whom I have put away? or which of my creditors is it to whom I have sold you? Behold, for your iniquities have ye sold yourselves, and for your transgressions is your mother put away. **(Isaiah 50:1)**

(5) A Backslider Loses His Inheritance In The Lord

Solomon lost his inheritance. In a promise made to King David, Solomon's father, his descendants were supposed to rule all over Israel, forever. Due to Solomon's disobedience, God cut down His promise of inheritance; instead of ruling over the twelve tribes of Israel, Solomon's son only ruled over the tribe of Judah.

> *"And the LORD was angry with Solomon, because his heart was turned from the LORD God of Israel, which had appeared unto him twice, And had commanded him concerning this thing, that he should not go after other gods: but he kept not that which the LORD commanded. Wherefore the LORD said unto Solomon, Forasmuch as this is done of thee, and thou hast not kept my covenant and my statutes, which I have commanded thee, I will surely rend the kingdom from thee, and will give it to thy servant... Howbeit I will not rend away all the kingdom; but will give one tribe to thy son for David my servant's sake, and for Jerusalem's sake which I have chosen."* (1 Kings 11:9-11, 13)

(6) The Lord Raises Up Enemies Against The Backslider

> *"And the LORD stirred up an adversary unto Solomon, Hadad the Edomite: he was of the king's seed in Edom... And God stirred him up another adversary, Rezon the son of Eliadah, which fled from his lord Hadadezer king of Zobah... And Jeroboam the son of Nebat, an Ephrathite of Zereda, Solomon's servant, whose mother's name was Zeruah, a widow woman, even he lifted up his hand against the king.* (1 Kings 11:14, 23, 26)

BACKSLIDING AND CURSES

If all that is listed above are not enough reasons for a backslider to quickly retrace his steps back to God, then hear this: "A backslider is under a curse from God." I want you to know that every time a Christian slides back into sin, he offends God, and curses are attached to some of the sins committed. This may explain why you always find yourself falling into a particular sin. And in spite of your desire to break free, you are unable to.

When you backslide, one or more curses are likely to stick to you. Even when you repent, these curses linger on – until you break them. If you leave them unattended, you may find yourself in a recurring cycle of sin. This is why some believers cannot get out of a particular sin, even when they have confessed. The curses attached to these sins have not been broken. Such people must present themselves for deliverance so that men of God can assist in breaking those curses. This is the cure for backsliding.

Everybody knows, for instance, that there are curses imposed on anyone who refuses to pay his tithes and offerings.

> ***"Will a man rob God? Yet ye have robbed me. But ye say, Wherein have we robbed thee? In tithes and offerings. Ye are cursed with a curse: for ye have robbed me, even this whole nation."* (Malachi 3:8, 9)**

But there are blessings for those who obey the injunction of paying tithes and offerings:

> ***"Bring ye all the tithes into the storehouse, that there may be meat in mine house, and prove me now herewith, saith the LORD of hosts, if I will not open you the windows of heaven, and pour out a blessing, that there shall not be room enough to receive it. And I will rebuke the devourer for your sakes, and he shall not destroy the fruits of your ground; neither shall your vine cast her fruit before the time in the field, saith the LORD of hosts. And all nations shall call you blessed: for ye shall be a delightsome land, saith the LORD of hosts.* (Malachi 3:10-12)**

Now if for some reasons you fail to pay your tithes or offering, you are automatically ***"cursed with a curse."*** Among other things, God will not bless you with anything good. He will allow the devourers to destroy the works of your hand.

If out of fear or the realization of the consequences of your mistake, you pay your tithe or offerings, let's say after two months, and you pray and ask God to bless you and open the windows of heaven for you, you may expect God to bless you because you have turned back from the path of disobedience. However, with God, the arithmetic doesn't quite work out like that.

Don't forget that you have already been "cursed with a curse." You have paid your tithes or offerings without first breaking the curse brought on by the initial disobedience. In spite of your repentance and restitution, the curses will linger until you break them. Before then, they will not allow you to enjoy the blessings of the tithes that you have now paid.

> **Break all curses after repentance.**
>
> *****
>
> **The curse itself must be removed for you to have progress in that area you were afflicted.**

Children of God need to know that they have to break the curses that come upon them in the course of backsliding, in order to move forward. After repentance, which is asking God for forgiveness and saying you are sorry, you need to go back to God and ask Him to remove the curses attached to the sins you committed. You also need to ask for restoration. However, due to ignorance, most believers just recite this cliché: "God, forgive me. I will not do it again. Thank you, Jesus," and they believe it is all over. Well, this is not always the case. It might not be over until you settle the matter of these curses.

Abraham, the patriarch of Israel was Sarah's husband. As narrated in **Genesis 20:1-8**, he relocate to a place called Gerar because of the famine. There, he lied that his beautiful wife was his sister. He did this act because he was afraid that someone might want to kill him in order to have his wife. News of Sarah's beauty, soon reached Abimelech, the king of Gerar. Sarah was brought to him, and he saw her and fell in love with her. "I must make her my wife," he announced immediately and ordered that she should be moved into the royal quarters. The day the king made the pronouncement that Abraham's wife was his own, a curse came upon him, but he did not know.

Sometimes, we may not know that our action have brought a curse on us, except the Holy Spirit reveals it – either through the Scriptures or by some other means. In the case of King Abimelech, the Lord spoke to him, "Why did you take another man's wife?" Abimelech was alarmed and proclaimed his innocence right away, "I didn't know that she was married, oh Lord! Abraham lied to me." And God said, "I know that you didn't know."

God knew that this man acted out of ignorance, yet a curse was placed upon him and his entire household, but when he pleaded with the Lord, he received mercy. God showed him what to do to be free from the curse, "Restore the wife back to the husband." Abimelech obeyed. He restored Sarah immediately, and even appeased Abraham with gifts of sheep, oxen, men and women servants, and a thousand pieces of silver. One would think that this is the end of the story, but it wasn't – there was more!

"Ask Abraham to pray for you," God advised Abimelech; otherwise, the curses that came upon his life and household would not be cancelled. Unless an anointed man of God interceded for him, he would suffer the full consequences of those curses. So what happened next?

> **"So Abraham prayed unto God: and God healed Abimelech, and his wife, and his maidservants; and they bare children. For the LORD had fast closed up all the wombs of the house of Abimelech, because of Sarah Abraham's wife. (Genesis 2:17, 18)**

HOW BIG IS YOUR SIN?

Backsliding is a terrible bondage, and it is important for believers who constantly find themselves in this position to present themselves for deliverance, where they can confess their sins and break the curses behind those sins.

You may ask, "Is it every time a believer finds himself in some "small" sins (like telling a "white lie" or forgetting once in awhile to pay his tithes and offerings), that he has to submit himself for deliverance? Or is a simple prayer of repentance sufficient?" I ask you, "Is there any small sin?" Sin is sin and anything that will hinder you from the holiness of God must be removed. You will need to repent every time.

Sometimes, from a human point of view, we consider some sins to be "small" which in actuality are not. The story of Adam and Eve in **Genesis 3:1-13** is a prime example. God told them not to eat the fruit of a particular tree, but they went ahead and ate that particular fruit. From a human point of view, we could say that their sin was "small"; after all, they did not commit murder, robbery, or any other criminal act. They merely disobeyed God's one instruction. Yet that "small" sin was the reason God turned them away forever. That "small" sin is the reason why humanity became accursed and is still suffering.

With God, there is no "small" sin – sin is sin! All sins mean disobedience to God; when you disobey God, there is punishment awaiting you. You should also know that some sins attract specific curses from God. You will discover them when you adequately study your bible, and the Holy Spirit will surely reveal others to you in your walk with the Lord.

THE CURE FOR BACKSLIDING

If you keep on falling into sin, there are three important steps for you to take:

(a) **Go to God in repentance**. Confess your sins and ask Him to forgive you.

(b) **Ask the Lord to remove the curses** that your sins have brought upon you. Spell out the curse if you know it. This is where the assistance of a deliverance minister comes in.

(c) **Make a restitution of your ways**. Backsliding is a common disease that afflicts the Christian, and it is better to deal with it decisively before it eats deep into your spirit and you lose your well-being and salvation.

But how do you know that you are backsliding? It is easy? I've already told you that it starts from the heart. Others around you may not know, but if you examine your heart, you will surely know if you are pleasing the Lord or not. Since the devil knows that what God is most interested in is a man's heart, he will try to cause your heart to draw away from the Lord. He will do this even if you are still very busy working for God. Once your heart is not right or perfect toward God, your service becomes useless, like that of King Amaziah:

"And he did that which was right in the sight if the LORD, but not with a perfect heart." (2 Chronicles 25:2)

Always examine your heart and check whether it is with the Lord or not. Check your spirit and not your preaching or your sermon. Check your heart and not your outward show of righteousness. Is your heart perfect towards God? Do you love Him in your heart? Do you desire Him more than any other thing? If your answers to these questions are "No," then let me inform you that you are surely backslidden. Satan has succeeded in shifting your interest and attention away from God.

But thanks be to God for Jesus Christ. He is the ultimate cure for backsliding, through His Blood that was shed on the Cross of Calvary. He is the only One Who can restore you.

Don't be comfortable in your backslidden state; it is very dangerous. And don't crucify yourself either; there is a solution. Find your way back to God through Jesus Christ. He is the 'Author' and 'Finisher' of your faith and He is ever willing to cleanse you with His precious Blood.

Shift your attention from those 'little idols' that you value more than God. Cry unto the Lord. Repent of your sins. God is willing to accept you.

"If my people, which are called by my name, shall humble themselves, and pray, and seek my face, and turn from their wicked ways; then will I hear from heaven, and will forgive their sin, and will heal their land." **(2 Chronicles 7:14)**

"Come, and let us return unto the LORD: for he hath torn, and he will heal us; he hath smitten, and he will bind us up." **(Hosea 6:1)**

Look only unto the cross where Jesus died. Fix your eyes on the Lord and do not allow any distraction. Jesus asked Peter to walk on water. He did so confidently at the beginning because he fixed his eyes on the Lord, relying solely on Him. The moment Peter looked away from Jesus, he began to sink. When he cried for help, the Lord stretched forth His hand and saved him.

The only thing that will keep us from falling is to set our eyes on the resurrected Christ. His resurrected power is the same forever.

"Jesus Christ the same yesterday, and to day, and for ever. **(Hebrews 13:8)**

Never allow anyone or anything to take your focus away from Him. I know a lot of people believe that once they are saved, they are saved forever; so whatever they do thereafter does not matter. Well, hear this: everything you do as a Christian matters. There is no room for complacency in your relationship with God.

You simply have to try to stay away from committing sin. However, if you have reached the stage where you fail to recognize that you are living in sin, then you have backslidden and are in serious problem. The cure is simple: find your way back to God.

In case you find it difficult to find your way back to God on your own, you need the assistance of a deliverance minister. Maybe a particular sin has become a part of you; you have prayed and done everything possible, yet you cannot get it out of your life. In such a case, you need someone to take you through the deliverance process; there may be a curse that needs to be broken.

SECTION E

Victory Over Unseen Forces

*"For God shall bring every work into judgment,
with every secret thing, whether it be good,
or whether it be evil."*
(Ecclesiastes 12:14)

*"And the LORD said unto Satan,
The LORD rebuke thee, O Satan;
even the LORD that hath chosen Jerusalem rebuke thee:
is not this a brand plucked out of the fire?"*
(Zechariah 3:2)

CHAPTER 12

UNSEEN FORCES FIGHTING AGAINST US

There are fierce battles being fought against us every day by forces that we cannot see with the naked eye. This fact remains a mystery for many growing Christians, although for the spiritually mature this may appear elementary. The truth is that because man is a spirit being living in a physical body, he often finds it hard to contend with forces that are not visible to the naked eye. However, these forces do exist, and the sooner a Christian acknowledges this, the better it is for him or her.

If a man knows the stuff his enemy is made of, then it becomes easier for him to fight back. Unfortunately, due to ignorance, many Christians spend their time fighting the wrong battles. This thereby creates tension and enmity where there shouldn't be; meanwhile, their problems remain unsolved.

From time to time, there have been Christian men proposing to send their wives away because according to them, the wives are witches and their progress in life has been ruined by their wives' demonic activities. Some children have abandoned their aged parents to hunger for the same reason; they are afraid that the "wicked old thing" might kill them and feast on them at their nocturnal meetings.

The fear of witches and wizards is so real in many countries and I have seen this to be true in many parts of Africa; it has destabilized many families, friendships, churches, and associations.

Some cannot eat food cooked by just anybody. They want to be sure that the person who prepared the food is above suspicion. Every old man or woman appears dangerous to them. They misinterpret the most innocent of actions. They are so careful that they do not consider any friendship as genuine; they deal with everyone, even Christians, with suspicion. Others are so obsessed that the only prayer they know how to prayer is for God to destroy their enemies.

I once stayed with a Christian brother who believed that almost every sister he encountered was an instrument of the devil. I was his guest for about a month and we attended prayer meetings together throughout that period. My friend saw all the sisters at these meetings as his enemies because he believed they were agents of the devil who were out to tempt him. Incredible, isn't it? But my friend is not alone in this kind of phobia.

I know of a Church that broke up because members of the congregation were pointing accusing fingers at each other.

Are we then to assume that there are no witches, wizards, or familiar spirits? On the contrary, that would be foolishness. It would be foolhardy not to acknowledge the dark forces of this world that are at work.

There are many dangerous men, women and children – all agents of the devil – roaming around the place, that it takes the mercy of God to remain protected. However, it is not the people that we should identify and fight. Rather, we should deal with the unseen forces that control them.

If you want to cut off the electricity supply from a light bulb, you do not break the bulb. You turn off the power from the light switch. Same way if you want to stop a running water faucet, you don't block the faucet. You simply turn off the lever that controls the faucet. If you want to stop a car's engine from running, you do not stand and speak to the engine, telling it to stop. No! You turn off the ignition. The same principle applies to the unseen battles being waged against us. Deal with the problem from the root source; take authority over that which controls the problem.

Why then do we set ourselves against human beings? Why then do we harbor such thoughts and fears about men of limited ability, men created the same way we were and who sleep and wake up the same way we do? They are just ordinary shells. However, we should be aware of the fact that there are evil forces that inhabit and drive them, making them do the outrageous, supernatural, and wicked things they do. It is these forces we should attack.

> *"Cease ye from man, whose breath is in his nostrils: for wherein is he to be accounted of?"* (Isaiah 2:22)

The fear of anything or anybody will destroy your life, even when you think you are simply being careful,

******

There is no fear in God.

Remember that these evil powers did not begin to manifest in this generation. In the time of Saul, the first king of Israel, the land was filled with wizards and those with familiar spirits. One day, the king rounded up these people and slaughtered them. The wicked spirits in them did not die, because the Bible records that when Saul needed divination, he still found someone with familiar spirits to consult.

> *"Then said Saul unto his servants, Seek me a woman that hath a familiar spirit, that I may go to her, and enquire of her. And his servants said to him, Behold, there is a woman that hath a familiar spirit at Endor... And the woman said unto him, Behold, thou knowest what Saul hath done, how he hath cut off those that have familiar spirits, and wizards, out of the land: wherefore then layest thou a snare for my life, to cause me to die?"* (1 Samuel 28:7, 9)

Suppose we kill all the wizards in the whole world today, will that be the end of wizardry? Certainly not! In the twinkle of an eye, the wizard spirits would find other victims to enter into or possess. Who then do we need to fight? Certainly not our wives, husbands, friends or parents. We need to fight the unseen forces fighting us through them.

"For though we walk in the flesh, we do not war after the flesh." **(2 Corinthians 10:3)**

"For we wrestle not against FLESH and BLOOD, but against PRINCIPALITIES, against POWERS, against the RULERS OF THE DARKNESS OF THIS WORLD, against SPIRITUAL WICKEDNESS IN HIGH PLACES."
(emphasis added, Ephesians 6:12)

The above passage is simple and clear. Human beings are not the ones we should fight against in our spiritual battles. Our real enemies are unseen forces.

The enemies we need to fight are:

(i) Principalities
(ii) Powers
(iii) The rulers of the darkness of this world
(iv) Spiritual wickedness in High places.

(1) Principalities

> These are demons. They have physical bodies and they form the highest level of government in the kingdom of darkness. Like the worldly forces, principalities have a well-arranged hierarchy like the army, the navy, and the air force. Principalities rule here on earth and they have more than 50,000 demons in their hierarchy, and under each "commanding demon," there are usually more than 20,000 demons.

(2) Powers

These groups have their own hierarchy and they work hand in hand with principalities. Powers operate in high places. They have their seat in the air from where they monitor lives and events.

(3) The Rulers of Darkness of This World and Spiritual Wickedness in High Places

These are evil spirits that are always wandering about, looking for human bodies to dwell in and use as their operating base. They live in the air and cannot easily function or carry out their acts of wickedness without a human body to use.

(4) Spiritual Wickedness in High Places

These evil spirits (like the Powers mentioned above) have their base in the air, and they mainly operate in the heavenlies. They are responsible for a wide range of deadly disasters, both natural and man-made that occur in the skies above. Their operations include (but are not limited to): airplane crashes, air mishaps and deaths in activities such as parachuting, sky diving, bungee jumping and so on, and natural disasters like hurricanes, tornadoes, heat waves, meteor showers and all other forms of deadly storms or weather.

Spiritual wickedness in high places are evil spirits that frustrate the believers especially in their prayer lives. They are responsible for causing a delay in the answers or responses to our prayers, thereby hindering our blessings, breakthroughs and miracles. A case in point can be seen in the book of Daniel, where an angel had to fight the Prince of Persia that was withholding the response to Daniel's prayers:

> *"Then said he unto me, Fear not, Daniel: from the first day that thou didst set thine heart to understand, and to chasten thyself before thy God, thy words were heard, and I am come for thy words. But the prince of the kingdom of Persia withstood me one and twenty days: but, lo, Michael, one of the chief princes, came to help me; and I remained there with the kings of Persia."* **(Daniel 10: 12-13)**

We do not need to go into a lot of arguments or explanations as to the identity of the 'Prince of Persia'. Theologians and Bible scholars have agreed that the 'Prince of Persia' is an evil (or demonic) spirit who operates in the heavenlies, hindering our prayers. This evil spirit is indeed the Spiritual Wickedness in High Places.

These evil spirits include witchcraft spirits, wizard manifestations, and familiar spirits (e.g., Marine spirits, etc.) Witchcraft spirits are the closest to human beings and they are so destructive because they manipulate their victims in so many ways. Jesus Christ referred to Satan as the *"Prince of this world"* **(John 12: 31)** and **(John 16: 11)**.

This does not imply that God, the Creator, handed over the world as a gift to the devil when he was cast down from heaven, along with one third of the angels. It only means that our Lord recognizes the fact that there is a spiritual kingdom here on earth over which Satan is the head.

> *"And there was war in heaven: Michael and his angels fought against the dragon; and the dragon fought and his angels, And prevailed not; neither was their place found any more in heaven. And the great dragon was cast out, that old serpent, called the Devil, and Satan, which deceiveth the whole world: he was cast out in the earth, and his angels were cast out with him."* **(Revelation 12:7-9)**

It was when the rebels who had lost their place in heaven got down here on earth, that they set up another spiritual kingdom with

Satan as the overall head. This kingdom is divided into four parts as seen in **Ephesians 6:12**. We are not just fighting principalities or powers, but all the four spiritual categories in the kingdom of darkness.

Many Christians are busy praying for God to kill all witches and wizards. If they die unrepentant, their souls will go to hell, but the evil spirits in them will leave and go on to possess other people.

Apostle Paul, through the Holy Spirit, did not say that when we overcome one of them, the battle is won. You cannot fight this battle and succeed with human strength.

Avoid giving the devil entry into your life through the gateways that will become open when you follow the world and its practices.

******

FEAR GOD!!!

"For though we walk in the flesh, we do not war after the flesh." **(2 Corinthians 10:3)**

This means that, though we live in physical bodies, the battles we are fighting are unseen. He also warns that:

"...the weapons of our warfare are not carnal, but mighty through God to the pulling down of strong holds." **(2 Corinthians 10:4)**

All different parts of the evil kingdom operate in their own peculiar ways. Apart from those who possess and torment human beings, some oversee national affairs; others are set against the Church, while some rule over the air. The enemy's plan that he wants achieve is: to kill, steal, and destroy.

HOW TO STAY FREE

Sometimes through carelessness and prayerlessness, the devil can gain entry into a Christian's life so that the Christian becomes obsessed with him. Demonic obsession describes the situation

> Stand tall in your army uniform – your armor of God.
>
> ******
>
> We are at war and any carelessness may result in death.

whereby evil spirits operate the physical and mental senses of an individual at different intervals of time, for example, through epileptic fits and other unusual manifestations. The devil usually practices obsession on its victims before possessing them.

There are different ways through which the devil can enter into a believer's life, but the main avenues are unclean living, fear, and participation in "white garment" churches where special sponges, soaps, and candles are used for ritual baths. Visiting witchdoctors, keeping charms, reading magical and other unwholesome books, consulting oracles, celebrating Halloween and consulting star readers, palm readers or reading horoscopes, are all gateways for evil spirits.

Demonic possession occurs when evil spirits enter and dwell in a person, taking over his will and mental power and using them as they choose. A believer cannot be possessed unless he is careless or he had been earlier subjected to possession by the devil before he accepted Christ.

From **Luke 8:30**, we see that a person can have from one evil spirit to a legion (3,000 to 6,000) in him. The extent to which afflicted people can be used by the devil depends on the number of evil spirits dwelling in them. Usually, many who are obsessed or possessed cannot tell when the demons entered into them until they begin to see the manifestations.

HOW TO FIGHT UNSEEN FORCES

The Holy Bible offers us a complete set of weapons, known as "the whole armor of God," which we should employ to fight the unseen forces that war against us.

"Put on the whole armour of God, that ye may be able to stand against the wiles of the devil. For we wrestle not against flesh and blood, but against principalities, against powers, against the rulers of the darkness of this world, against spiritual wickedness in high places. Wherefore take unto you the whole armour of God, that ye may be able to withstand in the evil day, and having done all, to stand." **(Ephesians 6:11-13)**

Paul, through the Holy Spirit, revealed to the Church the secrets of the unseen battles and how to fight them. He was the one whom the Holy Spirit also used to reveal the kingdom and authority of the devil. No wonder, when the evil spirit challenged the seven sons of Sceva in **Acts 19:13-15,** it said, *"...Paul I know..."* God had shown Paul their wiles, tricks, and other things concerning them. So on this subject, we can learn from Paul, the secrets that the Holy Spirit has kept in store for the Church.

Just as soldiers have to prepare adequately before going to war, it is equally necessary that we put on our complete 'battle attire' before approaching the field of battle. In other words, before a physical man stands up to fight an unseen force, he must put on "all the armor of God." **Ephesians 6:11** tells us that if we fail to put this armor on, then we are not fit to stand in the battle. The components of a Christian's armor are given in **Ephesians 6:14-18** and they are analyzed below:

(1) *"Stand therefore, having your loins girt about with truth, and having on the breastplate of righteousness."* **(Ephesians 6:14)**

Be honest, truthful, and live a holy and blameless life. Manifest the acts of righteousness according to the laws of the Kingdom of God. Today, many Christians do not believe in holiness, they claim "love covers a multitude of sins." Are such people free from the fear of the devil and the machinations of wizards? God expects every one of His children to be perfect even as He is perfect. It should be your daily aspiration to be like your Father who is in heaven.

"He that committeth sin is of the devil; for the devil sinneth from the beginning. For this purpose the Son of God was manifested, that he might destroy the works of the devil." **(1 John 3:8)**

Don't play with sin. The reason God sent Jesus Christ to us is to call us out of a life of sin, into a life of:

"... holiness without which no man shall see the Lord." **(Hebrews 12:14)**

(2) *"And your feet shod with the preparation of the gospel of peace."* **(Ephesians 6:15)**

You need to receive the baptism of the Holy Ghost after salvation and sanctification. Then preach the gospel everywhere you go, and also seek every opportunity to be a witness for Christ. If you fail to preach the gospel, you are already weakened by the unseen forces and you are not fit to go out for battle. The Bible states:

"For I am not ashamed of the gospel of Christ: for it is the power of God unto salvation..." **(Romans 1:16)**

(3) *"Above all, taking the shield of faith, wherewith ye shall be able to quench all the fiery darts of the wicked."* **(Ephesians 6:16)**

Faith is another part of the armor that you must put on. If you do not have it, you cannot be a soldier. In God's sight, without faith, you are not qualified and you will be defeated. If there must be a successful battle, you need the shield of faith. Paul says, by the Holy Spirit, that if you don't have faith, the fiery darts of the devil will hit you.

(4) *"...Take the helmet of salvation..."* **(Ephesians 6:17a)**

Make sure that you are washed in the Blood of the Lamb. You must be born again and your name must be written in the Lamb's Book of Life. Make sure that you have repented of your sins and invited Jesus Christ into your life through prayer and faith. Then you can testify to Satan that you are a child of God **(John 1:12)**. If you are not born again, the battle will always go contrary. Paul says that you will not be able to stand against the wiles of the devil. The seven sons of Sceva who tried to do that **(Acts 19:13-15)** were disgraced by the evil spirit.

(5) *"And take....the sword of the Spirit, which is the word of God."* **(Ephesians 6:17b)**

The Word of God must be found in your heart, mind, and mouth; the last two are very important. You can only be successful in battle when the Word of God is in you. This means you must study it, memorize the appropriate Scripture, and use it at any given time. It is your spiritual bullet.

> *"This book of the law shall not depart out of thy mouth; but thou shalt meditate therein day and night, that thou mayest observer to do according to all that is written therein: for them thou shalt make thy way prosperous, and then thou shall have good success."* **(Joshua 1:8)**

(6) *"Praying always with all prayer and supplication in the Spirit, and watching thereunto with all perseverance and supplication for all saints.* **(Ephesians 6:18)**

The last thing that will determine whether you will win or lose the battle is prayer. If you put on all the other parts of the armor but fail to pray, you are just like the soldier who dons his armor, guns, bullets, and every other necessary thing, only to fall asleep when he gets to the battle front. Prayer is the only thing that keeps us awake to fight the enemy.

"...men ought always to pray, and not to faint."
(Luke 18:1)

From Genesis to Revelation, people became successful because they prayed. Consider Moses, Joshua, Elijah, Elisha, Jesus Christ, Peter, and others. Today, people want the power of Daniel, but not the prayer life of Daniel. They desire the success of Jeremiah, but not his tears. We would like to say, like Paul, *"I have fought a good fight, I have kept the faith..."* but we don't want to have a taste of his experience in fasting and suffering.

Until the spirit and the flesh are willing to pray, we will continue to deny Christ. When both are willing, like it happened to Peter after the day of Pentecost, we can be sure of victory in each battle we face. You cannot fight unseen battles with visible weapons.

You will win all your unseen battles <u>ONLY</u> through the items that make up the whole armor of God:

(1) Be saved – **Ephesians 6: 17a**
(2) Be holy and fruitful - **Ephesians 6:14**
(3) Preach the gospel - **Ephesians 6:15**
(4) Stand on 'mountain-moving' faith - **Ephesians 6:16**
(5) Memorize and use the Word of God - **Ephesians 6:17b**
(6) Prayer will determine whether you will overcome or be defeated - **Ephesians 6:18**

Having done all to stand, do not go to sleep after the battle is won; the devil never sleeps. You must remain vigilant and continue using the whole armor of God. It is the only way you can remain standing until the Captain of our salvation blows the trumpet to call us home.

May you find yourself among the champions when life's battles are over, in Jesus' name, Amen!

CHAPTER 13

UNSEEN FORCES FIGHTING FOR US

These are dangerous times. It is an era of fierce battles, both in the physical and the spiritual. Virtually all of us – young and old, male and female – have suddenly discovered the importance of security. This is why security outfits are thriving everywhere. In Nigeria and other parts of Africa, houses are built with giant, prison-like walls and gates to ward off armed robbers, assassins, and other threats to life and property. Many rich men cannot move around without a band of bodyguards for protection.

A lot of men and women are compelled by the problems of life, to seek one form of protection or the other. This has, unfortunately, lured many into occultism, wizardry, witchcraft, and other demonic practices. Sadly, these people totally miss the point: they simply don't understand what true security is.

WHAT IS TRUE SECURITY?

If you are one of those people who are engaged in a frantic search for worldly security and protection, then read this story of a young man whom I encountered in a college of theology. He was deeply involved in occultism while seeking for power, long before he became a born again Christian.

According to him, his quest for power began at the tender age of twelve, when he was initiated into a cult. From then on, he didn't look back. He joined one group after another, and began to increase in power.

At a point, he was in more than seven separate occult groups. Later, with the demonic qualifications and influenced he acquired, he killed his mother and turned his father into a sick man. There was something about him that instilled fear in the hearts of men, including his teachers. He was a terror to all, both at home and at school.

He confessed to having attended meetings of the spiritual underworld in India, Paris, and London, in the sea, and at other improbable places. Due to his high position in the demonic hierarchy, it would take him only a minute or so to be transported to the venue of a meeting anywhere in the world.

In spite of his unparalleled truancy, he was always top of his class while in high (secondary) school. This, he explained, was because during examinations, he would use his evil powers to summon the necessary answers to the questions, which he would then copy. In a case where the answers were not forthcoming, he would influence the teachers to give him excellent grades, sometimes even the full marks, A+ all the way!

He had so much demonic power that he was able to kill many people and send several others on a journey of insanity. He very vividly recalled the terrible fate of some of his colleagues, who had ganged up against him. On that unfortunate day, they planned to ambush and beat him on his way home, but he turned the tables on them. He commanded snakes to materialize from the surrounding bushes and bite the boys. He left them in the throes of anguish and went on his way, as if nothing had happened.

At such a young age, he was drunk with the evil powers that he used

> **Speaking in boldness, knowing that the power of God that is within you is above any other; will cause you to manifest the glory of God here on earth.**

indiscriminately to ruin lives. He actually thought he was powerful. But thank God for His mercies. One day, this man discovered his limitations. He discovered the name of the all-powerful One, Jesus; the name that is greater than any other name; the name at which:

"...Every knee should bow, of things in heaven, and things in earth, and things under the earth; And that every tongue should confess that Jesus Christ is Lord, to the glory of God the Father." (Philippians 2:9-11)

It was just like any other day, when a colleague of his – a Christian girl – approached this fearsome character with the message of salvation. She told him, *"Forsake your evil ways and accept Jesus Christ as your Lord and Savior."*

The young man was surprised. *"Who is this Jesus and who is this girl to preach to me when some experienced pastors in town avoid me like a plague?"* There and then, he decided to deal with her effrontery and put her to shame. He called her out in the presence of some other colleagues and challenged her and "her Jesus" to a power duel.

"If this Jesus that you preach is more powerful, then I will accept Him. But if not...." he said with an air of pride. Everybody waited, holding their breath. They were afraid of the evil that might befall the girl and wondered what manner of madness drove her to arouse the "little god" in the first place.

With the supreme confidence of a man of authority, the young man moved somewhere and looked toward a nearby forest. He then commanded a particular tree to move and stand right in front of him. To everybody's amazement, the tree moved! He then asked her to tell her Jesus to send the tree back to the forest where it came from. Pandemonium broke out as other students started running away from the scene of this unusual display of power. Some teachers who had been attracted by the noise, stood at a safe distance to watch.

The sister was not fazed. She stood her ground. There and then, she looked up to the heavens and prayed: **"Lord Jesus, I have preached Your word to this young man whom You created with**

Your own hands. Now he throws a challenge to You. Father, I thank You because I know that You will prove to him and all others present here today that You are the Almighty God." She then said to her challenger, *"I am not going to obey your command. In the name of Jesus Christ, the Creator of all things, this tree will never obey you again, but it will stand here forever and ever."*

The man laughed. It was time to confound the girl and disgrace her once and for all. He immediately commanded the tree to return to its original base, but to his dismay, nothing happened. After much drama, he ran to his family house to equip himself for "battle."

By the time he came back, wearing a red regalia, a great number of students had gathered. His eyes became red as he summoned all his gods and evoked all the powers available to him. Still, nothing happened. He realized then that he had failed and that there was indeed a higher authority somewhere. And not just a higher authority, as he later learned that the young lady he had challenged was secure under the highest spiritual authority.

True authority is not found in any occult or secret powers. You can only find it in Jesus.

From the moment you accept Jesus Christ as your Lord and Savior, some fundamental changes occur in your life. Among other things:

- You become God's own child **(John 1:12,13)**.
- You are delivered from the powers of darkness and transported into the kingdom of Jesus, where Satan cannot operate, and you become a partaker in the benefits of the commonwealth of Israel **(Colossians 1:12,13)**.
- One other thing you will enjoy is divine protection.

All power and dominion belongs to God. Since you no longer own yourself, the battles of your life are no more yours. You now belong to God; the battles that confront you actually confront God, Who owns you. Think about it! Can any problem stand before the Almighty God Who is a consuming fire? Of course not!

Most of life's battles are fought in the spiritual real, and the earlier a Christian realizes this, the better it is for him or her. Without an iota of doubt, there are unseen forces, from the kingdom of darkness, fighting against us. You also need to know that as a Christian, there are also unseen forces, from the kingdom of God, fighting for us. It is only those who know this secret that can succeed in life's battles.

Once upon a time, a fetish priest and a Christian brother were both tenants living in the same house. One day and for no just cause, the fetish priest ordered the brother to vacate the house within seven days or face serious consequences. Of course, the Christian brother told him off, saying that his boast was empty. Instead of being afraid, the brother reported the matter to God in prayer. He did nothing in the physical to fight for himself.

On the seventh day, a strange thing happened. The first son of the fetish priest dropped dead, while the Christian brother was hale and hearty. Following this inexplicable disaster, the fetish priest went and prostrated before the brother and pleaded with him, "Please Sir, forgive me.... You don't have to move out of this house. Rather, let me be the one to move out instead..."

This kind of experience could happen to anyone fighting a person who is under the highest authority.

"The LORD shall fight for you, and ye shall hold your peace." **(Exodus 14:14)**

"No weapon that is formed against thee shall prosper; and every tongue that shall rise against thee in judgment thou shalt condemn. This is the heritage of the servants of the LORD, and their righteousness is of me, saith the LORD." **(Isaiah 54:17)**

The lives of those who truly know Jesus Christ as their personal Lord and Savior are secure under the highest authority, and because of this, their spiritual battles are no longer theirs but the Lord's. They will be at peace at all times, while God is fighting the enemies on their behalf. While they are asleep, God is awake, watching over them.

> *"He will not suffer thy foot to be moved: he that keepeth thee will not slumber. Behold, he that keepeth Israel shall neither slumber nor sleep."* **(Psalm 121:3, 4)**

All those who know that they are secure through the Blood of Jesus **(Exodus 12:13)** do not live in fear. They live in peace with all men and God does the fighting for them when necessary. Their eyes are set only on Jesus and nothing will take their attention away from following Him. There is no power, no kingdom here on earth, or in hell below, that is able to pluck them out of His secure hands.

> *"My sheep hear my voice, and I know them, and they follow me: And I give unto them eternal life; and they shall never perish, neither shall any man pluck them out of my Father's hands. My Father, which gave them me, is greater than all; and no man is able to pluck them out of my Father's hand."* **(John 10:27-29)**

An enemy sent a snake to kill a Christian sister while she was sleeping, but because "He that keepeth (her) shall neither slumber nor sleep," God woke her up in the nick of time to see the mighty snake come in through the locked door. She knew her rights, so instead of being afraid, she reminded the snake that she was secure under the highest authority, and spoke the powerful Word of God to it: *"It is written that no weapon that is fashioned against me shall prosper..."* Even before she finished speaking, the snake jumped up and slumped to the ground. It died without her touching it.

> *"He that dwelleth in the secret place of the most High shall abide under the shadow of the Almighty."* **(Psalm 91:1)**

The Lord is not called "THE MAN OF WAR" for nothing. If you look throughout the Bible, you will see that He proved His mettle countless times. There was no battle HE fought that He did not win; there is no battle He cannot win! He is the Lord of Hosts and Commander-in-Chief of the heavenly armies. You may not see His soldiers, but rest assured they are present, doing battle at the Lord's command. They drove Lucifer out of heaven when he declared war on God's domain.

Believe me when I say the battles that confront you will soon be won. Praise God!

> *"...but the people that do know their God shall be strong, and do exploits."* **(Daniel 11:32b)**

God is a God of war, but many people are ignorant of His presence and assistance in the all the spiritual battles they are fighting.

Many Christians are often deceived by the magnitude of their problems that they cannot discern the presence of the unseen forces of God fighting for them. They continue to worry about sickness, poverty, barrenness, fetish priests, demons, etc. Such Christians often die at the battlefield.

GOD'S UNSEEN FORCES

Instead of living in defeat, Christians should learn to focus on the presence of the Holy Spirit, the angels, the hosts of heaven and the chariots of fire that surround them. These are ever ready soldiers from the kingdom of God, always standing by ready to fight on behalf of the children of God in times of trouble.

(1) THE HOLY SPIRIT

The greatest of your defenders is the Holy Spirit – the third person in the Godhead. You cannot win a battle, whether physical or spiritual, without the help of the Holy Spirit. You can't win by your own might or by your power.

> *"Not by might, nor by power; but by my spirit, saith the Lord of hosts."* **(Zechariah 4:6)**

As a matter of fact, the Holy Spirit, who is the Spirit of the omnipotent, omniscient, and omnipresent God, fights all the battles that comes in the way of a Christian, and helps set his or her feet on the path of victory. Even before you know that a war is being waged against you, the Holy Spirit knows. Before you can see the battle, the Holy Spirit sees it and He uses His omnipotence to win the war even before you can lift a finger. What a comforting companion!

However, in order to enjoy the everlasting companionship of the Holy Spirit, you have your own role to play.

> *"Let us hear the conclusion of the whole matter: Fear God, and keep his commandments: for this is the whole duty of man."* **(Ecclesiastes 12:13)**

If you do all these when the forces – seen and unseen from the kingdom of Satan – wage war against you, the Holy Spirit will take care of the battle and you will hold your peace.

> *"So shall they fear the name of the LORD from the west, and his glory form the rising of the sun. When the enemy shall come in like a flood, the Spirit of the LORD shall lift up a standard against him."* **(Isaiah 59:19)**

Partial obedience to the Word of God cannot guarantee you the victory that comes from the Lord. The Holy Spirit requires nothing short of total submission from you in order to arise on your behalf.

In some cases, however, the Holy Spirit does not go into battle Himself. He delegates angels or any other heavenly hosts to fight your battles. It all depends on the strategy that the Almighty God wants to employ, but He will never leave you in the lurch.

(2) ANGELS

Hezekiah, king of Judah, was a man who served the Lord faithfully, but he had an enemy who was determined to destroy him and his kingdom. This enemy was the powerful king of Assyria, Sennacherib. What did Hezekiah do? He cried unto God. When your ways please God, there is no battle He won't fight for you.

How did God fight and win this battle for Hezekiah and the people of Judah? He sent an angel to slaughter 185,000 Assyrian soldiers in one night, the entire invading army!

> *"Then the angel of the LORD went forth, and smote in the camp of the Assyrians a hundred and fourscore and five thousand: and when they arose early in the morning, behold, they were all dead corpses."* **(Isaiah 37:36)**

Only one angel of the Lord achieved this mighty feat. It was also an angel that fought the battle of the Red Sea. When the mighty army of Egypt marched against the cornered Israelites:

> *"And the angel of God, which went before the camp of Israel; removed and went behind them; and the pillar of the cloud went from before their face, and stood behind them: And it came between the camp of the Egyptians and the camp of Israel; and it was a cloud and darkness to them, but it gave light by night to these: so that the one came not near the other all night."* **(Exodus 14:19-20)**

This was a deciding factor in the battle at the Red Sea. The angel gave the Israelites enough time and illumination to cross the sea. Yet, the same angel delayed the advance of the enemy – Pharaoh's mighty army – so that they could perish.

Daniel was a man who knew his God. When his enemies conspired together to destroy him, he said:

> *"My God hath sent his angel, and hath shut the lions' mouths, that they have not hurt me: forasmuch as before him innocency was found in me; and also before thee, O king, have I done no hurt."* **(Daniel 6:22)**

Faithfulness to God was what led Daniel into the lions' den. Daniel knew that there were unseen forces fighting for him, so he was not frightened by the faces of the lions, neither did he panic at their roaring. God did not send the angel to kill the lions, but rather to shut their mouths so that they could not hurt Daniel, and by doing this, people could acknowledge His presence in the den with Daniel. These same lions that did no harm to Daniel, later devoured his enemies. Praise the Lord! He still sends angels to safeguard the lives of those who belong to Him whenever the need arises.

> *"For he shall give his angels charge over thee, to keep thee in all thy ways..."* **(Psalm 91:11)**

There are angels fighting for us. The ability or inability to see them does not remove the fact of their presence.

(3) HEAVENLY HOSTS

From time immemorial, God has used the hosts of heaven to deliver His children from the harassment of the devil. Even now, God releases them for battle on our behalf when necessary.

In **Joshua 6**, when the immovable wall of Jericho confronted Joshua, Israel's leader, all human efforts had failed. This was an obstacle that stood between Israel and the Promised Land. The wall was eventually pulled down, not by the children if Israel, but by the heavenly soldiers sent by the God of Israel.

The faithful, unchanging God also showed Himself mighty during the siege on Samaria by the Syrian Army. The siege was so serious and the food shortage was so severe that the inhabitants of the town started feeding on their children's flesh. One glorious day, the Lord sent His heavenly hosts to break the siege.

> *"For the LORD had made the host of the Syrians to hear a noise of chariots, and a noise of horses, even the noise of a great host: and they said one to another, Lo, the king of Israel hath hired against us the kings of the Hittites, and the kings of the Egyptians, to come upon us. Wherefore they arose and fled in the twilight, and left their tents, and their horses, and their asses, even the camp as it was, and fled for their life."* **(2 Kings 7:6, 7)**

There are a great number of the heavenly hosts that are ever ready to fight for us when the enemy rears its troublesome head. Just call on God, tell him what you want Him to do and He will answer you.

There is no doubt that the hosts of heaven that are fighting for us are more than the unseen evil forces fighting against us, because it is written:

> *"Ye are of God, little children, and have overcome them: because greater is he that is in you, than he that is in the world."* **(1 John 4:4)**

(4) CHARIOTS OF FIRE

A chariot is an open, two-wheeled carriage draw by horses. They were used in ancient times mostly for fighting wars and in competitive racing. They were also used for traveling.

Just as His angels are in the thousands, the Bible states very clearly that God has chariots, and that He has them in thousands.

> *"The chariots of God are twenty thousand, even thousands of angels: the Lord is among them, as in Sinai, in the holy place."* **(Psalm 68:17)**

When the Lord is angry with our enemies:

> *"...Behold, the Lord will come with fire, and with his chariots like a whirlwind, to render his anger with fury, and rebuke with flames."* **(Isaiah 66:15)**

It is clear that God's chariots are chariots of fire.

When it was time for Elijah to depart, God sent one of his chariots to pick him up. As Elijah was discussing with Elisha, there appeared a chariot of fire, and horses of fire parted them. Elijah went up by a whirlwind into heaven, accompanied by a chariot of fire and Elisha saw him no more **(2 Kings 2: 11, 12)**.

The chariots of God, also known as the chariots of fire, are part of the weapons of warfare.

When the king of Syria was told that Elisha was in a town called Dothan, he sent a large army there – with horses and chariots. They reached the town at night and surrounded it. Ordinarily, Elisha would have had no way of escape because of the severity of the siege. However, we soon discover the contrary:

> *"And when the servant of the man of God was risen early, and gone forth, behold, an host compassed the city both with horses and chariots. And his servant said unto him, Alas, my master! How shall we do? And he answered, Fear not: for they that be with us are more than they that be*

> *with them. And Elisha prayed, and said, LORD, I pray thee, open his eyes, that he may see. And the LORD opened the eyes of the young man; and he saw: and, behold, the mountain was full of horses and chariots of fire round about Elisha."* **(2 Kings 6:15-17)**

Those who do not pray often, see problems rather than the Savior. Elisha's servant who may not have had his quiet time that morning saw enemies, defeat, and the chariots of the enemy.

The enemy had come against Elisha on chariots, but before their arrival, God's chariots were already there waiting for them. Elisha had spiritual insight, so he trusted in the Lord and was not worried. His servant, however, failed to see the armies of the Lord and was troubled.

The determining factor in the type of life you live is what you see – the heavenly hosts around you or the evil powers fighting against you. Whenever a Christian is faced with any spiritual battle, he needs not fear at all because God will send chariots of fire to render the necessary assistance. The greatest weapon of the devil is to send fear into your heart, so that you forget God's presence or His help.

Christians are not overcome by the devil because the chariots are dispatched against the devil. When you go out or come in, there are chariots of fire with you. When you are sleeping at night, there are chariots of God watching over you. The important thing is not whether you can feel or see them, but to believe that they are there with you.

The Bible says in **2 Kings 6:17** that the chariots and horses of fire were only around Elisha. This was because fear had taken Elisha's servant out of God's protection. Fear always takes a Christian out of God's presence and protection.

Beloved, you have no reason to be afraid of the array of demonic forces that are against you, for *"they that are with us are more than they that are with them."*

As long as you are living in the will of God, you have the Holy Spirit, the angels of God, the hosts of heaven, and the chariots of God or the chariots of fire, as you unassailable bodyguards. Remember, only one angel slew 185,000 Assyrian soldiers. The Lord has thousands of them at His beck and call. Don't give the enemy more credit than he deserves. The armies of God are unbeatable.

For unseen forces to arise on your behalf, however, you have to learn how to pray earnestly. The unseen chariots of God were waiting to hear Elisha's command. They did not take any action against the Syrian soldiers until Elisha prayed to God to smite the enemy with blindness. The only reason we are commanded to pray always is so that these unseen forces will always be active on our behalf.

Never forget that the enemy cannot match the unseen forces fighting on your behalf if you are a Christian.

CHAPTER 14

PULLING DOWN THE WALLS

In your battles against the kingdom of darkness, you will always win if you stay on the Lord's side. However, there is a great mistake many Christians make, which invariably delays their breakthrough, or makes them unable to reach their goals – despite the fact that God has already given them victory. The moment such Christians receive the promise of God on a given situation, they go to sleep, thinking that all is well. God expects you to pursue that promise until you take hold of it. If you relax at the wrong time, you are bound to lose the promise. When God has played His own part, He expects you to play yours. If you don't, you will never "possess your possession."

When God gives a promise to His people, or grants them a vision of a possession He has given them, more often than not there are obstacles or barriers that they have to overcome to be able to enter into that promise. If, however, they get discouraged on the way, and refuse to press on due to the obstacles, too bad! They will lose the promise, and that is what the enemy wants.

The story of the children of Israel at the verge of entering into the Promised Land is an apt metaphor for the kind of struggles that the people of God have to engage in, and the manner of obstacles and barriers they have to contend with to possess that which God has already given them.

Several generations before Joshua, the Lord had made a covenant with Abraham, the patriarch of Israel:

"In the same day the LORD made a covenant with Abram, saying, Unto thy seed have I have given this land, form the river of Egypt unto the great river, the river Euphrates: The Kenites, and the Perizzites, and the Rephaims, And the Amorites, and the Canaanites, and the Girgashites, and the Jebusites." **(Genesis 15:18-20)**

The time had come to enjoy the promise that God had made to Abraham, their ancestor, that is, the time to enter into the Promised Land, but there was a big problem. Jericho was the city through which the Israelites would go through to get to the Promised Land. According to **Joshua 6:1**, the gates of the city were kept shut and guarded to keep the Israelites out. No one could enter or leave the city. The gate of the city was not an ordinary gate. Mighty and seemingly impregnable as it appeared:

"...The LORD said unto Joshua, See, I have given into thine hand Jericho, the king thereof, and the mighty men of valour." **(Joshua 6:2)**

God was speaking here about a job He had already finished. Yet, physically speaking, there still was the matter of a certain wall – the unbreached wall of Jericho. Jericho was a fortified city. It was fenced all around with bricks. The thickness of the wall was such that horsemen used the topmost floor for races. The wall even accommodated several living quarters. It was impenetrable and intimidating. This was the manner of the wall that protected Jericho!

God spoke to Joshua, "SEE", He said. God did not say, "Joshua, I will take you to the wall of Jericho and then before you very eyes, pull it down so that you can march through and possess the land I promised you." Rather, He opened Joshua's eyes and gave him some spiritual insights. God made Joshua realize that the matter of Jericho had been settled in the spirit realm. Joshua knew what the mouth of the Lord had spoken and the vision he had seen. He believed in his God. However, if he had not taken a step of faith by walking, as the Lord had commanded him and the Israelites **in Joshua 6:3-5**, the physical wall of Jericho would never have fallen.

1. FAITH

Joshua took the first, most important step to pulling down the wall, which was having faith in that which the Lord had spoken.

> *"Now the just shall live by faith: but if any man draw back, my soul shall have no pleasure in him. But we are not of them who draw back unto perdition; but of them that believe to the saving of the soul."* **(Hebrews 10: 38, 39)**

God spoke to Joshua as He has done to many of us in different circumstances, about His goodness, love, and manifold mercies, and about victories. He has given us these blessings over the enemies of our lives. He has spoken through His Word (the Scriptures) and through dreams, visions, and through His prophets (our pastors or ministers).

A lot of us have also experienced the presence of God during praise and worship sessions, prayer time and during seasons of quiet time. In spite of these experiences, and despite the fact the God has spoken to us concerning specific situations, we still find ourselves bound to painful tasks, hurts, unfulfilled dreams and desires, and increased oppression by the devil, etc.

What should be made clear is that such bondage is not from God. They are linked to the spiritual barricades set up by the kingdom of darkness, to hinder, disrupt, postpone, or destroy God's promises to you. You should know that for every spiritual promise made to you by God, there is a spiritual wall that the devil has erected to keep you from receiving that which is already yours.

The most important step you need to take to pull down the wall that stands between you and your blessings – which could be success, prosperity, marriage, children, etc. – is to have absolute and unflinching faith in God. He does not lie! He can do all things, no matter how impossible they sound. Your enemy is just waiting for you to doubt the faithful promises of God. A doubter is a sinner, and a sinner cannot receive the promise meant for the righteous.

> *"Now the just shall live by faith: but if any man draw back, my soul shall have no pleasure in him. But we are not of them who draw back unto perdition; but of them that believe to the saving of the soul."* **(Hebrews 10: 38, 39)**

> *"For by it (faith) the elders obtained a good report."* **(Hebrews 11:2)**

Once you know what God has said about your situation, you have the spiritual access to enter, by His grace, into a vantage point of battle, from where you can pull down the strongholds of the enemy. You are the one who will accomplish the task; God has done His part. You do not expect Him to vacate His throne in the heavens and come down to earth to do what you should do for yourself. You need to exercise your faith even in deliverance.

2. ACTION

Remember that at the time God spoke to Joshua, Jericho had been given to him spiritually. In the physical, however, he was still outside the walls of the city.

> *"By faith the walls of Jericho fell down, after they were compassed about seven days."* **(Hebrews 11:30)**

It is only when we underrate God and doubt His ability to lift us up that we end up taking a longer path to reach our destiny. This is the simple truth. If you have prayed to God concerning a specific need and you maintain a right relationship with Him, then you need not be afraid. God will minister to you in that situation. All you need to do thereafter is to believe in Him and in His promises, and then move on to possess your possessions.

Expect the walls of resistance to be there, but also remember that Joshua did not complain about the difficulties to be encountered in pulling down the walls of Jericho. He rejoiced at the Lord's bidding and gave commands to the children of Israel to do that which the

Lord God had instructed. In like manner, you can command the ministering angels of God to enter the battle with you against the kingdom of Satan. Surely, the walls that obstruct your joy will fall down flat.

To hide is to give yourself over to shame and death; to surrender is to go into captivity and eternal bondage, bringing along with it the abortion or untimely death of your destiny.

God is a God Who makes a way where there is no way. He is the same God Who calls things that are not as though they are. He is able to give us more than we can ask or imagine. Even if your walls say: "THERE IS NO THOROUGHFARE HERE," by your unchanging resolution that ignites the love of God, you can overcome those walls. Though there may not be any physical thoroughfares, God will provide alternative, supernatural, and effective arrangements to enable you finish the race.

Arise, therefore, brethren! There are walls you have to contend with. Don't look back and don't move your feet away from the battle line. As long as you are on the Lord's side, the obstacles will melt away. And when they do, you will enter into the joy the Lord has given you.

SECTION F

Keys To Complete Deliverance

*"And when the LORD shall deliver them before thee;
thou shalt smite them, and utterly destroy them;
thou shalt make no covenant with them,
nor shew mercy unto them."*
(Deuteronomy 7:2)

*"And the LORD gave them rest round about,
according to all that he sware unto their fathers:
and there stood not a man of all their enemies before them;
the LORD delivered all their enemies into their hand."*
(Joshua 21:44)

CHAPTER 15

THE PROCESS OF DELIVERANCE

Every human being is born with a curse on his or her head. Adam and Eve, our ancestors, brought this upon us when they disobeyed God in the Garden of Eden and chose to obey Satan. God put the curse of disobedience on everybody born of man – and we all are. In **Genesis 3:13-19**, God pronounced these curses on men as well as on women. Additional curses followed in **Deuteronomy 28:15-68**. In essence, even before we are old enough to make our own mistakes, we would have started suffering from the consequences of the mistakes of our ancestors.

Given the population explosion from biblical times till date, the impact of these curses on the human population is unimaginable. What is certain is that the human race is a race of cursed people. Only through the new birth and pleading the Blood of Jesus can we be redeemed from these curses. The Bible says:

> *"Christ hath redeemed us from the curse of the law, being made a curse for us: for it is written, Cursed is every one that hangeth on a tree."* **(Galatians 3:13)**

If you are not born again, then you are a non-starter. I do not waste my time ministering deliverance to anybody who has not received Jesus Christ as his Lord and Savior, because I know that it is a waste of time. The blessings of God are not for dogs. As far as God is concerned, sinners are dogs. God has reserved His blessings for His children only:

"But he answered and said, It is not meet to take the children's bread, and to cast it to dogs." **(Matthew 15:26)**

The Bible is very clear on who the children of God are.

"But as many as received him, to them gave he power to become the sons of God, even to them that believe on his name: Which were born, not of blood, nor of the will of the flesh, nor of the will of man, but of God." **(John 1:12, 13)**

The children of God are those who have accepted Jesus as their Lord and Savior. They are those who have repented from their evil ways and now live in obedience to the Word of God. They are the people who are qualified to ask and receive any good thing including deliverance from God, Who owns and can do all things. What then are the keys to receiving deliverance from God, the only One Who can break the yoke of Satan?

The first step then is to receive and/or check your salvation, making sure that you are still in good standing with God.

THE PROCESS OF SALVATION

(a) Acknowledge the fact that you are a sinner.
(b) Think about the terrible things you have done and the life of sin you have lived, and sincerely repent of them.
(c) Confess your sins to the Lord and ask Him to forgive you.
(d) Forsake the life of sin and pray to God to give you the divine ability for overcoming sin and temptation.
(e) You must believe that Jesus is the Son of God; that He came to this world to die for your sins, and that His Blood has washed away all your sins.
(f) You must acknowledge that Jesus is your Lord and Savior, and thank Him for saving you.
(g) Seek baptism by immersion in water if you have not done that.

Forsaking your sins and accepting Jesus Christ as your Lord and Savior is the first and most important step to take in breaking family curses. After following these instructions, you are then given the opportunity to become a child of God. Now God will arise on your behalf and fight your battles.

In the preceding chapters, we have seen that apart from the general curse on the human family by God, it is possible for individual families to acquire curses and pass them down to generations after them through idol worship and other ungodly acts. Although, becoming born again is a great fundamental experience, it is not enough to break these acquired family curses. For a Christian to be free from such inherited curses, there are further steps that need to be taken:

Step One: Confess your sins and the numerous sins of your forefathers. Ask God to forgive you and to blot out these sins.

Step Two: Pray to God to remove all the curses that came upon you as a result of the sins committed by your parents and forbearers.

Step Three: Pray to God to remove the impact and consequences of these curses from your life, as they must have been affecting you in different ways. Ask God to lift the burden that these curses have heaped upon your head.

The most important thing to remember is that there is no curse that the Word of God cannot break.

> *"For the word of God is quick, and powerful, and sharper than any two-edged sword, piercing even to the dividing asunder of soul and spirit, and of the joints and marrow, and is a discerner of the thoughts and intents of the heart."*
> **(Hebrews 4:12)**

The Bible recommends that all we need to do is come...

> *"Let us therefore come boldly unto the throne of grace, that we may obtain mercy, and find grace to help in the time of need."* **(Hebrews 4:16)**

THE NEED FOR AN INTERCESSOR

Some have identified that they are suffering under one curse or the other and have tried to conduct deliverance ministrations for themselves without much success. After asking God to forgive their sins and remove the family curses and the consequences of these curses from their lives, they still find that they are not making headway in life. They have continued to experience the same problems, frustrations, and failures that their parents experienced.

This does not mean that God does not hear and answer prayers. It is just that you need to pray specifically, under the guidance or supervision of a deliverance minister to break those family curses.

Don't get me wrong! Jesus Christ is the ultimate Intercessor. He is our Great High Priest, and He pleads our case with the Father better than any human being can ever do.

The issue now is this: an offender or an accused person cannot stand for himself or bail himself out in the court of law. According to the Scriptures, the person who needs to break a family curse has committed a crime, and because of this, he is under the oppressive yoke of the devil. The Bible says that it is the anointing that breaks the yoke. Therefore, this person needs an anointed man of God to assist him in breaking the yoke.

There is nothing bad in praying for yourself, taking the steps already enumerated above, but the level of deliverance you will experience may depend upon the anointing of God in your life. Your deliverance may not be total, and that is dangerous.

It is advisable, therefore, as a follow-up to your prayers, that you invite a man of God into your situation and allow him to take you through a proper deliverance ministration. I am not saying here that your deliverance lies in the hands of a man (even a man of God). Only the Almighty God can deliver. What I am saying is that after reading a book on deliverance and praying, it is not sufficient for you to say, "I don't need the help of a deliverance minister." There is a wealth of anointing and experience that God has deposited in these servants of God. So you need a deliverance minister.

Let me use this practical illustration. You are feeling feverish, so you go down to a pharmacy to buy some medication for fever, having convinced yourself that you don't need to see a doctor. Now whom would you blame when you later find yourself lying on your deathbed, dying of typhoid fever? Of course, you will only have yourself to blame. If you had gone to the doctor at the initial stage, he would have prescribed the right medication that would have saved your life.

The same thing applies in ministering deliverance. There are servants of God who are gifted in this special area. They will be needed at the point of ministration to offer a word of knowledge and/or other gifts of the Spirit that you may not have, but which may be absolutely necessary to pinpoint your exact problem and reveal how to deal with it.

If curses are not properly broken, then there is a problem. The person will continue to suffer the consequences of those curses and yet live under the illusion that he or she has been delivered.

DISCERNING OF SPIRITS NEEDED FOR DELIVERANCE

A lot of people have presented themselves for deliverance on several occasions, and men of God have prayed for them. During ministrations, these people have manifested in different ways such as falling down, rolling on the floor, foaming at the mouth, and so on. After a period of time, they find that the same problems that they sought deliverance from were still very much a part of them. I believe that in such cases, the deliverance was not complete. Sometimes, it could be a case that the person in this category has several inherited curses that need to be broken. Having broken some of the curses, there could be more active curses in his life that he is not even aware of. This is why there is need for the gifts of wisdom, word of knowledge, and discerning of spirits in the servants of God who conduct deliverance ministrations. They should be able to detect and know those who are in need of further deliverance.

About twenty years ago, when I was still young in the ministry, a girl was brought to a fellow minister and myself for deliverance. We spent the whole night praying for her, but at the end of it all, I was convinced in my spirit that she was not delivered; I told my partner what was happening. Honestly, we did not know what to do next, so we decided to take a break and go to sleep. It was much later that God spoke to me concerning the exercise, and gosh, what an eye-opener it was!

The Lord stated that while we were praying, the evil spirits operating in the girl, changed position. With the active co-operation of the girl, the powers of darkness left all other parts of her body and hid in her left breast. She didn't want to release the demons; her father actually forced her to attend the ministration against her wish.

As men, there was no way we could touch or tamper with her body, and to complicate issues, we didn't even know that these forces were hiding somewhere in her body. So in this case, we were not able to help the girl. Everybody went home, and if God had not opened my eyes, I would not have been any wiser.

The point being made here is that men of God who handle deliverance ministrations should be able to hear and receive instructions from God on how to conduct such exercises. If the Holy Spirit is not in charge to reveal the power and antics of the devil, no deliverance will take place. If I were to handle that girl's case now, I would handle it differently. I would wait to hear from the Spirit of God what steps to take - right there on the spot. If the evil spirits decide to hide somewhere, I would wait for the Holy Spirit to show me the exact location, and then I would be able to speak directly to them: "Demons, I see you and I am aware that you are hiding there." And even if I could not touch her body, I could point and say, "I command you to get out of her breast."

Since the demons know that I could see them and address them directly, they'll be forced to leave the girl. She would be okay, assuming that she has already made a choice to be free of demons.

From my experience, deliverance is an individual thing; you have to desire it to have it. Hence before a family curse can be broken, willingness and cooperation have to be there on the part of the person being delivered.

Like the story of the girl I just narrated, I have seen that it is not everybody that goes for ministration that is actually ready to be delivered from demons. Some are forced – against their will by their parents, guardians, or spouses. Some do not believe that there is something unwholesome in their life that needs to be removed, but they just go for deliverance ministrations because they think it fashionable. Since others are doing it, they should do it too.

Many have gone for deliverance only because a minister or parent said they should, and so unwillingly, they go to meet with the deliverance minister. Such people can never experience the breakthrough that follows true and complete deliverance.

There is, however, a third category of people who are so overwhelmed and blinded by the forces of darkness (acting within them) that they do not see the need to treat the issue of their deliverance with seriousness. Such people do not co-operate with the men of God ministering to them.

When such people are given the deliverance forms to fill out in order to understand their historical or cultural background, they write all kinds of lies. During counseling, they hold back on important information about their lives and past religious activities, which could facilitate their deliverance.

It must be pointed out here that God is the only One Who can deliver us from curses and the oppressive yoke of the enemy; the Holy Spirit will not cooperate with those who do not cooperate with Him.

I advise anyone going for deliverance ministrations, to fast, pray, and rededicate themselves to God. It is good to pray that God should prepare you for the ministration and reveal the secrets of the demons and curses tormenting you. Deliverance is a spiritual warfare, so you need to ask the Holy Spirit to give you the spiritual stamina and the necessary utterance.

If you are silent over the secrets that should be divulged, you will discover that the doors will be shut against you spiritually. You must write down all the information you believe will help your case. The deliverance minister can only work with the facts they receive even when they discern that you are still not free; they cannot help you until you make up your mind to be free.

If the family curses operating in your life are broken properly, I can assure you that you will be free! Let me refer you back to the story of my life. My family background brought innumerable curses upon my head and I suffered the consequences of those curses until the day God had mercy on me. I prayed under the guidance and leading of the Lord, but I also sought out a minister friend of mine, an anointed man in the deliverance ministry, and I received my deliverance. From then onwards, it has been one success story after another. Failure has become a thing of the past.

There is no one born into a family like mine who would not have been cursed. Let me state here that the child of a fetish priest suffers the same fate as the child of an Islamic protégé, an occult practitioner, an idol worshipper, a member of the white garment church, occult church denomination like Mormons, etc. If your family ever served any other god apart from JEHOVAH, the God of Abraham, Isaac, and Jacob, the Father of our Lord Jesus Christ, in any fashion other than that which is laid down in the Word of God (The Holy Bible), then you should not be under any illusion at all; you have a whole heap of curses on your head which must be broken immediately. The consequences of not breaking them are too great and you will never succeed in life or maximize your full potential in life, because there are curses hanging over your head.

> **Your deliverance cannot save someone else. Everyone has to be set free individually. God sees us as individuals.**
>
> *******
>
> **Salvation is not a Joint process!**

YOUR DELIVERANCE CANNOT SAVE OTHERS

From experience, I have equally discovered that breaking a family curse, like all other aspects of deliverance, is a personal thing. Just like your being born again cannot save your child, spouse, brother or sister, your deliverance is strictly personal. It does not affect other members of your family.

If you are a parent to someone who is suffering from the hands of the devil as a result of curses that were brought upon that life by you, you cannot help him or her to break the curse totally. As a parent, you can stand in the gap to break the curse that came directly from you. Ask God for forgiveness and mercy. This will make it easier for your child to also break the curses in his/her life, because the curses are already broken in the life of the parent.

If you are a member of a cursed family and you go for deliverance prayers to break the curses and you are set free, there is little or next to nothing that your deliverance can do for other members of your family. For instance, when I got my deliverance in 1987, I had expected that my deliverance would affect the life of my younger brother, but no, it did not! While my life changed for the better by the grace of God, my younger brother continues to experience misery and failure in the tradition of the family.

One day, I called him and said to him, "Dear brother, we are born of the same mother, and I know why you are suffering." I told him how God had spoken to me about our faulty foundation, and then I explained the process of deliverance that I had just gone through. Since we came from the same foundation, I told him, "The only way out is for you to present yourself for deliverance." At first, he thought it was all a fantasy, but now, he knows better. He is now with me in the ministry, totally free in Christ Jesus, and he is now a pastor. Praise God!

Your deliverance cannot save your children from family curses. They will have to undergo their own 'curse-breaking' deliverance. This might sound incredible, but let us judge again from what happened in my nuclear family.

I had broken all family curses in my life and the Lord had given me total victory. Two years later, in 1989, I got married to a Christian woman, a fellow minister who had also gone through deliverance. We started a family right away; we first had a girl and then a set of twins (both boys). I was shocked when three months after the birth of the boys, God told me to pray for their deliverance!

I felt it was not necessary since we had prayerfully requested these children from God and He had given then to us; so what kind of deliverance would they need? I convinced myself that since they were God's children, they did not need any deliverance, and besides, my wife and I were already delivered. But the all-knowing God kept on telling me to minister deliverance to them. Thank God I did!

You will be amazed at the kind of serious manifestations I saw in my children while ministering to them. Then I understood what God meant, when He said:

***"…. For I the LORD thy God am a jealous God, visiting the iniquity if the fathers (not the immediate or biological father alone) upon the children unto the third and fourth generation of them that hate me."* (Exodus 20:5)**

Even though I was free and my wife was free, my children were liable for the sins of the past generations of their ancestors. Since they were still within the third and fourth generation, they still had the curses on them. This is why the issue of breaking inherited family curses is important.

Many Christians take things for granted. They feel that there is no need to take their children to Church, and that they do not need deliverance. This is carelessness or sheer ignorance on the part of such parents, and this is dangerous. Don't allow yourself to be cheated by the devil because of your ignorance.

***"Lest Satan should get an advantage of us: for we are not ignorant of his devices."* (2 Corinthians 2:11)**

We have inherited lots of curses because of our family background. We must break them so that they will stop operating in our lives.

Anything short of this will bring about a life of sorrow and failure. You can start that process today, by taking a step of faith and using the prayer guide below, as you trust God for your deliverance.

CHAPTER 16

HOW TO RECEIVE YOUR DELIVERANCE

*"Apply thine heart unto instruction,
and thine ears to the words of knowledge."*
(Proverbs 23:12)

Satan is a tenacious character. He does not like anyone escaping from his wicked clutches. In fact, he fights tooth and nail to discourage anybody from being delivered, but thank God, Satan is not omnipotent – only God is. Fortunately, God has sent His only begotten Son, Jesus Christ, to deliver those under the devil's yoke.

When the devil hears the name of Jesus Whom God had anointed to set us free, he trembles and bows. When Jesus confronts him on our behalf, the devil has no choice but to release us from his clutches.

You must possess the right keys and use them before you can receive your deliverance.

1. TRUE REPENTANCE

Repentance is the firm and determined decision by an individual to stop committing sin and to start living a righteous life. Repentance is the master key that opens all doors to the blessings of God. It is the key to the door of salvation, healing, prosperity, promotion, baptism of the Holy Spirit, deliverance, etc. Without repentance, we have no right standing with God:

"... all have sinned and come short of the glory of God." (Romans 3:23)

The act of repentance begins with the acceptance of the fact above. If indeed, you are convicted in your heart that you are a sinner, you will experience a true and godly sorrow, the kind of sorrow that will make you hate the life of sin, the kind of sorrow that will make you forsake sin.

A lot of people mistake remorse for repentance; they are two different things. Remorse comes from being sorry for one's wrongdoing. It is a shallow feeling, a sense of regret. It is not a lasting feeling, neither is it deep enough to affect one's attitude to the things of God. True repentance, on the other hand, deeply affects the individual. As explained earlier, it causes godly sorrow and conviction in that person, making him forsake sin and totally turn away from a life of disobedience to God.

True repentance is having our spiritual eyes opened and turning away from darkness to light, and from the power of Satan to God. True repentance is an individual DECISION, an act of self will. No one can repent on your behalf; you must want to repent on your own and do it truthfully.

There is nothing God can do for a person who has not made up his mind to be saved. There can be no lasting deliverance where there is no true repentance.

2. CONFESSION OF SINS

The confession of sin is part of repentance, and it is also a wonderful way by which an oppressed person can be delivered and healed.

> *"Confess your faults one to another, and pray one for another, that ye may be healed. The effectual fervent prayer of a righteous man availeth much."* **(James 5:16)**

Confession is a major key to healing and deliverance. I will advise those seeking deliverance never to hide anything from those ministering to them. If they do, they will be wasting their time. Demons love it when you don't confess all of their activities in your life. It gives them room to hide when they know you are concealing them. Expose the devil to let him know that you don't want him in your life. If you conceal him by keeping quiet and not speaking the truth, you are deceiving yourself and not the minister, whose effectual fervent prayer can set you free. If you do not follow these steps, you cannot receive true deliverance.

3. HOLINESS

Once you become a Christian, you are expected to leave your life of sin behind and live holy. Many people want to experience lasting deliverance yet they continue to wallow in sin. They want to live their lives as dictated by the flesh and expect to be protected by God. This cannot be! You cannot eat your cake and have it.

> *"Neither yield ye your members as instruments of unrighteousness unto sin: but yield yourselves unto God, as those that are alive from the dead, and your members as instruments of righteousness unto God. For sin shall not have dominion over you: for ye are not under the law, but under grace."* **(Romans 6:13-14)**

We are called unto holiness, and living holy is the best way of receiving and retaining our deliverance. The nature of God is holiness and when we live our lives in holiness, nothing can harm us. If you want lasting deliverance, you need to present yourself to God in absolute purity.

4. HONESTY

We must be absolutely honest in our dealings with God and also with one another. Failure to be honest provides an avenue for Satan to enter and maintain a hold on our lives. People who fall into this category are not released when they need deliverance. In fact, they cannot get true deliverance unless there is total honesty on their part. We must, however, be transparent if we are to receive true deliverance.

5. FORGIVENESS

This is a cardinal part of deliverance. Failure to forgive is one of the principal reasons why some people are not released from demonic oppression. Jesus' reply emphasized that forgiveness has no end.

We may suffer demonic torture if we do not, from our hearts, forgive those who trespass against us. Unwillingness to forgive will hinder your prayers of deliverance, or any other prayers for that matter.

> *"And when ye stand praying, forgive, if ye have ought against any: that your Father also which is in heaven may forgive you your trespasses. But if ye do not forgive, neither will your Father which is in heaven forgive your trespasses."* **(Mark 11:25, 26)**

I have seen tremendous deliverance happen in the lives of people as a result of true forgiveness. I recall one occasion on a popular prayer mountain in Western Nigeria, where I went to pray. There was a woman who came to wait on the Lord for seven days; the Holy Spirit told me that if she did not forgive someone who had offended her, she would not be delivered from the yoke under which she was laboring. The woman left and made peace with the person who had offended her, and God answered her prayers immediately.

6. BREAK ALL CURSES AND COVENANTS

You cannot receive total deliverance if you are still under demonic covenants or curses. You must renounce all demonic covenants. You must, with your mouth, break all inherited and personal curses.

7. BE HUMBLE AND SUBMISSIVE

Allow the Holy Spirit to complete His work in you. Don't feel that you know it all. During ministration, if you are asked to kneel down, stand up or lift up your hands, don't feel you know more than the minister; just obey! Pride will lead you down a path of destruction. Be humble and submissive. Do not behave like Naaman, the commander of the Syrian Army **(2 Kings 5)**. Pride! Naaman could have lost his deliverance to pride were it not for his servants who prevailed on him to be submissive and obey Elisha's instructions. The Bible records:

> *"And his servants came near, and spake unto him, and said, My father, if the prophet had bid thee so some great thing, wouldest thou not have done it? How much rather then, when he saith to thee, Wash, and be clean? Then went he down, and dipped himself seven times in Jordan, according to the saying of the man of God: and his flesh came again like unto the flesh of a little child, and he was clean."* **(2 Kings 5:13-14)**

His leprosy disappeared. He got his deliverance because he obeyed the man of God!

Be submissive to the leading of the Holy Spirit. This is very important in receiving your deliverance.

CHAPTER 17

HOW TO KEEP YOUR DELIVERANCE

The moment you obtain your deliverance, it is something you must guard jealously. It will be too bad if you lose it. Like most good things in life, it is much easier to receive deliverance than to keep it. I have seen too many people who had been delivered in the past, but who are suffering today under the yoke of Satan. Why? They could not retain or maintain their deliverance. The saddest part is that such people are worse off than they were at the beginning.

This is not meant to frighten you, but the truth is that the demons, which were chased out of you today, can come back tomorrow if you don't know how to keep them off. The Bible says that when they do, they won't return alone. They will come back with *"more wicked"* associates and together they would wreck your life all over again.

> *"When the unclean spirit is gone out of a man, he walketh through dry places, seeking rest, and findeth none. Then he saith, I will return into my house from whence I came out: and when he is come, and he findeth it empty, swept, and garnished. Then goeth he, and taketh with himself seven other spirits more wicked than himself, and they enter in and dwell there: and the last state of that man is worse than the first..."*(Matthew 12:43-45)

If, in the past, you succeeded in chasing out one demon, and you give him the opportunity to come back, he will, but he will come back with seven other demons that are more wicked than himself. This means that instead of just one, you now have a total of eight demons oppressing you. If you are delivered from the eight demons and you still don't know how to keep your deliverance, the eight demons will return to your life, and each of them will invite seven other demons – meaning you will now have a legion of demons oppressing you! Without being told, you will know that you are in a worse state than you were at the beginning.

Keeping demons out of your life dear brethren is a most important task. To be able to do this, however, there are some guidelines you must follow, and they are listed below.

(1) MAINTAIN A HOLY LIFE

The devil can easily regain entrance into your life when you return to a life of sin. Your best bet, therefore, is to stay holy, as the Lord commands:

"...Be ye holy; for I am holy." **(1 Peter 1:16)**

Sin is the opposite of holiness. Sin is rebellion against God. It is disobedience to God. It means failure to do the will of God. Sin can only bring God's anger upon the sinner, and if God is angry with you, how will demons not have dominion over you? Sin can only lead to a life of bondage.

"Stand fast therefore in the liberty wherewith Christ has made us free, and be not entangled again with the yoke of bondage." **(Galatians 5:1)**

When you live a holy life, then your heart will be pure. Demons will have no hiding place in you, because the Holy Spirit will be in control.

(2) BE FILLED WITH THE HOLY SPIRIT ALWAYS

A man who is filled with the Holy Spirit is filled with the power of the Almighty God. It is not possible for demons to repossess such a man.

> *"But ye shall receive power, after that the Holy Ghost is come upon you..."* (Acts 1:8)

The power of Satan cannot contend with the power of God. However, if you allow the presence of the Holy Spirit to depart from you due to unrighteousness, then you leave yourself open to the attacks of demons. They can oppress or repossess you.

If an evil spirit goes out of you, it travels around looking for a new home. If it cannot find one, it goes back to its former house (you). If it finds the house empty, it goes and calls some other (more) wicked spirits to come and live there. If, on the other hand, there is no empty space, if the Holy Spirit is now resident and you are filled with the Word and knowledge of Christ, then the evil spirit will not have the audacity to come anywhere near you anymore.

(3) PUT ON THE WHOLE ARMOR OF GOD

You can keep your deliverance if you wear the complete armor that God has given you. Then you will be able to stand against the power and wiles of Satan.

> *"Stand therefore, having your loins girt about (1) <u>TRUTH</u>, and having on the breastplate of (2) RIGHTEOUSNESS; And your feet shod with the preparation of the (3) <u>GOSPEL OF PEACE</u>; Above all, taking the shield of (4) <u>FAITH</u>, wherewith ye shall be able to quench all the fiery darts of the wicked. And take the helmet of (5) <u>SALVATION</u>, and the sword of the Spirit, which is the (6) <u>WORD OF GOD</u>."* (emphasis added, Ephesians 6:14-17)

Check these spiritual gears and put them all on. Make sure they are always complete, and then you can laugh at any demon that may come calling at your doorstep.

(4) FELLOWSHIP WITH BELIEVERS

Christians are enjoined to meet with each other in fellowship.

> *"Not forsaking the assembling of ourselves together, as the manner of some is; but exhorting one another: and so much the more, as ye see the day approaching."* **(Hebrews 10:25)**

If you cultivate the habit of fellowshipping with the brethren, the possibility of your backsliding diminishes. Such avenues provide opportunities for encouraging each other in the Lord. Do not look at such meetings as mere Christian duty. The consequences for not partaking in them may be grave, as Satan is always around the corner to draw you out of the presence of God through his wiles. When you are in the midst of Christian brothers and sisters who are constantly exhorting you, you will most likely be able to stand firm.

> *"Iron sharpeneth iron; so a man sharpeneth the countenance of his friend."* **(Proverbs 27:17)**

(5) AVOID OCCULT BOOKS, FILMS, SYMBOLS, AND PRACTICES

What you read, watch, or keep in your home, has an effect on your life. Many people don't know this so they feed their minds with occult books such as: ***The Secret of the Psalms, The Sixth and Seventh Books of Moses, various books on astrology, and so on.*** They defile their eyes with demonic films, watch pornography, visit diviners, and keep occult symbols and clothing (e.g., zodiac signs, rings, posters, paintings, etc.) in their homes and this has caused unbelievable problems in their lives. Avoid these things. They are sure avenues for demons to come back into a life that has been delivered. If you still have the desire for them, do what the early Christians did:

> *"Many of them also which used curious arts brought their books together, and burned then before all men: and they counted the price of them, and found it fifty thousand pieces of silver."* **(Acts 19:19)**

Also avoid pagan practices because the Lord hates them. Moses had this much to say:

> *"When thou art come into the land which the LORD thy God giveth thee, thou shalt not learn to do after the abominations of those nations. There shall not be found among you any one that maketh his son or his daughter to pass through the fire, or that useth divination, or an observer of times, or an enchanter, or a witch. Or a charmer, or a consulter with familiar spirits, or a wizard, or a necromancer. For all that do these things are an abomination unto the LORD: and because of these abominations the LORD thy God doth drive them out from before thee."* **(Deuteronomy 18:9-12)**

Destroy all demonic materials within your reach and run away from occult practices before they attract demons back into your life. Don't count the monetary cost; you will have more to lose if you keep them.

(6) MEDITATE ON THE WORD OF GOD

The devil's major target for attack in man is the mind. When you begin to think negatively, what you are thinking about is likely to happen to you. Negative thinking brings negative results.

> *"Finally, brethren, whatsoever things are true, whatsoever things are honest, whatsoever things are just, whatsoever things are pure, whatsoever things are lovely, whatsoever*

things are of good report; if there be any virtue, and if there be any praise, think on these things." **(Philippians 4:8)**

Meditate on God's Word and put every wrong though into captivity in obedience to Christ.

(7) PLEAD THE BLOOD OF JESUS

There is victorious power in the Blood of Jesus Christ. Before any deliverance ministration, we usually sing and plead the Blood of Jesus before going into the ministration itself.
(Read more on this topic in the next chapter).

(8) CONFESS YOUR DELIVERANCE OFTEN

Always give a testimony of your deliverance. It keeps you in remembrance and boosts your faith whenever the devil tries to confuse you. Confessing your deliverance to others is a powerful tool against the world of darkness. Always remember the Scripture above.

(9) AVOID OLD HABITS

Old sinful habits got you into bondage the first time, so avoid them. It could be the cigarettes you smoke, the beer you drink, the friends you keep, the bribe you take (or give), the women you love, etc. It could be any of your old ways that the Lord does not approve of.

"... Behold, thou art made whole: sin no more, lest a worse thing happen to you." **(John 5:14)**

(10) BE BOLD

"For God hath not given us the spirit of fear; but of power, and of love, and of a sound mind." **(2 Timothy 1:7)**

Therefore, you have no reason whatsoever to fear the wiles of Satan. Just stay away from sin and be bold.

"There is no fear in love; but perfect love casteth out fear: because fear hath torment. He that feareth is not made perfect in love." **(1 John 4:18)**

If you are living in God's perfect will, what do you have to be afraid of, anyway? When the devil rears his ugly head in your life, look at him eyeball to eyeball and call him a liar. Stand firm against him. You have no reason to be afraid. God has given you the power to defeat him and his cohorts through Jesus Christ, our Lord and Savior.

(11) PRAY ALWAYS

Due to the importance of prayer, the Bible enjoins us to:

"Pray without ceasing." (1 Thessalonians 5:17)

The lyrics of a certain song go like this:"

> *"Prayer is the Key, prayer is the key*
> *Prayer is the master key.*
> *Jesus started with prayers,*
> *And ended with prayers.*
> *Prayer is the master key."*

Prayer is a two-way communication between man and God; you are constantly having a conversation with your Father in heaven. He will teach you the way you should go so that you will not fall into the hands of Satan.

***"I will instruct thee and teach thee in the way which thou shalt go: I will guide thee with mine eye."* (Psalm 32:8)**

As you actively begin to walk in the way that the Lord has commanded you to, I pray that your deliverance will be permanent, in Jesus' name. Amen!

CHAPTER 18

POWER IN THE BLOOD OF JESUS

Throughout this book, I have sought to shed some light on the nature of the forces of darkness and the evil works they perpetrate. My own family background and faulty foundations helped me to appreciate firsthand, the kind of havoc these forces wreak in the lives of people. In fact, where one is not careful, there is a likelihood of being overwhelmed with fear when faced with the full measure of what these forces are capable of doing. However, such fear arises when one is ignorant of the overcoming power in the Blood of Jesus.

Ordinarily, blood is a mysterious substance. The very sight of blood brings to mind all kinds of serious connotations, especially as it is so intricately tied to life and death.

"For the life of the flesh is in the blood..." **(Leviticus 17:11)**

Truly, there is power in the Blood. Many do not understand the magnitude of this power; neither do they appreciate the implications of the shedding of the Blood of Jesus for the human race.

"... All power is given unto me in heaven and in earth." **(Matthew 28:18)**

ALL POWER! Not some power or just a little power, but total, all encompassing, overcoming power, in all heaven and earth, and all because of the Blood that was shed at the Cross of Calvary. This same Blood is now made available to you and me for cleansing and deliverance.

BENEFITS OF THE BLOOD

It is an all-purpose remedy with limitless benefits. In fact, no deliverance ministration is complete without applying the overcoming power in the Blood of Jesus. Here are some facts about the Blood of Jesus, as well as the benefits to be derived from its application to specific problems, situations, and circumstances during deliverance.

(i) THE APPLICATION OF THE BLOOD

In the Old Testament times, the prophets had to sprinkle the blood (of animals) in the temple before they could enter in the sacred place, known as the "Holy of Holies." They did this for cleansing, and to invite the presence of the Almighty God.

On the night of the Passover, the Jews were told that in order to stay safe and alive, they had to apply the blood of the animals they had sacrificed on the top posts and sides of the door frames of their houses. The "destroyer" passed over every house that had this blood on it, but slew the firstborn of all the houses that were without the blood (i.e., the Egyptians).

The Bible says that these events that happened in the Old Testament were foreshadows of the real Blood of Jesus Christ that was to be used in the New Testament. The Bible in the New Testament also supports the sprinkling of this same Blood of Jesus. We can plead it and cover ourselves with it just like the priests in the Old Testament did. This is because Jesus Christ has made a sacrifice on our behalf, a sacrifice of His precious Blood, once and for all.

(ii) AVERTS DIVINE JUDGMENT

a. The Blood of Jesus Christ was shed for the remission of the sins of man, thereby bringing about reconciliation between God and man. The Blood of Jesus, therefore, averts God's judgment upon man.

b. **Averts The Judgment By Demons**

Before we became born again, many of us had enjoyed all sorts of benefits from demons and other agents of the kingdom of darkness. Some of us got children, wealth, or even protection from these evil forces. These oaths, agreements, and covenants that we entered into with the demons are binding. The moment we betray the kingdom of darkness by declaring Jesus as Lord and switching over to the kingdom of Light, the demons are within their rights to cry "breach of contract"! It is only by applying the Blood of Jesus Christ that we can avert the judgment of these demons.

c. **Averts The Judgment By Man**

In our day-to-day interactions with our fellow man, we do things that bring down curses on our heads. We may have cheated a business associate or jilted a young lady to whom you made fervent promises of marriage. You could even have offended those in authority over us, such as husbands or parents, and so on, causing them to curse us. The only way these judgments pronounced upon us by these aggrieved parties can be averted is by pleading the Blood of Jesus.

(iii) IT PROMISES BETTER THINGS

The Blood of Jesus promises better things because it is life.

> *"And to Jesus the mediator of the new covenant, and to the blood of sprinkling, that speaketh better things than that of Abel."* **(Hebrews 12:24)**

Demons respect the Blood of Jesus more than the "miracle of handkerchiefs" – which are so popular these days because the BLOOD OF JESUS IS LIFE (whenever you call the Blood, Jesus Himself stands to back it up). Even though the name of Jesus is powerful, it won't work without the Blood which is life itself. The name of Jesus is authority, but the Blood of Jesus is multi-purposed in application.

(iv)   DELIVERANCE FROM THE CLUTCHES OF SATAN

For those trapped under demonic oppression or sold out to the kingdom of darkness, the Blood of Jesus purchases them and buys back their freedom.

> *"Forasmuch as ye know that ye were not redeemed with corruptible things, as silver and gold, from your vain conversation received by tradition from your fathers; But with the precious blood of Christ, as of a lamb without blemish and without spot."* **(1 Peter 1:18-19)**

(v)   FORGIVENESS AND RECONCILIATION UNTO GOD

Our God is a holy and righteous God. He cannot behold sin. Man who has sin in his very nature has to be blameless to be able to have communion with Him. God in His infinite mercy has provided a way out for man through the Blood of Jesus. The book of **Matthew** tells us that the Blood of Jesus was shed for the remission of sins.

> *"For this is my blood of the new testament, which is shed for many for the remission of sins."* **(Matthew 26:28)**

This same Blood of Jesus reconciles sinful man with God...

> *"And all things are of God, who hath reconciled us to himself by Jesus Christ, and hath given to us the ministry of reconciliation."* **(2 Corinthians 5:18)**

As a result of the Blood of Jesus, we have confidence that when we plead the Blood and are washed in it, we can approach the throne of Grace in prayer, with the assurance that God will hear us.

(vi) JUSTIFICATION FROM THE GUILT OF SIN

Sin usually places upon man a heavy burden of guilt. The Blood puts right all errors in the lives of those who have faith in Jesus Christ.

> *"Being justified freely by his grace through the redemption that is in Christ Jesus: Whom God hath set forth to be a propitiation through faith in his blood, to declare his righteousness for the remission of sins that are past, through the forbearance of God."* **(Romans 3:24-25)**

(vii) CLEANSING AND SANCTIFICATION

Sanctification, which is the second work of grace, simply means 'to make holy and be separated unto God.' Sanctification destroys the root of sin from the life of a Christian. One of the most effective ways of achieving sanctification is through the Blood of Jesus Christ. **(Hebrews 9:3-14; 10:19-20; 1 John 1:7, 9)**

(viii) DELIVERANCE FROM SICKNESS

It is the will of God for us to be in good health. Sickness and diseases are not part of God's script for our lives. So if you are afflicted in your body, by pleading the Blood of Jesus, you can be made whole. You can overcome that ailment – whatever it might be – by the Blood of Jesus Christ.

(ix) THE BLOOD OF JESUS PROTECTS

The Blood of Jesus offers total protection. Whenever the devil harasses you, plead the Blood of Jesus and the evil spirit will be handicapped. We can use the Blood in a variety of ways: we can sprinkle, plead, cover ourselves, or even wet a whole house with the Blood of Jesus. We can sprinkle the Blood on all that we own or have.

(x) BREAKING OF COVENANTS

Covenants are binding agreements between two parties. They could be holy or demonic. When they are demonic, they take a heavy toll on the lives of people. These covenants come in different forms: blood, food, marriage, etc. In order to be free from such evil and powerfully binding covenants, we need a more powerful tool. No tool is stronger than the Blood of Jesus.

(xi) PREPARATION FOR THE SECOND COMING OF JESUS

Heaven is for those who are constantly on guard, watching, so that they are not casually swallowed up by "small" sins. When we fall into sin, we should not wait till we go to Church on Sunday before confessing these sins to God and pleading the Blood of Jesus to cleanse us. This is because we don't know whether we will be alive come Sunday. We must constantly plead the Blood of Jesus at every point of our lives when we sin against God, because we don't know when Jesus Christ will return. **(Matthew 24:27, 37-44)**

The Blood of Jesus is a strong force that no demon can withstand; it has the power that no human can fathom. The Blood is more potent than the blood of 20,000 goats. There is complete victory over problems through the Blood of Jesus. When you don't know what to say in prayer, plead the Blood of Jesus for a long time, and every opposing force will disappear.

Those who are possessed should plead the Blood of Jesus continuously; the kingdom of darkness will be troubled. If you pronounce "the Blood of Jesus" in places of occult activity or worship, you immediately trigger confusion in their camp.

Let me relate a true story to underscore the reality of the overcoming power in the Blood of Jesus: A minister of God was involved in a serious automobile accident and it seemed that all hope for his survival was lost; his body was severely mutilated. The doctors had virtually abandoned his case. At that point, a minister friend of his who heard about the crash came rushing to the hospital. When he saw how critical his friend's condition was, he begged the doctors and nurses to allow him to pray over his friend.

For a long time – about an hour – he just pleaded the Blood of Jesus. At some point in time, the room physically heated up with the power of God. Not long after this spiritual operation, the dying minister opened his eyes and testified that during that period of intense heat in the room, he saw doctors, in the spirit realm, fixing up parts of his body.

To God be the glory, the minister who had been abandoned by the medical doctors as a hopeless medical case was made whole.

There is power in the Blood of Jesus Christ!

CHAPTER 19

BIBLICAL CURSES

Below is a list of curses that need to be broken off of your generation. To break these curses, according to **Galatians 3:13**, ask the Lord to forgive you (and your ancestors going back ten generations on both sides of your bloodline) for the sins and iniquities that allowed these curses to come upon you, in JESUS' NAME.

- Those who curse or mistreat Jews **(Deut. 27:26; Gen. 12:3, 27:29; Num. 24:9)**.
- Those willing deceivers **(Joshua 9:23; Jer. 48:10; Malachi 1:14; Gen. 27:12)**.
- An adulterous woman **(Numbers 5:27)**.
- Disobedience of the Lord's commandments **(Deut. 11:28; Dan. 9:11; Jer. 11:3)**.
- Idolatry **(Jer. 44:8; Deut. 5:8-9, 29:19; Exodus 20:5)**.
- Those who keep or own cursed objects **(Deut. 7:25; Joshua 6:18)**.
- Those who refuse to come to the Lord's help **(Judges 5:23)**.
- House of the wicked **(Proverbs 3:33)**.
- He who gives nothing to the poor **(Proverbs 28:27)**.
- The earth by reason of man's disobedience **(Isaiah 24:3-6)**.
- Jerusalem is a curse to all nations if the Jews rebel against God **(Jer. 26:6)**.

- Thieves and those who swear falsely by the Lord's name **(Zech. 5:4)**.
- Ministers who fail to give the glory to God **(Mal. 2:2; Revelation 1:6)**.
- Those who hearken unto their wives rather than God **(Genesis 3:17)**.
- Those who lightly esteemed their parents **(Deut. 27:16)**.
- Those who make graven images **(Deut. 5:8, 27:15; Exodus 20:4)**.
- Those who willfully cheat people out of their property **(Deut. 27:17)**.
- Those who take advantage of the blind **(Deut. 27:18)**.
- Those oppressing strangers, widows, and the fatherless **(Deut. 27:19; Exodus 22:22-24)**.
- He who lies with his father's wife **(Deut. 27:21; Exodus 22:19)**.
- He who lies with his sister **(Deut. 27:22)**.
- Those who smite their neighbors secretly **(Deut. 27:24)**.
- Those who take money to slay the innocent **(Deut. 27:24)**.
- He who lies with a beast **(Deut. 27:21: Exodus 22:19)**.
- Adulterers **(Job 24:15-18; Deut. 22:22-27)**.
- The proud **(Psalm 119:21)**.
- Those who trust in man and not the Lord **(Jeremiah 48:10)**.
- He who keeps back his sword from blood **(Jer. 48:10; 1 Kings 20:35-42)**.
- Those who reward evil for good **(Proverbs 17:13)**.
- Illegitimate children **(Deut. 23:2)**.
- Children born from incestuous unions **(Genesis 19:36-38)**.
- Murderers **(Exodus 21:14)**.
- Those who murder indirectly **(Exodus 21:14)**.
- Children who strike their parents **(Exodus 21:15)**.
- Kidnappers **(Exodus 21:16; Deut. 24:7)**.
- Those who curse their parents **(Exodus 21:17)**.
- Those who cause the unborn to die **(Exodus 21:22-23)**.
- Those who do not prevent death **(Exodus 2:29)**.
- Those involved in witchcraft **(Exodus 22:18)**.
- Those who sacrifice to false gods **(Exodus 22:20)**.

- Those who turn people away from the Lord **(Deut. 13:6-9)**.
- Those who follow HOROSCOPES **(Deut. 17:2-5)**.
- Those who rebel against pastors **(Deut. 17:12)**.
- False prophets **(Deut. 18:19-22)**.
- Women who were not virgins before marriage **(Deut. 22:13-21)**.
- Parents who do not discipline their children but honor them above God **(1 Samuel 2:17, 27-36)**.
- Those who curse their rulers **(1 Kings 2:8-9; Exodus 22:28)**.
- Those who teach rebellion against the Lord **(Jeremiah 28:16-17)**.
- Those who refuse to warn others against sin **(Ezekiel 3:18-21)**.
- Those who defile the Sabbath **(Exodus 31:14; Numbers 15:32-36)**.
- Those who sacrifice human beings **(Leviticus 20:2)**.
- Participants in séance and fortune telling **(Leviticus 20:6)**.
- Homosexual and lesbian relationships **(Leviticus 20:13)**.
- Sexual intercourse during menstruation **(Leviticus 20:18)**.
- Necromancers and fortune tellers **(Leviticus 20:27)**.
- Those who blaspheme the Lord's name **(Leviticus 24:15-16)**.
- Those who are carnally minded **(Romans 8:6)**.
- Sodomy (oral and anal sex) **(Genesis 19:13, 24-25)**.
- Rebellious children **(Deut. 21:18-21)**.
- Possibly from murder or non-productivity, a fugitive vagabond **(Genesis 4:11; Matthew 5:21-22)**.
- Possible curse upon improper family structure – destruction of family priesthood – with special attention given to the relationship between father and children **(Malachi 4:6)**.
- An undeserved (causeless) curse shall not come **(Proverb 26:2)**.
- Any sin worthy of death is also curse by the Lord **(Deut. 21:22-23)**.

CHAPTER 20

PRAYER OF PREPARATION BEFORE DELIVERANCE

Dear God, in the name of JESUS,

According to **Romans 10:9**, I confess with my lips that JESUS is Lord and in my heart I believe that You raised Him from the dead.

According to **Luke 13:3**, I repent of my past sins and I admit and confess that I have sinned (mention the sin) and I believe that You are faithful and just to cleanse me from all unrighteousness.

I call upon You, Lord JESUS, to cleanse me from all sin and unrighteousness by Your Blood **(1 John 1:7)**. And, as Your Word says in **Romans 10:13**, "Everyone who calls upon the name of the Lord shall be saved."

I confess, repent, and ask for forgiveness from occult practices such as (witchcraft, fortune telling, horoscopes, astrology, Halloween, etc.).

I renounce Satan and all occult practices, and I break all curses associated with those practices. According to **Galatians 3:13**, Christ purchased our freedom (redeeming us) from the curse (doom) of the Law (and its condemnation) by becoming a curse for us. For it is written (in the Scriptures), "Cursed is everyone who hangs on a tree (crucified)" **(Deuteronomy 21:23).**

I confess, repent, and ask for forgiveness of all sins listed in **Deuteronomy 27 and 28**, and I break the curses associated with those sins.

I confess, repent, and ask for forgiveness of my iniquities and my father's iniquities according to **Leviticus 26:40**, and I break the curses associated with those iniquities.

I break and loose myself from all evil soul ties with my mother, father, brother, sister, spouse, former spouse, former sex partners, etc.

Lord JESUS, I forgive my mother, father, brothers (mention their names), sisters (mention their names) and anyone else who has ever hurt name. **Matthew 6:15, 18:21, 22, 35; Luke 11:4** (our Lord's prayer)

I break and loose myself and my family from all curses that have been or are being placed upon us: curses of witchcraft, psychic thoughts or prayers, ungodly intercessory prayers, and words spoken in anger, and I return these curses back to the sender(s) sevenfold, and I bind them with the Blood of Jesus.

In JESUS' Name. Amen!

PREPARING FOR WARFARE

1. We are dealing with principalities, powers, rulers of the darkness of this age, and spiritual hosts of wickedness in the heavens.
2. This is an organized kingdom with delegated authorities, world rulers, and wicked spirits.
3. We must sound the trumpet, clothe ourselves for battle, take up our spiritual weapons, identify our enemy, and attack.

4. Satan has limitations, methods of attack, and schemes. He tempts us, accuses us, and deceives us.
5. Research the past, repenting of all sins, forgiving all others, recognizing God's purpose, ministering with all compassion and praying with all prayers.
6. The boot camp of spiritual warfare is in our local churches, working with the sheep and ministering deliverance to them one by one.
7. Ground level warfare is casting demons out of people.
8. God sets the battle plan.
9. We have authority to pull down strongholds. It was given to The Twelve, The Seventy, and to The Church.
10. We are to pull down strongholds, bind and loose with authority.
11. Christ's Church, through the exercise of her authority, can change the course of history.
12. You should continue in spiritual warfare until victory comes. Be prepared to wrestle with the enemy. Keep your faith. Remain steadfast in prayer and warfare.
13. Our strength in the Lord is derived through spiritual exercises: daily prayer and Bible study, fasting, fellowship with other believers, praise, worship, our testimony, and walking in holiness.
14. We must forgive everyone, no matter what they did to us or when they did it.
15. We must sanctify ourselves as individuals, and cleanse the Church corporately in the Blood of Jesus.
16. After cleansing, speak to the principalities and powers in the authority of the Name of Jesus.
17. Put aside jealousy, doctrinal questions, and other factors that separate Christians and churches from each other. Pull down ignorance, fear, and prejudice.
18. Help those who are bound by blindness, disease, poverty, and fear in the mental, physical, spiritual, and material areas.

CHAPTER 21

SCRIPTURES
AND
RENOUNCING DECLARATIONS

In agreement with the Word of God, you are going to stand against every demonic agreement in/over your life. The Lord has given you a promise that even Satan cannot break. The Word of God is real.

> *"As soon as they hear of me, they shall obey me: the strangers shall submit themselves unto me. The strangers shall fade away, and be afraid out of their close places."* **(Psalm 18:44-45)**

Every stranger in your destiny, marriage, finances, and others shall submit unto you.

RENOUNCING COVENANTS

> *"Shall the prey be taken from the mighty, or the lawful captive delivered? But thus saith the LORD, Even the captives of the mighty shall be taken away, and the prey of the terrible shall be delivered: for I will contend with him that contendeth with thee, and I will save thy children.*

And I will feed them that oppress thee with their own flesh; and they shall be drunken with their own blood, as with sweet wine: and all flesh shall know that I the LORD am thy Saviour and the Redeemer, the mighty One of Jacob." **(Isaiah 49:24-26)**

DECLARATIONS

1. I claim and withdraw all the grounds given or yielded to Satan by my ancestors.
2. Let the fire of God consume everything that has been transferred into my life as a result of the demonic laying of hands by false prophets, in the name of Jesus!
3. Father, consume every covenant that is affecting my life, in the name of Jesus!
4. I electrify the ground where satanic covenants have been established against me (things that have been buried such as the placenta, blood of animals...), in the name of Jesus!
5. I break every hidden covenant that Satan is using against my destiny, in the name of Jesus!
6. I command every demon attached to any curse in my life to depart, in the name of Jesus!
7. I break the backbone of every satanic addiction in my life, in the name of Jesus!

CHAPTER 22

SCRIPTURES FOR DELIVERANCE AND SPIRITUAL WARFARE

The Word of God is the greatest weapon of deliverance. There are certain Scriptures that can be used as a weapon for your deliverance. You must keep on confessing these Scriptures so that you can obtain and retain your deliverance.

Any bondage that emanates from the kingdom of darkness can be nullified through the Word of God. The Word of God will open your eyes to whatever it takes to obtain your deliverance.

Confessing the Scriptures below will arm you with the weapons needed for obtaining victory in spiritual battles. These Scriptures will also open the gates of deliverance to those held captive through curses, covenants, and satanic bondage. You need to read these Scriptures over and over again, until you are completely set free. These verses will also grant you spiritual immunity.

> "And I will feed them that oppress thee with their own flesh; and they shall be drunken with their own blood, as with sweet wine: and all flesh shall know that I the LORD am thy Saviour and the Redeemer, the mighty One of Jacob."
>
> **Isaiah 49:26**

"And I will deliver thee out of the hand of the wicked, and I will redeem thee out of the hand of the terrible."
Jeremiah 15:21

"The Spirit of the Lord is upon me, because he hath anointed me to preach the gospel to the poor; he hath sent me to heal the brokenhearted, to preach deliverance to the captives, and recovering of sight to the blind, to set at liberty them that are bruised, To preach the acceptable year of the Lord."
Luke 4:18-19

"For the LORD thy God walketh in the midst of thy camp, to deliver thee, and to give up thine enemies before thee; therefore shall thy camp be holy: that he see no unclean thing in thee, and turn away from thee."
Deuteronomy 23:14

"Let the redeemed of the LORD say so, whom he hath redeemed from the hand of the enemy; And gathered them out of the lands, from the east, and from the west, from the north, and from the south. They wandered in the wilderness in a solitary way; they found no city to dwell in. Hungry and thirsty, their soul fainted in them."
Psalm 107:2-5

"And from the days of John the Baptist until now the kingdom of heaven suffereth violence, and the violent take it by force."
Matthew 11:12

"No weapon that is formed against thee shall prosper; and every tongue that shall rise against thee in judgment thou shall condemn. This is the heritage of the servants of the LORD, and their righteousness is of me, saith the LORD."
Isaiah 54:17

"But the LORD your God ye shall fear; and he shall deliver you out of the hand of all your enemies."
2 Kings 17:39

"When I cry unto thee, then shall mine enemies turn back: this I know; for God is for me."
Psalm 56:9

"Shall the prey be taken from the mighty, or the lawful captive delivered? But thus saith the LORD, Even the captives of the mighty shall be taken away, and the prey of the terrible shall be delivered: for I will contend with him that contendeth with thee, and I will save thy children."
Isaiah 49:24-25

"And I will make thee unto this people a fenced brasen wall: and they shall fight against thee, but they shall not prevail against thee: for I am with thee to save thee and to deliver thee, saith the LORD."
Jeremiah 15:20

"For thou hast broken the yoke of his burden, and the staff of his shoulder, the rod of his oppressor, as in the day of Midian. For every battle of the warrior is with confused noise, and garments rolled in blood; but this shall be with burning and fuel of fire."
Isaiah 9:4-5

"And there was delivered unto him the book of the prophet Esaias. And when he had opened the book, he found the place where it was written, The Spirit of the Lord is upon me, because he hath anointed me to preach the gospel to the poor; he hath sent me to heal the brokenhearted, to preach deliverance to the captives, and recovering of sight to the blind, to set at liberty them that are bruised."
Luke 4:17-18

"Thou art my hiding place; thou shalt preserve me from trouble; thou shalt compass me about with songs of deliverance. Selah."

Psalm 32:7

SCRIPTURES FOR SPIRITUAL WARFARE

- **Matthew 10:1** – Power against unclean spirits, to cast them out.
- **Matthew 12:24-29** – First bind the strong man and then we will spoil his house.
- **Matthew 16:18-19** – And I will give unto thee the keys of the kingdom of heaven.
- **Matthew 28:18-20** – All power is given unto me in heaven and in earth.
- **Mark 11:22-23** – He shall have whatsoever he saith.
- **Mark 16:15-20** – In my name shall they cast out devils.
- **Luke 9:1-2** – Power and authority over all devils.
- **Luke 10:17-20** – Even the devils are subject to us through thy name.
- **Luke 11:21-22** – He taketh from him all his armor wherein he trusted.
- **2 Corinthians 2:10-11** – We are not ignorant of his devices.
- **2 Corinthians 4:3-4** – The god of this world hath blinded the minds of them which believe.
- **2 Corinthians 10:3-6** – Mighty through God to the pulling down of strongholds.
- **Ephesians 1:19-23** – Far above principality, power, might, dominion, and every other name.
- **Ephesians 2:6** – Made us sit together in heavenly places in Christ Jesus.
- **Ephesians 6:10-18** – Against principalities, powers, rulers of the darkness of this world, spiritual wickedness in high places.
- **Colossians 2:15** – Having spoiled principalities and powers.
- **1 John 3:8** – That he might destroy the works of the devil.

CHAPTER 23

WARFARE PRAYERS FOR SELF-DELIVERANCE

Father in heaven, in the name of JESUS,

I (Name) _____(Name)

of _____
(ADDRESS)

(Mother's Name) _____

(Father's Name) _____

present myself to you today – spirit, soul, and body; for cleansing through the Blood of Jesus, from all curse in my family. I renounce all known and unknown curses as well as unholy covenants in JESUS NAME. I apply the Blood of Jesus to my whole system for purification from all curses. Christ has redeemed me from the curse of the law. Therefore, I am free in JESUS NAME. Amen.

    You can make further confessions on your own; this is just a guideline. Pray and believe that God is faithful. If you call upon Him, He will answer you. Believe that He has cleansed you and begin to thank Him

For additional and more specific prayer points, ask for my workbook (Demonic Covenants and Curses Workbook).

(I) REPENTANCE AND CONFESSION

"Thank You, Lord, for dying for my sins, for Your glorious resurrection, and for making me a new creature in CHRIST JESUS, by faith in Your precious Blood."

According to **Romans 10:9** – I confess with my lips that JESUS is Lord and in my heart I believe that you raised him from the dead.

According to **Luke 13:3** – I repent of my past sins and I admit and confess that I have sinned, and I believe that You are faithful and just to cleanse me from all unrighteousness.

I call upon You, Lord JESUS, to cleanse me from all sin and unrighteousness by Your Blood **(1 John 1:7)**.

As your Word says in **Romans 10:13**, "everyone who calls upon the name of the Lord will be saved."

1. I am the BODY OF CHRIST. I overcome evil with good **(1 Cor. 12:27; Rom. 12:21)**.

2. I am of God. I have overcome the world. He who is in me is greater than he who is in the world **(1 John 4:4)**.

3. I am established in righteousness. I am far from terror and oppression. I shall not fear. I walk through the valley of the shadow of death. I will fear no evil. CHRIST is with me. His rod and His staff comfort me **(Isa. 54:14; Psa. 23:4)**.

4. My righteousness is from THE LORD. No weapon formed against me shall prosper. I condemn tongues that rise against me. This is my heritage as a servant of THE LORD **(Isa. 54:17)**.

5. No evil shall befall me. No plague shall come near me or my dwelling. He gives His angels charge over me. They keep me in my ways **(Psa. 91:10-11)**.

6. I delight in the LAW OF THE LORD; I meditate in it day and night. I am like a tree planted by the rivers of water bringing forth abundant fruit in season. My leaves do not wither. Whatever I do prospers **(Psa. 1:2-3)**.

7. JESUS CHRIST gave Himself for my sins. I have been delivered from this world according to the WILL OF GOD **(Gal. 1:4)**.

8. I have been given authority over the power of the enemy to trample on serpents and scorpions. Nothing shall by any means hurt me. I possess the keys of the KINGDOM OF HEAVEN. Whatever I bind on earth is bound in Heaven. Whatever I loose on earth is loosed in Heaven. I bind principalities, powers, rulers of darkness, and hosts of wickedness that oppose me, my family, and the work of God. I loose THE HOLY GHOST, mighty warring angels, and the BLOOD OF JESUS CHRIST to cover, protect, bless, and minister to me, my family, and those doing THE WORK OF GOD **(Luke 10:19; Matt. 16:19; Eph. 6:12)**.

9. I take the shield of faith. I quench the fiery darts of the wicked one. I overcome by THE BLOOD OF THE LAMB and word of my testimony. I love not my life unto death. My life belongs to CHRIST JESUS **(Eph. 6:16; Rev. 12:11)**.

10. I submit to GOD, resist the Devil and he flees from me. I draw near to GOD. He draws near to me baptizing me with the Holy Ghost and fire **(James 4:7-8; Matt. 3:11)**.

11. I am in the way of righteousness. I find life. There is no death in or around me. CHRIST redeemed me from the curse of the law. He became a curse for me. I walk in the blessings of THE HOLY SPIRIT. I am truly blessed **(Prov. 12:28)**.

12. THE SPIRIT that raised JESUS CHRIST from the dead dwells in me. He gives life to my mortal body. No sickness or infirmity has any place in me. CHRIST was bruised for my iniquities,

the chastisement of my peace was upon Him, and by His stripes I am healed **(Rom. 8:11; Isa. 53:5).**

13. I am the temple of the LIVING GOD. I do not let THE WORD OF GOD depart from my eyes. I keep it in the midst of my heart. It is life to me and health to my flesh **(Prov. 4:21-22).**

14. I am sowing bountifully as I have purposed in my heart, not grudgingly nor of necessity but as a cheerful giver. It is given to me good measure, pressed down, shaken together, and running over. It is put into my bosom. It is measured back to me with the same measure I use. He who sows sparingly will reap sparingly. He who sows bountifully will reap bountifully. You are making grace abound toward me. I always have sufficiency. I have an abundance for good works **(Luke 6:38; 2 Cor. 9:6-8).**

15. CHRIST came so that I can have life and have it more abundantly. I delight myself in THE LORD. He gives me the desires of my heart **(John 10:10; Psa. 37:4).**

16. My GOD is supplying my needs according to His riches in glory by CHRIST JESUS. He is my shepherd. I shall not want **(Phil. 4:19; Psa. 23:1).**

(II) BREAKING EVIL COVENANTS & CURSES FROM THE BLOODLINE!

"Then I will set my face against that man, and against his family, and will cut him off, and all that go a whoring after him, to commit whoredom with Molech, from among their people. And the soul that turneth after such as have familiar spirits, and after wizards, to go a whoring after them, I will even set my face against that soul, and will cut him off from among his people." (Leviticus 20:5-6)

This is not automatic; it must be applied like salvation, healing, Holy Ghost baptism, and so on. If you don't confess God's Word with your mouth and believe in your heart, nothing will happen.

Now it is time to break the curses of our bloodline. When these curses are broken, I have found out that the demon is ready to get out because he doesn't have a place to stay anymore.

First of all, begin to worship the Lord. You are His tabernacle. You are a dwelling place for the Lord. God Almighty dwells in you. You are His vessel.

Now pray these prayer points with me:

1. I break the curses of idle words and abominations that caused generations before me to go after the gods of this world, in the name of Jesus!
2. I break the curse of idolatry and paganistic practices, and command them to lose their hold on my life, in the name of Jesus!
3. I break the curses of "the wanderer and the vagabond." I break every curse of rebellion, disobedience, and not obeying the Word of God. I command selfishness and greed to lose their hold on me, in the name of Jesus!
4. I break the curse of the city where I was born and everything that has affected me from that city, in the name of Jesus!

5. I break every curse on my fields, lands, and inheritance. I break every curse on the fruit of my body, on my children and on my generation, in the name of Jesus!
6. I break every curse concerning the work of my hands, the increase of my wealth and the blessings of my land, in the name of Jesus!
7. I break all curses on my going out and my coming in, on my sitting down and my rising up, in the name of Jesus!
8. I break the curse on my basket and my storehouse, in the name of Jesus!
9. I break every curse set up by Satan, to bring defeat into my generation, in the name of Jesus!
10. I command all lawlessness and rebellion to cease, in the name of Jesus!
11. I break the curse of confusion. I command the spirit of confusion, the spirit of Babylon – the harlot system, the whorish nature of the flirtatious woman that goes whoring after other gods, to lose its hold on my life right now, in the name of Jesus!
12. I come against the curse of Babylon. I go back four generations and break its hold on my life, in the name of Jesus!
13. I come against all rebuke, blasphemy, and every curse of damnation that has been spoken my bloodline for the past four generations, in the name of Jesus!
14. I break everything that took away my self-worth, in the name of Jesus!
15. I come against the spirit of destruction and perishment. I command this curse of destruction to be loosed from my generation, in the Mighty name of Jesus!
16. I command the curse of all forms of evil: backbiting, slander, contention, anger, hatred, and so on, to come out, in the name of Jesus!
17. I come against every pestilence. I break the curse of poverty and command it to lose its hold on my life, in the name of Jesus!
18. I break the curses of stealing and deceit, incest, illegitimacy, and sodomy. I come against the spirits of pride and self-righteousness. I command all religious spirits to lose their hold

on my life. Everything that has been stolen from me, I command an immediate restoration, in the name of Jesus!
19. I break the curses of consumption and fever, inflammation, fiery heat, sword and drought, blasting and mildew, which continue to pursue me. I come against all diseases and infirmities, in the name of Jesus!
20. I break the curse of brass – not hearing, no sight, no vision, in the name of Jesus!
21. I command condemnation to lose its hold on my life, in the name of Jesus!
22. I break the curse of powdered soil and dust from the heavens, in the name of Jesus!
23. I break the curse that causes me to be struck down by my enemies. I command the spirits of failure and lack of vision to lose its hold on my life, in the name of Jesus!
24. I break the curse of premature death and the curse of boils, blood diseases, and tumors, in the name of Jesus!
25. I lose the curse of cancer from my body, in the name of Jesus!
26. I command bitterness (the roots of bitterness), resentment and unforgiveness to lose its hold on my life. I break the curse of molestation and frigidity, in the name of Jesus!
27. I break everything that would make me the tail (i.e., beneath always), in the name of Jesus!
28. I come against depression, insanity and retardation, in the name of Jesus!
29. Under the covering of the Blood of Jesus, I break the curse of scurvy, itching, all skin diseases, herpes, psoriasis, and all infirmities or conditions that don't heal. I come against the torment of itching and nervousness, in the name of Jesus!
30. I break the curse of shingles, madness, and insanity, in the name of Jesus!
31. I break the curse of blindness and no spiritual insight, in the name of Jesus!
32. I come against the spirit of dismay, despair, mental anguish and mental depression, in the name of Jesus!

33. By the Power in the Blood of Jesus, I cancel everything that has bruised my life as a result of generational curses, in the name of Jesus!
34. I call on heaven and earth to witness that I will no longer be bound by poverty. I come against the enemy coming in and robbing me of all things that are precious and good, in the name of Jesus!
35. I break the curse of lust, promiscuity, adultery, fornication, bestiality, and perversion. I cancel your assignments in my life, in the name of Jesus!
36. I break the curse of sore boils in the knees and legs – causing a lack of balance. I decree healing from the crown of my head to the soles of my feet, in the name of Jesus!
37. I break the curse of all the diseases of Egypt, and all types of diseases which could run in my bloodline: arthritis, diabetes, hypertension, heart trouble, nervousness, and all other blood-related diseases, weakness in the knees, rheumatism, neck and back aches, and pain in the spinal cord, in the name of Jesus!
38. I break the curse of edema and swelling. I command heart attack and stroke to be broken off from my bloodline, in the name of Jesus!
39. I break the curse that would allow the enemy to pursue and overtake me, in the name of Jesus!
40. I break all curses of mind control and witchcraft in my bloodline; and I command every demon to lose its hold over my life, in the name of Jesus!
41. I break every curse pronounced into my life by false prophets, and I command that all false teachings and errors that I have heard and accepted be cancelled and removed from my life, in the name of Jesus!
42. I break the curse of unbelievers in my household: from the lives of my father, mother, siblings, children, husband or wife, in the name of Jesus!
43. I break the curse of laziness and I command the spirit of passivity to lose its hold on my life, in the name of Jesus!
44. I command the witch, the warlock, and the generation that has been filtered with these evils, to depart, in the name of Jesus!

45. I break the curse of the spirit of Jezebel, and I lose that theatrical spirit that always wants to be seen and heard, in the name of Jesus!
46. I break the curse of verbal and physical abuse (many times as children, we were whipped or beaten and verbally abused, and this has left a mark on our personality). I come against the spirit of abuse and I break the curses of damnation, in the name of Jesus!
47. O Lord, baptize me with the fire of deliverance, in the name of Jesus!
48. I bind all demonic spirits attached to covenants and curses, and command you to come out of my life, in the name of Jesus!
49. Father, let the Blood of Jesus erase all my sins that opened the doors to the curses recorded in the Bible, in the name of Jesus!
50. By the Power of resurrection, I reverse every negative decree already signed against me, and that can affect me in any form, in the name of Jesus!
51. Father, reverse every negative order, placed over my destiny, in the name of Jesus!
52. Holy Spirit, wherever my name has been written or is mentioned, let Your voice respond on my behalf, in the name of Jesus!
53. Holy Spirit, confuse my enemies in their own camp, in the name of Jesus!
54. Let the Power of God tear down everything the devil has put together concerning my name, in the name of Jesus!
55. Under the new covenant which is the covenant of the Blood of Jesus, I renounce all the evil works I have done in the lives of innocent people through my membership with these demonic associations, and I ask the Almighty God to forgive me and cleanse me with the Blood of Jesus, in the name of Jesus!
56. I request the Blood of Jesus to flush out my system, purify my body, and cleanse me from all evil things I have eaten in any of the demonic cults or associations, in the name of Jesus!
57. Wherever my name has been initiated either consciously or unconsciously, I withdraw and cancel my name from their registers with the Blood of Jesus, in the name of Jesus!

Now begin to thank and praise the Lord: *"Lord, I worship You. I empty myself and surrender my all to You, Lord. Come into my life, Lord Jesus, and fill me afresh. I give You my everything, Lord, in the Mighty name of Jesus! Amen."*

(III) RENOUNCING EVIL INITIATIONS, DEDICATIONS, AND OCCULTISM

"There shall not be found among you any one who maketh his son or his daughter to pass through the fire, or that useth divination, or an observer of times, or an enchanter, or a witch. Or a charmer, or a consulter with familiar spirits, or a wizard, or a necromancer. For all that do these things are an abomination unto the LORD: and because of these abominations the LORD thy God doth drive them out from before thee. Thou shalt be perfect with the LORD thy God. For these nations, which thou shalt possess, hearkened unto observers of times, and unto diviners: but as for thee, the LORD thy God hath not suffered thee so to do." **(Deuteronomy 18:10-14)**

Prayer Points

1. I confess, repent and ask forgiveness for my involvement in occult practices such as: witchcraft, fortune telling, horoscopes, astrology, water witching, etc.
2. I renounce Satan and all occult practices and I break all curses associated with those occult practices. According to **Galatians 3:13** – Christ purchased our freedom [redeeming us] from the curse [doom] of the Law [and its condemnation] by [Himself] becoming a curse for us, for it is written [in the Scriptures], Cursed is everyone who hangs on a tree (crucified); **Deuteronomy 21:23**.

3. I confess, repent, and ask forgiveness of all sins listed in **Deuteronomy 27 and 28** and break the curses associated with these sins.
4. I confess, repent, and ask forgiveness of my iniquities and my fathers' iniquities according to **Leviticus 26:40** and I break the curses associated with these iniquities.
5. I break and loose myself from all evil soul ties with my mother, father, brother, sisters, spouses, former spouses, former sex partners, etc.
6. Lord JESUS: I forgive my mother, father, brothers (name), sisters (name) and _____ and anyone else who has ever hurt me. **(Matthew 6:15, 18:21, 22, 35; Luke 11:4 – Lord's prayer)**
7. I break and loose myself and my family from all curses that have been or are being placed upon us: curses of witchcraft, physic thoughts or prayers, ungodly intercessory prayers and words spoken in anger; and I return these curses back to sender(s) sevenfold and bind them by the Blood of JESUS, in the name of Jesus!
8. I have sought supernatural experience apart from you and I have disobeyed your Word. Lord, forgive my foolishness, in the name of Jesus!
9. I renounce all these things and ask for the cleansing of my body, soul, and spirit, in the name of Jesus!
10. I renounce witchcraft and magic: both black and white, in the name of Jesus!
11. I renounce Ouija boards and all other occult games, in the name of Jesus!
12. I renounce all séances, clairvoyance, mediums, second sight and mind reading, in the name of Jesus!
13. I renounce all fortune telling, palm reading, tea-leaf reading, crystal balls gazing, Tarot and other card reading. I renounce all astrology and interest in horoscopes, in the name of Jesus!
14. I renounce the heresy of reincarnation and all healing groups involved in metaphysics, in the name of Jesus!
15. I renounce all hypnosis under any excuse or authority, in the name of Jesus!

16. I break any curse placed on me from any occult source, in the name of Jesus!
17. I renounce all curiosity about the future or the past and which is outside Thy will, in the name of Jesus!
18. I renounce water witching or dowsing, levitation, body lifting, table tipping, psychometry, and automatic writing, in the name of Jesus!
19. I renounce astral projection and other demonic skills, in the name of Jesus!
20. I renounce all literature I have ever read in any of these fields, and vow that I will destroy such books in my own possession, in the name of Jesus!
21. In the name of Jesus Christ, I break all psychic heredity, and any demonic hold upon my family line as a result of the disobedience of any of my ancestors. I also break any bonds of physical or mental illness, in the name of Jesus!
22. I also break all demonic subjection to my mother, father, grandparents, or any other human being, in the name of Jesus!
23. In the name of JESUS CHRIST I renounce everything psychic and occultic.
24. I renounce every cult that denies the Blood of CHRIST, in the name of Jesus!
25. I renounce every philosophy that denies the divinity of CHRIST, in the name of Jesus!
26. I call upon the Lord to set me free, in the name of Jesus!

(IV) DELIVERANCE FROM GENERATIONAL CURSES

> *"Christ hath redeemed us from the curse of the law, being made a curse for us: for it is written, Cursed is every one that hangeth on a tree: That the blessing of Abraham might come on the Gentiles through Christ Jesus; that we might receive the promise of the Spirit through faith."* **(Galatians 3:13-14)**

WHAT IS A GENERATIONAL CURSE?

A generational curse is a curse that has been activated into one's life from birth, aligning that person to the same calamities affecting his or her generation. It is a curse you don't work for; it automatically takes over the life of a person.

A generational curse is transferred from one member of the family (e.g., a parent) to another within the same bloodline. It justifies the visitation (of the consequences) of the sins of one's ancestors upon their children (in future generations).

A generational curse operates within the bloodline of a person.

GENERATIONAL CURSES

> *"Thou shalt not make unto thee any graven image, or any likeness of any thing that is in heaven above, or that is in the earth beneath, or that is in the water under the earth. Thou shalt not bow down thyself to them, nor serve them: for I the LORD thy God am a jealous God, visiting the iniquity of the fathers upon the children unto the third and fourth generation of them that hate me; And shewing mercy unto thousands of them that love me, and keep my commandments."* **(Exodus 20:4-6)**

Going backwards, each of us has: Two parents, four grandparents, eight great grandparent and sixteen great-great grandparents; that is a total of thirty ancestors from which curses could possibly be derived or generated from.

Prayer Points

1. Holy Ghost, scatter all powers inherited from my parents, propelling my life toward a direction not commissioned by God, in the name of Jesus!
2. I destroy all evil powers implementing evil decrees into my life, in the name of Jesus!
3. I command all powers of darkness assigned to implement failure in my life to come out (of my life), in the name of Jesus!
4. I scatter every gathering of the ungodly against me (physically or spiritually) from my conception till this present day, in the name of Jesus!
5. Every form of evil information brought against me from the kingdom of darkness; I cancel you, in the name of Jesus!
6. I abort every operation of the forces of darkness commissioned against me to monitor my progress in life, in the name of Jesus!
7. (Lay your right hand on your head and your other hand on your stomach) Every evil operation, evil nature, and evil habits inherited from my lineage; lose your hold, in the name of Jesus!
8. Every initiation, dedication and manipulation that has yoked me into all forms of generational bondage be broken now and forever, in the name of Jesus!
9. Let every incantation, evil decrees and curses uttered against me from my birth; become impotent, in the name of Jesus!
10. All curses affecting the members of my family, lose your grip and hold over my life, in the name of Jesus!

11. I paralyze the activities of every strongman ruling over my generation and working against my progress, in the name of Jesus!
12. Let every generational curse that is affecting my destiny be broken, in the name of Jesus!
13. I renounce all curses originating from my ancestors; I denounce the power of those curses, in the name of Jesus!
14. I break all evil pronouncements propelling my life to the same type of failure, misfortune, poverty, and material lack suffered by my ancestors, in the name of Jesus!
15. Holy Ghost, disconnect me from all curses placed upon my ancestral family that is now affecting my progress, in the name of Jesus!
16. By the power in the Blood of Jesus, I paralyze all foundational curses working against my divine destiny, in the name of Jesus!
17. By the power in the Blood of Jesus, I break all generational curses of poverty, mutilating against my breakthroughs, in the name of Jesus!
18. By the power in the Blood of The Lamb, I paralyze every parental curse hindering my progress, in the name of Jesus!
19. By the power in the Blood of the Lamb, I break the generational curse of idolatry working against my life, in the name of Jesus!
20. I release myself and my family from all collective captivity of idolatry in the place of my birth, in the wonderful name of Jesus!
21. By the power in the Blood of Jesus, I release myself and my family from every collective captivity of innocent blood that was shed by my parents up to ten generations ago, in the name of Jesus!
22. I break the power of every foundational curse placed on the place of my birth, in the name of Jesus!
23. By the power in the Blood of Jesus, I paralyze every curse of "aborted destinies" in my family line, and I declare that "I am not your CANDIDATE," in the name of Jesus!

(V) RENOUNCING ALL MEMBERSHIP OF EVIL ASSOCIATIONS

"Shall the prey be taken from the mighty, or the lawful captive delivered? But thus saith the LORD, Even the captives of the mighty shall be taken away, and the prey of the terrible shall be delivered: for I will contend with him that contendeth with thee, and I will save thy children. And I will feed them that oppress thee with their own flesh; and they shall be drunken with their own blood, as with sweet wine: and all flesh shall know that I the LORD am thy Saviour and thy Redeemer, the mighty One of Jacob." (Isaiah 49:24-26)

"Be ye not unequally yoked together with unbelievers: for what fellowship hath righteousness with unrighteousness? and what communion hath light with darkness? And what concord hath Christ with Belial? or what part hath he that believeth with an infidel? And what agreement hath the temple of God with idols? For ye are the temple of the living God; as God hath said, I will dwell in them, and walk in them; and I will be their God, and they shall be my people. Wherefore come out from among them, and be ye separate, saith the Lord, and touch not the unclean thing; and I will receive you. And will be a Father unto you, and ye shall be my sons and daughters, saith the Lord Almighty." (2 Corinthians 6:14-18)

"From henceforth let no man trouble me: for I bear in my body the marks of the Lord Jesus." (Galatians 6:17)

"Therefore is any man be in Christ, he is a new creature: old things are passed away; behold, all things are become new." (2 Corinthians 5:17)

In agreement with the Word of God, we are going to stand against every demonic activity over our lives, for the Lord has given us His promises in His Word that Satan cannot break.

Prayer Points

1. I reject, revoke, and renounce my membership with: Christian Science, The Holy Order of Man, Unification Church, Mormonism, Jehovah's Witnesses, Rosicrucian, marine spirits, water spirits, Queen of the coast, and Star readers. Voodoo priest, Halloween groups, familiar spirits, witches and wizards, spirits of the dead and all other occult societies, in the name of Jesus!
2. I reject and renounce all demonic names given to me from any evil association, in the name of Jesus!
3. I resign from my position in any evil association and I withdraw my services and responsibilities permanently, in the name of Jesus!
4. I reject all yokes and burdens that I had accepted previously or presently, in the name of Jesus!
5. I command all evil agents of – Christian Science, The Holy Order of Man, Unification Church, Mormonism, Jehovah's Witnesses, Rosicrucian, marine spirits, water spirits, Queen of the coast, and Star readers. Voodoo priest, Halloween groups, familiar spirits, witches and wizards, spirits of the dead, spirit of Jezebel and all other occult societies – to come out of my life, in the name of Jesus!
6. I call on heaven and earth to witness this day that I am totally separated from any evil association, in the name of the Father, and of the Son, and of the Holy Ghost, in the name of Jesus!
7. I renounce any covenant that knowingly or unknowingly to me still binds me to any of these evil associations, in the name of Jesus!
8. I break all inherited evil covenants that I entered into consciously or unconsciously, which opened the door to gain access into my life, in the name of Jesus!

9. I bind all demons and evil spirits attached to these covenants and command them to come out of my life, in the name of Jesus!
10. I resist every attempt to return back to these evil associations, because I am now under a new covenant – the covenant of the Blood of Jesus, in the name of Jesus!
11. Holy Spirit, break down the faulty foundations of my life and rebuild a new one in Christ Jesus, in the name of Jesus!
12. By the Power in the Blood of Jesus, I disown any evil power attached to my life, and I replace them with the Power of the Holy Ghost, in the name of Jesus!
13. In the name of Jesus, I remove every satanic embargos, tags, hindrances, obstacles and/or blockages that have been put in the way of my progress by my involvement with these demonic associations.
14. I command all doors of blessings and breakthroughs that have been shut against me because of my involvement with these demonic associations, to be opened, in the name of Jesus!

(VI) PRAYERS AGAINST THE MANIPULATION OF FAMILIAR SPIRITS AND WITCHCRAFT

"Thou shalt not suffer a witch to live." **(Exodus 22:18)**

"Regard not them that have familiar spirits, neither seek after wizards, to be defiled by them: I am the LORD your God." **(Leviticus 19:31)**

(Also read 1 Samuel 28:7-23)

Witchcraft is commonly defined as the use of magical powers to influence, control, or manipulate people or events. It is commonly known as sorcery, and has been an integral part of the folklore of many societies for centuries.

Prayer Points Against Witchcraft Activities

1. I deactivate the power of every satanic food that I have eaten in my dream, in the name of Jesus!
2. Every arrow of darkness militating against my destiny, I return back to sender, in the name of Jesus!
3. I reverse all evil pronouncements aimed at me into blessings, in the name of Jesus!
4. By the Power in the Blood of Jesus, I break all witchcraft curses working against my ministry, in the name of Jesus!
5. By the Power in the Blood of Jesus, I break all witchcraft curses working against my family, in the name of Jesus!
6. By the Power in the Blood of Jesus, I break every conscious or unconscious initiation into witchcraft by my grandparents, parents, or by myself, in the name of Jesus!
7. By the Power in the Blood of Jesus, I paralyze all witchcraft curses from my foundation that are working against my job/career/business, in the name of Jesus!
8. I break the power of every "placental manipulation" of my destiny by any familiar spirits, in the name of Jesus!

9. Arrows of the Almighty God! Arise and persecute my persecutors, pursue my pursuers, attack my attackers and torment my tormentors, in the name of Jesus!
10. Finger of God! Arise; destroy my destroyers and arrest my arrestor, in the name of Jesus!
11. By the Power in the Blood of Jesus, I recover all that I have lost to the powers of the night either physically or through immorality in my dreams, in the name of Jesus!
12. I break every link to witchcraft in my life, in the name of Jesus!
13. I break every power of witchcraft from my mother's and/or father's family that has been affecting my life, in the name of Jesus!
14. Holy Ghost, destroy all the central control towers of witchcraft activities over my destiny, in the name of Jesus!
15. Satan, I take authority over your kingdom and over all your programs against my life, in the name of Jesus!

Prayer Points Against Familiar Spirits

1. I disown every familiar spirit, in the name of Jesus!
2. I refuse to be under any familiar spirit that is presently ruling over my family, in the name of Jesus!
3. By the power in the Blood of Jesus, I break every evil covenant or dedication to the place of my birth, in the name of Jesus!
4. I break the power of limitation through every familiar spirit working against my destiny, in the name of Jesus!
5. By the Power in the Blood of Jesus and by the Power of the Holy Ghost, my family and I will make heaven, in the name of Jesus!

(VII) DELIVERANCE FROM SPIRIT HUSBAND OR WIFE

"Blotting out the handwriting of ordinances that was against us, which was contrary to us, and took it out of the way, nailing it to his cross." **(Colossians 2:14)**

A "spirit spouse" is a specific person with a particular face who relates with you consistently as a husband or a wife. In most cases, the spirit husband or wife may appear with someone else's face. The relationship of a "spirit spouse" is not limited to dreams alone. A lady once told me that whenever she is preparing to get married, a well dressed man will appear to her in her dream, warning her not to ever get married, and that if she did, her husband (in the physical) will die. (The rest of this story and other stories can be found in this book).

Prayer Points

1. I renounce every marital vows or agreements entered into by my ancestors or my immediate parents on my behalf, now or before my birth, in the name of Jesus!
2. I break and deactivate all vows or covenants entered into with a spirit husband or wife, in the name of Jesus!
3. By faith, I withdraw every engagement material, visible or invisible, presented to the spirit world on my behalf, in the name of Jesus!
4. I command the fire of God to burn to ashes the spiritual wedding gown (or tuxedo), rings, photographs, marriage certificate, and all other materials used for the wedding, in the name of Jesus!
5. I break every demonic blood covenant as a result of having sex, food, or ceremonies in my dream with a spirit husband or wife, in the name of Jesus!
6. Let all demonic children which I have had (consciously or unconsciously) in the spirit realm, be consumed by fire, in the name of Jesus!

7. By the power in the Blood of Jesus and under the new covenant, I withdraw my sperm, my blood, my destiny, and any other part of my body deposited on the altar of a spirit husband or wife, in the name of Jesus!
8. I receive spiritual authority to break all marital vows and covenants, and to affect an everlasting divorce between the spirit husband or wife and myself, in the name of the Father, the Son and the Holy Ghost!
9. I call on heaven and earth to witness this day that I return all demonic properties in my possession back to the spirit world, including symbols, dowry, kola, and whatsoever was presented on the satanic altar or shrine for the marriage ceremony, in the name of Jesus!
10. Let the Blood of Jesus purge my system of all wrongful sex and all demonic deposits, in the name of Jesus!
11. Let the flood light of the Holy Ghost, search my body and expose and destroy every demonic mark, tag, or embargo deposited in my life, in the name of Jesus!
12. I command every strange image, object, or symbol deposited by the spirit husband or wife, to come out of my life, in the name of Jesus!
13. I send my body to the heavenly surgical room for a complete operation to repair, restore, or put right any damage done to any part of my body and/or my earthly marriage, by the spirit husband or wife, in the name of Jesus!
14. I reject and renounce the demonic name given to me by the spirit husband or wife, and I soak myself in the Blood of Jesus and cancel every demonic mark attached to such names, in the name of Jesus!
15. I request the Judge of heaven and earth to issue a standing decree order of restriction to every spirit husband or wife, harassing me in my dreams, in the mighty name of Jesus!
16. I destroy every demonic power assigned to destabilize my earthly marriage and ability to bear children, in the name of Jesus!

17. May the Lord rebuke every demonic agent commissioned from the spirit husband or wife to cause misunderstanding between my spouse and I, in the name of Jesus!
18. By the Blood of Jesus, I renounce every marital creed and stipulation done in the spirit world that is affecting my earthly marital vows and stipulations, in the name of Jesus!
19. With immediate effect, I abandon and disown any spiritual children attached to my name from the spirit husband or wife, in the name of Jesus!

(VIII) RENOUNCING ALL HIDDEN AND GENERAL CURSES

"Christ hath redeemed us from the curse of the law, being made a curse for us: for it is written, Cursed is every one that hangeth on a tree: That the blessing of Abraham might come on the Gentiles through Christ Jesus; that we might receive the promise of the Spirit through faith." **(Galatians 3:13-14)**

What Is A Curse?

A curse is a violent expression of evil (intent) upon others. It is a word, phrase, or sentence calling for punishment, injury or destruction of something or on somebody. It is uttering a wish of evil against someone.

A curse is an evil pronouncement propelling one's life in a direction not originally intended. Curses are words put together to torment a person with great calamity.

A curse is an invisible barrier that keeps people away from the plan of God for their lives. Curses are oral pronouncements that bring about harm.

Curses could be:

- Self inflicted, based on disobedience to the Word (and Spirit) of God
- Inherited
- Transferred
- Pronounced on an individual by wicked people.

When hidden curses are in place, you find yourself taking wrong steps and decisions, and the spirit of failure will be in full operation.

Prayer Points

1. I break and cancel every curse placed upon me by my parents, either due to their carelessness, in anger or by mistake, in the name of Jesus!
2. By the resurrection power, I deactivate the power of all curses affecting my ancestral family as a result of their sin and disobedience to God, in the name of Jesus!
3. I break and cancel every curse, evil pronouncement, spells, hexes, enchantment, bewitchment, and incantations placed upon me by the kingdom of darkness, in the name of Jesus!
4. I break and revoke every blood and soul-tie covenants and yokes attached to those curses, in the name of Jesus!
5. I purge myself of all evil foods I have eaten with the Blood of Jesus and I purify myself with the fire of the Holy Ghost, in the name of Jesus!
6. Father, please forgive me and may the Blood of Jesus cleanse me from every disobedience that introduced curses into my life, in the name of Jesus!
7. Holy Ghost, revoke every caterpillar and cankerworms that are destroying my finances as a result of the curses in the book of Malachi, in the name of Jesus!
8. Lord, let the Blood of Jesus speak for me regarding any of the curses recorded in the Bible that is affecting my progress, in the name of Jesus!
9. Holy Spirit, deliver me from all self-inflicted curses that were pronounced either consciously or unconsciously, in the name of Jesus!
10. I retrieve and cancel every word I have spoken at any time of my life that has brought judgment upon me, in the name of Jesus!
11. All power implementing evil curses over my life, you are defeated, in the name of Jesus!
12. I return back to sender every curse pronounced over my life by demonic agents of darkness, in the name of Jesus!
13. I plead the Blood of Jesus over all evil pronouncements affecting my destiny, in the name of Jesus!

14. By the Power in the Blood of Jesus, I break all self-imposed curses working against my progress, in the name of Jesus!
15. O God of Elijah, arise and deliver me from every curse of polygamy in my foundation, in the name of Jesus!
16. By the Blood of Jesus, I break every curse used by the strongmen of my father's house, in the name of Jesus!
17. By the Blood of Jesus, I break every curse used by the strongmen of my mother's house, in the name of Jesus!
18. By the Power in the Blood of Jesus, I break every curse of untimely death working in my family line, in the name of Jesus!
19. By the Power in the Blood of Jesus, I break every curse of wrong marriages in my family line – I decree that I am not your Candidate, in the name of Jesus!
20. By the Power in the Blood of Jesus, I terminate every curse of stubborn limitations in my family line, in the name of Jesus!
21. Under the covenant of the Blood of Jesus, I stand to neutralize and deactivate the power of every curse inflicted on me at any point in time because Christ has redeemed me from the curse of the law.

(IX) BINDING AND LOOSING

"Verily, verily, I say unto you, He that believeth on me, the works that I do shall do also; and greater works than these shall he do; because I go unto my Father." **(John 14:12)**

*"**Heavenly Father**, forgive us for our failure to align ourselves perfectly to Your will. We also ask for forgiveness from known sin and rebellion, emotional stress and trauma, submissions to an ungodly cover, inherited curses, worldly art and music, ownership of unclean objects, failure to cleanse property and places, unforgiveness, idolatry and a lack of separation from the things of the world.*

We ask for forgiveness, confess our contact with the occult, close doors to Satan, break curses, renounces psychic bondage, cut off evil soul-ties, lose the mind, restore the fragmented soul, confess the sins of our fathers, surrender to Jesus and renounced all manner of evil, in the name of Jesus!"

Prayer Points

1. I lose myself from the bonds of Satan around my neck, in the name of Jesus!
2. By the Power of the Holy Ghost, I tie down the enemies in the spirit realm, in the name of Jesus!
3. I reverse the words of those who cursed me, send evil against me and sent evil against the work of the Lord. I send all their evil back to them seven times, in the name of Jesus! May the Lord Jesus bring them to their knees to repentance, so that they might be saved, healed, filled, and delivered, in the name of Jesus!
4. I reverse every assignment, trap, snare, wiles, and evil plan or attack against me by Satan and his angels, demons, imps, principalities, powers, rulers of the darkness of this world, spiritual hosts of wickedness in heavenly places or evil spirits of any kind. I silence their words and/or curses, in the name of Jesus!

5. I clothe all satanic networks with confusion as with a mantle. I cancel all assignments against me. By the Power of the Blood of Jesus, I render all curses null and void, in the name of Jesus!
6. I ask the Lord to send legions of angels to minister to me, protect me, fight for me, minister healing and restoration, and to surround me, in the name of Jesus!
7. O God, help me to be strong in the Lord and in His power, to exercise the authority over the devil which You have given me, to stand against the devil, to daily put on the whole armor of God, to pray without ceasing – intercede and to fight the good fight of faith, in the name of Jesus!
8. I use our weapons of warfare against the kingdom of darkness and I return all curses and demons back to sender, in the name of Jesus!
9. Satan, I close every door you may have opened for evil contacts to come into my life, in the name of Jesus! Because Jesus Christ became a curse on the cross for me, blotting out the handwriting of ordinances against me.
10. I break all curses dating back to the time of Adam and Eve in the Garden of Eden, and I destroy all legal grounds that the enemy has (and uses) to work with in my life, in the name of Jesus!
11. I break all demonic soul-ties, and I bind all powers of the evil spirits and lose myself from their hold, in the name of Jesus!
12. I ask for the necessary spiritual gifts – especially the gift of discernment, in the name of Jesus!
13. Having been given power and authority over Satan and his army, I ask for the anointing of the Holy Spirit to come upon me now, in the name of Jesus!
14. I command the angels to turn the minds of the demons upside down, to chase and harass them, to bruise, crush, and flatten the heads of the serpentine spirits and to snip off the tails of the scorpion spirits, in the name of Jesus!
15. I order the princes and rulers of darkness to be bound with chains and thrown down before the other spirits, with the words "Jesus Christ Is My Lord" written in red letters on their foreheads, in the name of Jesus!

16. I command the lesser spirits to attack the traitors in the camp and throw them out, in the name of Jesus!
17. I command every demonic accusation against me to face God's judgment, in the name of Jesus!
18. I send the warrior angels with swords to chain the rulers of darkness and throw the fire of God on them, in the name of Jesus!
19. Satan, you have been defeated by Jesus, so you **MUST OBEY** His commands!
20. I bind all powers of darkness operating over my area of location; I break the assignments from the powers of darkness in the heavens and I command the ruling spirits to cast out their underlings, in the name of Jesus!
21. I command the angel of the Lord to assist in my deliverance as directed by God, in the name of Jesus!
22. I break evil curses, vexes, hexes, jinxes, psychic powers, bewitchment, potions, charms, incantations, spells, witchcraft and sorcery, in the name of Jesus!
23. I break all cords, snares, controls, and bondages from my life and I ask that the Power of God will be manifested in me. I command the demons that have been harassing my life to go to Tartarus, with the other fallen angels, in the name of Jesus!
24. I agree with the Covenant of the Blood of Jesus and I use the Psalms as imprecations and pronouncements against the enemies of God. I call down the wrath of God upon all spiritual foes, in the name of Jesus!
25. I come against unholy spirits, fallen angels, demons, devils, evil empires, and the entire kingdom of Satan within humans and animals. I come against councils, principalities, powers, world rulers, and wicked spirits in heavenly places, in the name of Jesus!
26. I come against chiefs and kings, princes, kingdoms, dominions, generals, rulers, captains, centurions, and strongmen assigned over my life, and I command them to be destroyed, in the name of Jesus!
27. I pray for healing from the damages in my life caused by these demons, in the name of Jesus!

28. I bind all remaining demons or their operations until they are all cast out or they leave of their own accord, in the name of Jesus!
29. I ask angels to be stationed on my properties to stand guard or keep watch, in the name of Jesus!
30. I allow godly Spirits from the Lord to operate in my life, in the name of Jesus!
31. I agree to cleanse my being, possessions, and home of all unclean objects, in the name of Jesus!

(X) LORD, ENTHRONE MY ESTHER!!! BREAK EVERY CONSPIRACY AND INSTIGATE PROMOTION

Esther, Chapters 1-9; Job 1:6-12

Who Is An "Esther"?

An "Esther" is a man or woman assigned to you by God for your breakthrough, someone whom God has sent ahead of you to save your life. An "Esther" is a man or woman who can represent you in a place where decisions are to be made for or against you;, someone whom God has raised for your help in a place where you are powerless.

Your Esther is someone who will defend you in a meeting (or a place) you have no legal right to attend. He or she is ready to give his or her life for your own. An Esther is an instrument of God, ordained by Him to rise up and fight for you in the camp of the enemy.

Prayer Points

1. Father, help my opposition to hasten me to my promotion, in the name of Jesus!
2. By the authority of heaven, we cancel every negative investigation being conducted about me, in the name of Jesus!
3. The Lord will fight my battle today, in the name of Jesus!
4. O Lord, save me from satanic harassment, in the name of Jesus!
5. O God, arise on my behalf and show Yourself mighty in every situation of my life, in the name of Jesus!
6. Let every conspiracy of opposition against my life hasten my promotion, in the name of Jesus!
7. Let the Blood of Jesus arise and silence every blood crying out against my progress, in the name of Jesus!
8. Every spiritual "Haaman" in this land, elevate me with speed, in the name of Jesus!

9. Father, it is my turn to see Your hand and Your glory over my situation in this land, in the name of Jesus!
10. Father, let the hosts of heaven represent me in all legal matters, in the name of Jesus!
11. Father, by the Blood of Jesus, reverse every evil decree standing against my position, in the name of Jesus!
12. Lord, let the mark of favor be upon my entire life, in the name of Jesus!
13. Holy Spirit, deactivate every operation of Satan over this Church, in the name of Jesus!
14. I command any negative decree attached to my name in any computer to 'Crash,' in the name of Jesus!
15. Holy Ghost, terminate every evil decree against my name, in the name of Jesus!
16. Let every negative letter already written against me, concerning my status, marriage, children, and finances, be terminated, in the name of Jesus!
17. In my ministry, every Haaman shall be dethroned and every Esther shall be enthroned, in the name of Jesus!
18. By the Blood of Jesus, I dethrone very spiritual Haaman commissioned by the kingdom of darkness against my destiny, home, career, and family, in the name of Jesus!
19. Holy Spirit, let every Haaman of my life, ruling my destiny, be dethroned, in the name of Jesus!
20. Lord, give me peace in the midst of stormy seas, in the name of Jesus!
21. Holy Spirit, let my enemy experience monumental defeat, in the name of Jesus!
22. Father, let my Haaman hasten his devices to move me to greater places, in the name of Jesus!
23. Holy Spirit, turn every satanic demotion into promotion in my life, in the name of Jesus!
24. Holy Ghost, dethrone my Haaman, and enthrone my Esther, in the name of Jesus!
25. Holy Spirit, enthrone all my "Esthers" that have been dethroned, in the name of Jesus!

26. Every altar that has been arranged by my enemies for my defeat, Holy Spirit, turn them around to their shame, in the name of Jesus!
27. By the order of heaven, let every effort of Haaman turn out to be my promotion, in the name of Jesus!
28. Father, let every promotion and blessing that Haaman is sitting on (spiritually), be removed from under him, in the name of Jesus!
29. By the authority of heaven, I reverse every evil decree released to put me to shame or to hinder my progress in this country, in the name of Jesus!
30. Father, my Haaman shall make mistakes that will promote me, in the name of Jesus!
31. Holy Ghost, let there be a hundredfold return of everything that the enemy has stolen from or denied me, in the name of Jesus!
32. Holy Ghost, disappoint my enemies, in the name of Jesus!
33. Holy Ghost, replace every letter of shame, demotion, and disappointment written by Haaman, with letters of promotion, elevation, and success, in the name of Jesus!
34. Father, let Haaman's strength and energy spent on my destiny be wasted and in vain, in the name of Jesus!
35. Holy Spirit, erase my name from every negative program that has been set against me, in the name of Jesus!
36. Wherever Haaman has taken my name to, Lord, let Your favor speak for me, in the name of Jesus!
37. Lord, let the Blood of Jesus erase every mistake, misdeed, and negative words that I have spoken, and let Your favor speak for me, in the name of Jesus!
38. Let every conspiracy of Haaman over this ministry be brought to naught, in the name of Jesus!
39. Thank You Lord, for answered prayers, in the name of Jesus!

(XI) LORD FIGHT FOR ME

Nehemiah 1:1-11, 2:4-8, 5:19, 6:14-16

Prayer Points

1. O Lord, forgive us for our sins and the sins of our fathers, in the name of Jesus!
2. O Lord, help us to return back to You and keep Your commandments, in the name of Jesus!
3. O Lord, let Your favor and mercy be upon us, in the name of Jesus!
4. My God will commission me this year for His divine purpose, in the name of Jesus!
5. Hear me, O my God! Let the hands of my enemies be weakened in the work that they are carrying out against me; it will not be done, in the name of Jesus!
6. O Lord, expose my enemies and bring their plot against me to nothing, in the name of Jesus!
7. O Lord, strengthen my hands to perform the work you have assigned to me, in the name of Jesus!
8. Remember me, O God, for good, in the name of Jesus!
9. The Lord will build a wall around me, in the name of Jesus!
10. O Lord, deal with my enemies for me while I am doing the work You committed into my hands, in the name of Jesus!
11. My enemies will be shocked and amazed to see how God will surprise me, in the name of Jesus!
12. O Lord, redeem me by Your great power and by Your strong hand according to Your promise, in the name of Jesus!
13. O Lord, give me favor in the sight of my helpers, in the name of Jesus!
14. O God of heaven, cause me to prosper, in the name of Jesus!
15. O Lord, remember Your servants, and spare them in Your mercy, in the name of Jesus!
16. Hear me O my God, for I am despised, turn my enemy's reproach onto their own heads, in the name of Jesus!

17. O Lord, send my enemies into the land of captivity, in the name of Jesus!
18. I bless Your name O Lord, for Your goodness upon my life and I thank You for answered prayers, in the name of Jesus!

(XII) SCRIPTURAL DECLARATION OF VICTORY THROUGH THE BLOOD OF JESUS

Throughout this book, I have sought to shed light on the nature of the forces of darkness and the evil work they perpetrate. My own family background and faulty foundations helped me appreciate firsthand what havoc these forces wreak in people's lives. In fact, where one is not careful there is the likelihood of being overwhelmed by fear when faced with the full measure of what these forces are capable of doing. Such fear, however, arises when one is ignorant of the overcoming power in the Blood of Jesus.

Blood is ordinarily a mysterious substance. The very sight of blood brings to mind all kinds of serious connotations especially as it is so intricately tied to life and death. In the history of creation, it is recorded that God formed man from dust. He had no life in him until God breathed upon him and he became a living soul. Immediately the spirit came upon man, blood started to carry his life. **Leviticus 17:11** tells us that:

"For the life of the flesh is in the blood..."

Now if blood carries life, we can conclude that life's very essence is in the blood. The Bible records that when God was establishing His covenant with Noah and telling him what he could and could not eat, he specifically warned him in **Genesis 9:4** against eating any meat that still had blood in it because *"the life is in the blood."*

"But flesh with the life thereof, which is the blood thereof, shall ye not eat."

Speaking with specific reference to the Blood of the Jesus, **Revelation 12:11** states that:

"And they overcame him by the blood of the Lamb, and by the word of their testimony; and loved not their lives unto the death."

Truly, there is power in the Blood. But many do not understand the magnitude of this power; neither do they really appreciate the implications of the shedding of the Blood Jesus for the human race. In order to grasp the true essence of the overcoming power in the Blood of Jesus, we only need to retrace God's divine plan in bringing the Savior to earth.

Prayer Points

1. Through the Blood of Jesus, I am redeemed out of the hand of the devil **(Ephesians 1:7).**
2. Through the Blood of Jesus, all my sins are forgiven **(Psalm 107:2).**
3. The Blood of Jesus, God's Son, continually cleanses me from all sin **(1 John 1:7).**
4. Through the Blood of Jesus, I am justified, made righteous, *just as if I'd* never sinned **(Romans 5:9)**.
5. Through the Blood of Jesus, I am sanctified, made holy, and set apart unto God **(Hebrews 13:12)**.
6. My body is the Temple of the Holy Spirit, redeemed and cleansed by the Blood of Jesus **(1 Corinthians 6:19-20)**.
7. Satan has no place in or power over me through the Blood of Jesus and the Word of God **(Revelation 12:11)**.
8. In Him (Jesus) we have redemption (deliverance and salvation) through His Blood, the remission (forgiveness) of our offences (shortcomings and trespasses), in accordance with the riches and the generosity of His gracious favor, which He lavished upon us with every kind of wisdom and understanding (practical insight and prudence) **(Ephesians 1:7-8)**.
9. Let the redeemed of the Lord say so, whom He has delivered from the hand of the adversary **(Psalm 107:2)**.
10. But if we are (really) walking and living in the Light as He (Himself) is the Light, we have (true) unbroken fellowship with one another and the Blood of Jesus Christ, His Son, cleanses (removes) us from all guilt and sin (keeps us clean from sin in all of its forms and manifestations) **(1 John 1:7)**.

11. Therefore, since we are now justified (acquitted, made righteous and brought into a right relationship with God) by Christ's Blood, how much more (certain) shall we be saved by Him from the indignation and wrath of God **(Romans 5:9)**.
12. Therefore, Jesus also suffered and died outside the (city's) gate, in order that He might purify and consecrate (sanctify) the people through (the shedding of) His own Blood and set them apart as holy (unto God) **(Hebrews 13:12)**.
13. Do you not know that your body is the temple (the very sanctuary) of the Holy Spirit Who lives with you, Whom you have received (as a Gift) from God? You are not your own **(1 Corinthians 6:19)**.
14. You were bought with a price (purchased with preciousness and paid for, made His own). So then, honor (your) God and bring glory to Him in your body **(1 Corinthians 6:20)**.
15. And they have overcome (conquered) him by means of the Blood of the Lamb and by the utterance of their testimony, for they did not love or cling to life even when faced with death (holding their lives cheap till they had to die for their witnessing) **(Revelation 12:11)**.
16. In the name of Jesus, O Lord, baptize me with the fire of deliverance, in the name of Jesus!
17. All demonic spirits attached to all covenants and curses, I bind you and command you to come out of my life, in the name of Jesus!
18. Father, let the Blood of Jesus Christ erase all my sins that opened the doors to the curses recorded in the Bible, in the name of Jesus!
19. By the Power of resurrection, I reverse every negative decree already signed against me, and that can affect me in any form, in the name of Jesus!
20. Father, reverse every negative order placed over my destiny, in the name of Jesus!
21. Holy Spirit, let Your voice respond on my behalf wherever my name is written or mentioned, in the name of Jesus!
22. Holy Spirit, confuse my enemies in their own camp, in the name of Jesus!

23. Let the Power of God tear down everything the devil has put together concerning my name, in the name of Jesus!
24. Under the new covenant that is the covenant of the Blood of Jesus, I renounce all the evil works I have done in the lives of innocent people through my membership with these demonic associations, and I ask the Almighty God to forgive me and cleanse me with the Blood of Jesus, in the name of Jesus!
25. I request the Blood of Jesus to flush out my system, purify my body and cleanse me from all evil things I have eaten in any of the demonic cults or associations, in the name of Jesus!
26. Wherever my name has been initiated either consciously or unconsciously, I withdraw and cancel my name from their registers with the Blood of Jesus, in the name of Jesus!
27. By the Power in the Blood of Jesus, I withdraw any part of my body or blood deposited on their evil altars, in the name of Jesus!
28. I withdraw pictures, objects, presentations, food, sacrifices, money, children, wife, husband, clothes, images, and any other personal belongings from the altars of the forces of darkness, in the name of Jesus!
29. I return any weapon (physical or spiritual) belonging to the kingdom of darkness that I was a part of, and I also return any other properties for the execution of satanic duties at my disposal, in the name of Jesus!
30. Holy Spirit, build a wall of fire around me and let there be a permanent disconnection between the satanic kingdom and me, in the name of Jesus!
31. By the Blood of Jesus, I cancel and erase every evil mark, incision, tattoo, and writing inserted on my body as a result of my participation with the forces of darkness, in the name of Jesus!
32. I break all covenants that I have undertaken for my children, grandchildren, and generations after me, in the name of Jesus!
33. By the Power in the Blood of Jesus, I renounce and denounce every dedication of my destiny to any river, mountain, or idol in the place of my birth, in the name of Jesus!

34. By the Power in the Blood of Jesus, I renounce and denounce every initiation into occultism by my parents and/or grandparents, in the name of Jesus!
35. By the Power in the Blood of Jesus, I cancel every dedication or covenant with family idols, evil trees, forests, markets, road junctions, and so on, in the name of Jesus!
36. Anyone monitoring me through a satanic glass or device, I command that glass or device to be broken, in the name of Jesus!

(XIII) POSSESSING YOUR POSSESSIONS
Scripture Reading – Genesis 28

Confessions

"And I will give thee the treasures of darkness, and hidden riches of secret places, that thou mayest know that I, the LORD, which call thee by thy name, am the GOD of Israel." **(Isaiah 45:3)**

God has given us dominion to rule over all. This includes:

- The power or right of governing and controlling, i.e., sovereign authority.
- Rule, control, dominate.
- Lands or domains, subject to sovereignty or control.
- Government. A territory constituting a self-governing commonwealth and being one of a number of such territories united in a community of nations, or empire: formerly applied to self-governing division of the British Empire, as well as Canada and New Zealand.

Dominion has been defined as:

I. Sovereign or supreme authority, the power of governing and controlling, independent right of possession, use, and control, sovereignty, supremacy.
II. Superior prominence, predominance, ascendency.
III. That which is governed territory over which authority is exercised, the tract, district, or county, considered as subject, as the dominions of a king. Also used figuratively as the dominion of the passions

Prayer Points

1. Let the anointing of special favor fall upon my life, in the name of Jesus!
2. My star, arise and shine, and fall no more, in the name of Jesus!
3. O Lord, like Joseph, move me from the prison to the palace, in the name of Jesus!
4. O God of Elijah, bury my failures, in the name of Jesus!
5. If I have left my place of blessing, O Lord, take me back there – by fire, in the name of Jesus!
6. O Lord, as You parted the Red Sea, separate affliction from my destiny, in the name of Jesus!
7. My heavenly Father, open my eyes to see my breakthroughs, in the name of Jesus!
8. Let my season of divine intervention appear, in the name of Jesus!
9. O Lord, open my eyes to behold wondrous treasures, in the name of Jesus!
10. O Lord, cancel my journey of backwardness, in the name of Jesus!
11. I command my glory to appear, in the name of Jesus!
12. Angels of God, pursue my helpers and lead them to me, in the name of Jesus!
13. Every Haaman assigned to kill me shall die in my place, in the name of Jesus!
14. I command every satanic engineer and engine assigned against me to be destroyed, in the name of Jesus!
15. I arrest the traffic of demons directed against me, in the name of Jesus!
16. I command you, power of the night, from attacking my life, to turn around and begin to attack yourself, in the name of Jesus!
17. O Lord, as You killed all the firstborn of the Egyptians, kill every power that wants to terminate my destiny, in the name of Jesus!
18. I command every power defiling my body to die, in the name of Jesus!
19. Fire of God, arise and locate the camp of my enemies, in the name of Jesus!

20. I command any power redirecting my star to die, in the name of Jesus!
21. Let anyone staying awake to do me harm, receive an angelic slap, in the name of Jesus!
22. Let the Blood of Jesus wash off every strange touch of evil in my life, in the name of Jesus!
23. Any material carved against me, begin to attack the manufacturer, in the name of Jesus!
24. I command every altar that is raised up against me to crumble now, in the name of Jesus!
25. Every priest of the night ministering against me, receive the spirit of confusion, in the name of Jesus!
26. All my blessings that have been taken to the grave by any evil dead relative, arise and locate me, in the name of Jesus!

Begin to thank God for answering your prayers. Sing a song of praise about the Blood of Jesus. Confess and claim the promises in **Galatians 3:13-14** and **Revelation 12:11**.

Claim your total deliverance as you cover yourself, your family, your ministry, your job, your prosperity, and everything that concerns you with the Blood of Jesus, in the name of Jesus! Amen.

(XIV) REALIGN YOURSELF BACK INTO GOD'S PRESENCE

"And David recovered all that the Amalekites had carried away: and David rescued his two wives. And there was nothing lacking to them, neither small nor great, neither sons nor daughters, neither spoil, nor any thing that they had taken to them: David recovered all." **(1 Samuel 30:18-19)**

1. Lord, I thank You for Your presence in my life, in the name of Jesus!
2. O God, I want to be concerned with Your issues, in the name of Jesus!
3. Father, give me an understanding of Who You are, in the name of Jesus!
4. Open my eyes to see what matters to You the most, in the name of Jesus!
5. Lord, help me to recover what matters to You, in the name of Jesus!
6. Lord, I take up Your yoke, and I reject my yoke, in the name of Jesus!
7. Help me to obey You in order to have a better life, in the name of Jesus!
8. Lord, do something new in my life today, in the name of Jesus!
9. O Lord, give me insights into Your purpose for my life, in the name of Jesus!
10. My God, teach me how to fight the good fight of faith, in the name of Jesus!
11. O God, send down help from above, in the name of Jesus!
12. Holy Ghost, connect me to that man or woman whom You have positioned for my promotion, in the name of Jesus!
13. Father, search my heart and visit my spirit man. Show me who I am and let me know Who You are, in the name of Jesus!
14. Thank You for answering my prayers, in the name of Jesus!

(XV) INTERCESSORY PRAYERS FOR THE BODY OF CHRIST

1. I terminate every agent that Satan is using against the Church, in the name of Jesus!
2. Let all satanic efforts within the Church be consumed by the fire of the Holy Ghost, in the name of Jesus!
3. Holy Ghost, as a result of this prayer, connect me to every man or woman anywhere in the world that you have programmed to help me, in the name of Jesus!
4. O Lord, be merciful unto us and fight our battles, in the name of Jesus!
5. Father, we have been scattered around by our unfaithfulness. In Your mercy, gather us together with Your mighty hands, in the name of Jesus!
6. Remember Your servant (Rev. James) O Lord, and do not wipe out the good deeds he has done for the Kingdom of his God, in the name of Jesus!

(XVI) DAILY SCRIPTURAL DECLARATIONS AND CONFESSIONS

"O LORD, our Lord, how excellent is thy name in all the earth! who hast set thy glory above the heavens." **(Psalm 8:1)**

"Great and marvelous are thy works, Lord God Almighty; just and true are thy ways, thou King of saints.
Who shall not fear thee, O Lord, and glorify thy name? for thou only art holy: for all nations shall come and worship before thee; for thy judgments are made manifest." **(Revelation 15:3-4)**

Pause to express your thoughts of praise and worship.

Confession

1. The Lord has pleasure in the prosperity of His servant. Abraham's blessings are mine **(Psa. 35:27; Gal. 3:13-14).**

2. I have the SPIRIT OF TRUTH. He guides me in the paths of righteousness. Whatever He hears, He will speak and tell me things that are to come **(John 16:13; Psa. 23:3).**

3. I trust in THE LORD with my heart. I lean not on my own understanding. In my ways I acknowledge Him. He directs my paths. I am filled with the WISDOM OF GOD. I asked GOD for this wisdom. He gives wisdom to me liberally without finding reproach **(Prov. 3:5-6; James 1:5).**

4. I let THE WORD OF CHRIST dwell in me richly. To me the doorkeeper opens. As GOD'S SHEEP, I hear His voice. He calls me by name and leads me out. He goes before me. I follow after GOD; I know His voice. I do not know the voice and will not follow a stranger; I will flee from him. **(John 10:3-5; Col. 3:16).**

5. THE FATHER OF GLORY is giving me the SPIRIT OF WISDOM AND REVELATION in the KNOWLEDGE OF CHRIST. The eyes of my understanding are enlightened. I know what is the hope of His Calling and the riches of the glory of His Inheritance in the saints. I have been given the MIND OF CHRIST through THE WORD OF GOD. I am not conformed to this world but transformed by the renewing of my mind, proving what is that good acceptable PERFECT WILL OF GOD **(Eph. 1:17-18; 1 Cor. 2:16; Rom. 12:2).**

6. I am filled with the knowledge of His Will in wisdom and spiritual understanding. I walk worthy of THE LORD, pleasing Him, being fruitful in good work and increasing in the KNOWLEDGE OF GOD. I walk in faith not by sight. I realize I am His workmanship created in CHRIST JESUS for good works, which GOD has already prepared beforehand that I should walk in them **(Col. 1:9-10; 2 Cor. 5:7; Eph. 2:10).**

7. THE LORD is my light, salvation, and strength. Of whom shall I be afraid? I am strengthened with patience, long suffering, joy, and might according to CHRIST JESUS' GLORIOUS POWER. For the JOY OF THE LORD is my strength **(Psa. 27:1; Col. 1:11; Neh. 8:10).**

8. What can I say to these things? If GOD is for me, who can be against me? His divine power has given me things that pertain to life and godliness, through the knowledge of Him who called me by glory and virtue! Through these I become a partaker of His divine nature. I have escaped the corruption that is in the world **(Rom. 8:31; Peter 1:3-4).**

9. I enjoy redemption and forgiveness of my sins through CHRIST'S BLOOD. I overcome the Devil, world, and what I face. Whatever is born of GOD overcomes the world. This is the victory that overcomes the world: my faith. I believe that JESUS IS THE SON OF GOD. Greater is He that is in me than he that is in the world. I can do all things through CHRIST which strengthens me **(Col. 1:14; 1 John 4:4, 5:4-5; Phil. 4:13).**

10. I do not forget GOD'S LAWS. I let my heart keep His commands. I have length of days, long life, and peace. Mercy and truth do not forsake me. They are bound to my neck and written on the tablet of my heart. I find favor and high esteem in the sight of GOD and man. I am surrounded by divine favor. THE LORD will perfect me **(Prov. 3:1-4; Psa. 138:8)**.

11. I go into the world and preach the Gospel. He who believes and is baptized is saved. These signs follow me. In the NAME OF JESUS CHRIST, I cast out demons and speak with new tongues. I take up serpents. If I drink anything deadly, it will not hurt me. I lay hands on the sick and they recover. The Lord works with me confirming THE WORD through accompanying signs. Whatever I ask in the NAME OF JESUS, He gives me. I ask and receive THE PERFECT WILL OF GOD to be done in my life. His joy and my joy are full **(Mark 16:15-18; John 16:23-24)**.

12. What GOD has promised me is coming to pass. I am His workmanship created in CHRIST JESUS for good works. GOD prepared beforehand that I should walk in them. The Kingdom Of Heaven is at hand. I heal the sick, cleanse the lepers, raise the dead, and cast out demons. Freely I have received. Freely I give. I am complete in Him who is the head of all principality and power **(Eph. 2:10; Matt. 10:7-8; Col. 2:10)**.

13. **I am accepted:** GOD's child, CHRIST's friend, justified, united with THE LORD, one with Him in spirit, bought with a price, belong to GOD, member of CHRIST's body, saint, adopted as GOD's child, direct access to GOD through JESUS CHRIST, redeemed, forgiven of sins, and complete in CHRIST.

14. **I am secure:** free from condemnation, assured that things work together for good, free from condemning charges, cannot be separated from the love of GOD, established, anointed, sealed by GOD, hidden with CHRIST in GOD, confident that the good work that GOD has begun will be perfected, citizen of Heaven,

not given a spirit of fear, given power, love, and a sound mind, find grace and mercy in time of need, and born of GOD.

15. **I am significant:** salt, light of earth, branch of the true vine, a channel of His life, chosen, appointed to bear fruit, personal witness of CHRIST's, GOD's temple, minister of reconciliation, GOD's coworker, seated with CHRIST in the heavenly realm, GOD's workmanship, may approach GOD with freedom, confidence, and can do all things through CHRIST who strengthens me.

About The Author

Rev. James A. Solomon is a man who is truly gifted with an extraordinary anointing on the subject of Spiritual Warfare, Healing, and Deliverance. It is very rare to find ministers and servants of God who still operate powerfully in the Spirit of God prophetically and in truth, and still serving in the Church in this day and age.

Rev. Solomon is the President of Jesus People's Revival Ministries Inc., as well as the General Overseer and Senior Pastor of Jesus Family Chapel, with 28 branches in Nigeria, the United Kingdom, and several other countries. The international headquarters for both ministries is based in Atlanta, Georgia, in the United States of America.

In his efforts to serve the whole body of Christ beyond his own ministries, he also zealously serves as director for the West African Regional Directorate of the International Accelerated Missions (I.A.M.), a network of missionary churches based in New York.

He is a well, sought-after deliverance minister who has and still serves the Body of Christ in this very area of ministry. He visits and ministers in many local churches; testimonies of victory and freedom from bondage and the kingdoms of darkness abound so much that they serve as testimony to God's call on his life in this area of ministry.

Rev. Solomon started from very humble beginnings in his native country of Nigeria, West Africa, way back in the 1980s. With his team of ministers and due to popular demand, he has taken the revelation of Spiritual Warfare and Deliverance to massive venues such as the stadium domes in the major cities of Nigeria. He has also conducted a series of conferences, and organizes quarterly Deliverance Night Services in the United Kingdom, Europe, Canada, Japan, and all over the United States. Many have received freedom from satanic bondage and oppression at these quarterly deliverance services. He is in high demand as a guest minister in many crusades and conferences.

He currently resides in Atlanta, Georgia with his family. He is married to Rev. Mrs. Florence A. James and they are blessed with 4 children.

He has also authored several other books and publications.

For further studies, some of his other books are listed here for your reference. To purchase, please visit www.jesuspeople1.net or call 770-817-1376 (USA).

LIST OF BOOK TITLES
BY
REV. JAMES A. SOLOMON

1. CANCELLING SATANIC RESOLUTIONS.
2. DIVINE FAVOR.
3. EXCUSE ME, MY CASE IS URGENT!
4. THE SECRET OF SUCCESS IN CHURCH GROWTH.
5. LORD, SEND A REVIVAL.
6. MY BAD CREDIT VS A PERFECT CO-SIGNER.
7. THE CALL OF GOD.
8. THE DANGERS OF LATENESS, PROCASTINATION AND DELAY.
9. VICTORY OVER THE ENEMY OF MY STAR.
10. LORD, HEAL MY WITHERED HAND.
11. WHAT IS YOUR NAME?
12. WHO NEEDS DELIVERANCE (DELIVERANCE MANUAL).
13. CLEAR YOUR DOUBTS IN KNOWING GOD'S WILL.
14. THE ALMOST CHRISTIAN
15. DEMONIC MANIPULATIONS IN YOUR DREAM

CPSIA information can be obtained
at www.ICGtesting.com
Printed in the USA
BVHW030004090323
659972BV00006B/294